SOCIOLOGY FOR THE TWENTY-FIRST CENTURY

SOCIOLOGY FOR THE TWENTY-FIRST CENTURY

Continuities and Cutting Edges

EDITED BY Janet L. Abu-Lughod

WITH A FOREWORD BY
Felice Levine
AND AN AFTERWORD BY
Immanuel Wallerstein

*A Joint Project of the American Sociological Association
and the International Sociological Association*

THE UNIVERSITY OF CHICAGO PRESS
Chicago and London

JANET ABU-LUGHOD is professor emerita of sociology and historical studies in the Graduate Faculty of the New School for Social Research and of Northwestern University.

The University of Chicago Press, Chicago 60637
The University of Chicago Press, Ltd., London
© 1999 by The University of Chicago
All rights reserved. Published 1999

08 07 06 05 04 03 02 01 00 99   1 2 3 4 5
ISBN: 0-226-00191-1 (cloth)
ISBN: 0-226-00193-8 (paper)

Library of Congress Cataloging-in-Publication Data

Sociology for the Twenty-first Century : continuities and cutting edges
   / edited by Janet L. Abu-Lughod.
       p. cm.
     "Preliminary versions of almost all of the chapters in this book were presented at a small closed working conference held in Toronto during two extended (8 A.M. to 10 P.M.) but exciting days of August 1997"—Acknowledgments.
     Includes bibliographical references.
     ISBN 0-226-00191-1 (cloth : alk. paper). — ISBN 0-226-00193-8 (pb : alk. paper)
     1. Sociology—North America.   2. Sociology.   I. Abu-Lughod, Janet L.
HM477.N7S63   1999
301'.097—dc21   99-22434

♾ The paper used in this publication meets the minimum requirements of the American National Standard for Information Sciences—Permanence of Paper for Printed Library Materials, ANSI Z39.48–1992.

CONTENTS

It is a pleasure to be able to write a foreword for the book *Sociology for the Twenty-first Century: Continuities and Cutting Edges* only two years after the launch of this project. In deciding to undertake this effort in collaboration with the International Sociological Association (ISA), the American Sociological Association (ASA) sought to stimulate reflection and fresh ideas for the discipline at an important juncture in its history. Collective endeavors to foster sociological inquiry happen far too infrequently; to accomplish one with great success is even more rare.

Since this book focuses on the how and what of sociology as it is and can be, it is worth reflecting on how this product itself took form. As the subtitle *Continuities and Cutting Edges* implies, this is a book grounded in the heritages of sociology but not constrained by them. Too often projects aimed at taking stock and looking ahead tend to celebrate the past more than analyze it and to allude to the future more than engage with it. This book avoids these pitfalls. For those producing sociology or studying the sociology of our science, this work is worth reading.

Immanuel Wallerstein had the initial vision to launch a program of far-reaching thought about sociology's past and future. Vintage Wallerstein, of course, his ambition was on a grand and international scale. From the time of his election as president of ISA in 1994 (he was at the time the ASA representative to ISA), he wanted this international organization to play a vital role between world congresses in advancing the substance and scholarship of the field. A sociologist of action as well as ideas, Wallerstein traveled the globe during his first two years in office seeking to foster regional conferences aimed at assessing the discipline and identifying opportunities as seen from the perspective of every region of the world. He thought that, if this project could be pursued between ISA meetings, the contributions from these endeavors could form the basis of important discussion and debate at the 1998 ISA World Congress.

His outreach and his "house calls" included discussions with Alejandro Portes (then prior ASA representative to ISA), Neil Smelser (then ASA president-elect), and me. As ISA president and ASA representative to ISA, Wallerstein asked that the ASA take the lead in convening a conference and planning the project for the North America region. We were excited about this idea and sought a team leader who would bring imagination, versatility, skill, and tenacity to such a project.

It is fortunate indeed that Janet Abu-Lughod assumed this role. She is one of those rare scholars who transcend boundaries in their work, their sociological interests, and their spirit of inquiry. Because this initiative was a joint project of the ASA and ISA, it was a happy coincidence that Abu-Lughod was at that time a member of ASA Council and the seated ASA alternate to ISA. There was not a better person to take the lead.

I remember the e-mail when Wallerstein indicated that he had approached Abu-Lughod and that she had said yes to leading this project. Abu-Lughod's yes meant infectious enthusiasm and energy—which were both requisite to attracting others to participate and to produce. Her immediate and intense engagement in this project was refreshing and remains high. From the outset, Portes, Wallerstein, and I recognized that external funding would be necessary to convene a North American conference. In short order, Abu-Lughod and I dedicated the 1996 Christmas–New Year's period to the development of a proposal that the ASA submitted to the Russell Sage Foundation. Happily, its president, Eric Wanner, realized that we would need a fast-track decision if we were to meet our timeline of a conference in August 1997 and a preliminary published report in time for the ISA Congress in July 1998. By the end of January, we learned that Russell Sage would provide a grant.

As researchers and scholars well know, funding may seed a project, but making it a success necessitates deliberative and creative steps. The original title for the project was, aptly, "Millennial Milestone," and there were indeed many milestones that needed to be traversed to accomplish the project and produce a quality book. First, Abu-Lughod needed to undertake the hard intellectual work of conceptualizing the project and developing the right questions that could usefully inform a research conference. Second, she needed to attract contributors who have substantial ideas to bring to the table but who could also listen and learn from others. Third, she needed to be sure that written papers could be circulated prior to the conference, so that the meeting itself could move beyond the papers and provide the basis for important discussion and exchange. Fourth, she needed to ensure that a publishable report with a cross section of papers would be available for distribution at the 1998 World Congress. Fifth, she needed to keep the momentum going if a polished and complete volume was to be available to launch the new millennium. Abu-Lughod did all of this with great ease and with great depth.

In some sense, the success of a book project like this cannot be measured solely by the quality of the knowledge or the timeliness of its delivery. Key also are the modes of thinking that it stimulates and the questions that it asks. Abu-Lughod and the contributors to this volume have sought to ask "why" about the progress and problems of our past and the trajectories for the future. If these questions help to spawn other questions and new ideas, they will have left a legacy of significance for sociology and for social science beyond the year 2000.

FELICE J. LEVINE
Executive Officer, American Sociological Association

The broad task assigned us—nothing less than to take stock of the
legacy and future of sociology in North America—was a forbidding
one. It was evident from the start that no single conference assessing
the present state of sociology in our region, much less its future concerns, could possibly hope to exhaust the entire field. To avoid a dis-
parate laundry list of topics, a limited number of broad issues were
singled out for deeper exploration. And, as convener of the meetings,
I realized that to invite a random selection of even the "best" scholars
now involved in all the diverse areas in which sociologists work would
be to forfeit an opportunity to develop a constructive evaluation of the
field at some of its newer margins.

To encourage focused papers and discussions, my original position
paper outlined five general problematics and, within each, posed certain cutting-edge questions that I thought creative sociologists in
North America were addressing—or at least needed to address. This
paper was circulated to a limited number of individuals, along with
an invitation to prepare an essay on a specific topic in which I knew
he or she had deep interest and research expertise. The chapters in
this book represent thoughtful and original responses to the questions
raised in the original position paper—although, as the reader will soon
discover, the authors, all of whom wrote their essays independent of
one another, reached conclusions that led to a remarkable synergism.
Each contribution took from the past what it deemed usable, but each
also highlighted lacunae in earlier sociological works, even those of
the highest quality, and explored how changing realities in the contemporary social world now require important reconceptualization. All
subscribed to the underlying purpose of our conference: to acknowledge our intellectual roots but not to allow them to blind us to changing realities.

Two of the five problematics selected for our conference will surprise
no one, since they have had fundamental significance in the field from
the time of sociology's birth: namely, disjunctions within the realm of

theory (general laws versus changing social formations and facts versus values), and the often-cited antinomies in methods of inquiry and analysis referred to in shorthand as "macro-micro" and "quantitative-qualitative." Part 1 of the book includes six chapters that address these broad theoretical and methodological issues, for I strongly believe that theories and methods are inextricably intertwined.

The remaining foci were selected because they represented what I considered to be issues of increasing future centrality to the societies (and the field of sociology) in North America, namely:

1. the consequences of an increasingly entailed "global system" where the congruencies between the boundaries of mutually exclusive territorial units (the nation-state system), on the one hand, and the apparently deterritorialized nature of monetary transactions and interlocked transnational capitalist enterprises, on the other, have broken apart;
2. the ways that social scientists and legal structures have been led to reconceptualize racial and ethnic categories and relationships in response to the heightened and diversified immigration that has been taking place in the United States and Canada in recent decades, which is, in part, a result of this new structure of the world system; and
3. the possibilities for both intimate social relations and effective social movements in an "age of information," where older forms of social interactions based upon physical/spatial proximity are now supplemented if not supplanted by despatialized connections in cyberspace that not only affect economic-financial regulation and transnational identities, but transform the mechanisms for organized democratic politics.

These problematics are not necessarily those most central to sociological concerns throughout the rest of the world, nor do they exhaust the varied interests and fields of North American sociology.[1] But they do capture some of the pressing preoccupations of globally oriented and future-minded sociologists, as seen from the North American perspective.

What the North American regional conference sacrificed in terms of range, then, it gained in terms of focus. The advantage of following this strategy was that the two-day working conference enjoyed a certain coherence and animated depth, as does the volume presented here. Because the topics were intellectually linked and could be grouped for sequential presentation, and because, with few exceptions, the papers had been distributed and read in advance, there was lively communication during the ensuing discussions. Furthermore, there were over-laps and linkages among the essays that had been prepared indepen-dently for the separate sessions, suggesting a certain confluence of diagnoses, if not resolution of differing positions. In my introductory chapter I shall try to make these linkages more explicit.

Throughout, we have tried to identify some of the cutting-edge ques-tions that creative sociologists in North America are now beginning to address. Many of these questions hark back to those raised when the field of sociology was in its infant stage a century ago. But the old answers no longer suffice. To take from the past what is usable may be important, but it is also absolutely essential that past conceptualiza-tions do not blind us to new realities.

Note

1. For example, we did not address problems of economic and social development in other regions of the world, assuming that these would be addressed in other regional conferences, nor did we try to cover all the socioeconomic and political issues (i.e., edu-cation, health, crime) that are currently pressing within the United States and Canada. Further, I made a conscious decision not to single out gender as a separate problematic, in the firm belief that so basic a variable would emerge as significant in many of the essays, which it did.

ACKNOWLEDGMENTS

Preliminary versions of almost all of the chapters in this book were presented at a small closed working conference held in Toronto during two extended (8 A.M. to 10 P.M.) but exciting days of August 1997. In January of that year I accepted the invitation of Immanuel Wallerstein, then president of the International Sociological Association, to organize the sessions and to invite thirty participants from the United States, Canada, as well as representative international observers from Spain, Russia, India, and Germany who had participated in similar meetings for their own regions. I would like to express deep appreciation to Immanuel Wallerstein for placing such confidence in me, for helping me to identify appropriate international participants, and for serving as a gracious and fully participating "host."

Ours was one of a dozen regional conferences held throughout the world in 1996–97 to prepare for the 1998 biennial meetings of the International Sociological Association. The mandate for our regional meeting was to consider the heritage and future of sociology in North America as the millennium approached, but within that incredibly broad agenda I was given enormous latitude to organize the proceedings and to invite papers to address significant issues of continuity and change in sociology.

This assignment offered a rare opportunity. It seemed an appropriate moment to take stock of a limited number of sociological themes that had particular salience as the year 2000 approached. In addition, and for almost the first time, here was a rare opportunity to bring francophone and anglophone Canadian scholars together with their U.S. colleagues to explore mutual concerns and to find out whether, and in what ways, we differed in our preoccupations and approaches.

The American Sociological Association agreed to serve as the local cosponsor, and, in this connection, it received financial support from the Russell Sage Foundation to cover the costs of hospitality during the event. I would therefore like to acknowledge the valuable assistance received from these sources. Felice Levine and Janet Astner of the

American Sociological Association gave constant support, both to the intellectual agenda and to the complex practical arrangements required to bring together so many far-flung participants. It was my luck and pleasure that they assigned ASA intern Chris Hickey to handle the liaison between the conference and the executive office of the ASA. Hickey served ably in that capacity, as did Behrouz Moazami, a graduate student at the New School for Social Research, who assisted me on the New York side. In addition, all participants remain deeply indebted to the Russell Sage Foundation and its director, Eric Wanner, without whose financial support the luxury of our uninterrupted and collegial discussions would have been impossible.

The Graduate Faculty of the New School for Social Research assisted in so many ways it is difficult to enumerate them. A sabbatical leave in the fall of 1997 gave me the time to prepare the brief ISA volume and the longer manuscript for submission to the University of Chicago Press. On a material level, the university made it possible for me to remain in constant touch with the authors and gave me access to all the "machines" so necessary in the era of technology. On a more symbolic level, the New School provided encouragement and other no less important psychic benefits.

But my greatest gratitude is reserved for dear friends (old and newfound) and colleagues—all distinguished scholars—who squeezed precious time from their unbelievably overloaded schedules to prepare thoughtful and original essays on topics I had suggested in the detailed position paper that accompanied their invitation to participate.[1] With only two exceptions, provisional versions of the papers were completed on time and could therefore be distributed to all participants in advance of our assembling. This stimulated an extremely lively set of discussions, guided by the remarks of assigned discussants for each of the sessions. I would like especially to thank Danielle Laberge, Barry Wellman, Arnaud Sales, Sharon Zukin, and Gerda Wekerle for the thoughtful ways they focused our attention on key issues during four of the sessions and regret only that their remarks could not be included in this volume. In one case, however, the remarks by a sixth designated discussant had already expanded into a rough draft of a paper. The extended remarks of Tomás Almaguer, delivered from a handwritten text, were so detailed and significant that we asked him to prepare the full chapter that has been included in this book.

All essays were original contributions written specifically for our conference. Directly after the conference, early versions of six papers, plus my own very different introductory remarks, were sent to Maria

Luz-Moran of the ISA Secretariat in Madrid, who was charged with collating the various regional reports. These papers were made available by the ISA for distribution at its biennial meeting held in Montreal in August 1998. We are grateful to the International Sociological Association for the advanced right to include these preliminary essays, which in most cases have been considerably revised, as chapters in our book.

And finally, I want to express my appreciation to the editors of the University of Chicago Press and to the three anonymous readers whom they asked to evaluate the completed manuscript. While gratifyingly enthusiastic, the extended comments of the readers were scarcely perfunctory. We have taken many of their suggestions to heart and have revised various chapters in line with their constructive criticisms. A special, warm word of thanks is due to associate editor Matthew Howard, who not only shepherded the process through to its happy conclusion but sent so many interesting e-mails that I was always cheered and often amused by what otherwise might have been a dry exercise.

JANET ABU-LUGHOD
New School for Social Research
December 1998

Note

1. The high acceptance rate and the enthusiastic responses were very gratifying, indicating that many shared my interest in critical new ideas at the cutting edge of the discipline. Only a handful of those invited declined because of prior commitments. It was especially distressing to me that none of the four distinguished African American scholars I had invited was free to attend; it was unforeseen at the time of scheduling that our sessions would conflict with meeting times for the Caucus of Black Sociologists.

Theory(ies) and Method(s)

CHAPTER ONE

The Heritage and Future of Sociology in North America

JANET L. ABU-LUGHOD

Part 1: Theory(ies)/Method(s)

A century ago, North America was experiencing its fourth wave of settlers and intellectual ideas,[1] drawn across the currents of the Atlantic and deposited on a shore that, while rapidly Europeanizing in cultural roots, was ripe to generate a different synthesis—one born out of a different soil, a different history, and a different mix of peoples and institutional arrangements. And just about a hundred years ago, the first departments of sociology were being established on the North American continent, drawing upon the legacy of nineteenth-century Western European (chiefly German and French) social thinkers.[2] This implanting of sociology in the New World was intensified by highly selective "reverse migrations," as American scholars made pilgrimages abroad to seek out more advanced training, especially in Germany.

The transmission of social thought from Europe, however, went through a highly selective screening in early American sociology. The writings of Comte, Darwin, Durkheim, Simmel, Spencer, Tönnies, and eventually Weber gradually came to constitute the canons of sociological theory, whereas other European thinkers who addressed similar issues of social organization and transformation were overlooked. Thus, Karl Marx's detailed analysis of the objective workings of the capitalist system was conspicuously absent during those early days when sociology was being "codified" in the United States. In the more than a thousand pages of *Introduction to the Science of Sociology* (1921)[3] jointly assembled by Robert Park and Ernest Burgess as the first American textbook/readings in sociology, there were only a few oblique references to the work of Marx, all of them en passant or merely bibliographic.[4] It was not until after World War II that Marxist analysis and ideas from the Frankfurt school began to infuse the subfield of political economy, adding a structural appreciation of the operation of capitalism and its unique culture to the insights of historically minded and globally oriented thinkers.

Today, the field of sociology, as it is conventionally taught in North American universities, still bears the heavy imprint of its early European heritage, although more so in a subfield called "theory" than in many other areas of substance and practice. Max Weber, Émile Durkheim, Georg Simmel, and, to a lesser, later, and more variable extent, Karl Marx, now have their canonical (iconic) place in all graduate programs in sociology. However, their works are usually taught in the form of explication de texte, rather than as "tools" and "exemplars"; they are seldom critiqued as visions limited by their embeddedness in faulty data, historical specificity, and particular ideology.

The hidden (and not so hidden) subject of their inquiries, from which they drew their most trenchant conclusions, was of course the transformation of a specifically Western European society from its relatively unique feudal agrarian origins (Anderson 1974) into an industrializing set of countries occupying hegemonic/imperial positions in the world. However, there has been some tendency to suppress this historical specificity when their still-important concepts are applied, often uncritically, to the societies of the American continent, and insufficient attention has been paid to later "real world" developments that their theories could only hope to have foreshadowed.

This book begins with a question: If the transition from feudalism to modern capitalism was never, or no longer is, a central issue in North America,[5] in what new ways can old theories still be used? Chapter 2 by Randall Collins and chapter 3 by Gideon Sjoberg explore, albeit in different ways, the usefulness of old (and new) theories to illuminate the large-scale shifts now occurring in contemporary North American societies. They conclude that the institutions and practices of capitalism, bureaucracy, corporate power, and the state, whose nascent developments were first identified in Western and Central Europe by Marx and Weber, among others, have over time become even more pronounced and oppressive in their manifestations. Both suggest that these increases in scale and markedly greater concentrations of power make it more imperative to contain their abuses.

In chapter 2 Randall Collins asks point-blank whether any of the classic theoretical concepts of sociology, so deeply rooted in the specific social conditions of Western Europe between 1840 and 1930, can still apply to the world of 1990–2050. His answer is a qualified yes, with the caveat that although the nascent phenomena first dissected by nineteenth-century European theorists are still with us, their institutional forms have transmuted in Western societies well beyond their origins to become even more complex and gigantic in scale. Furthermore, many of them now appear to be spreading throughout the rest of the world. Collins singles out four classic "lines of sociological theory" that command continued attention: capitalism, bureaucratization, mass mobilization, and state power. He notes with approval that "the sociological tradition of studying economics as embedded in and mutually interacting with political and cultural structures ... has always ... focused on the right questions,"[6] even though the exact manner in which these forces now interact requires further exploration. His chapter thus sets an agenda not only for this book but for sociology in the next century.

However, his essay, similar to earlier macrosociological theories, focuses primarily on the activities of dominating institutions. Other chapters in part 1 recast this view by exploring these changes from the perspectives and practices of both institutional agents and the recipients of their power. For example, Gideon Sjoberg and Dorothy E. Smith take Collins's agenda to a more contextual level by examining the mechanisms through which bureaucracies in the private economy and the public sphere operate to control the levers of power (what Smith calls "relations of ruling") and by tracing how these institutions interact with their "clients" and even "victims."

Implicit in their chapters is a common concern for those affected by the vast powers now concentrated in state institutions and capitalist firms. Eschewing "value-free" or at least perspective-neutral social science, both make a plea for a "new" sociology that empowers citizens through sociology's capacity to lay bare "how the system works." Both assume an inevitable connection between ends and means and, at least implicitly, defend the responsibility of social scientists to use their knowledge to bring about a more humane society. In this, Sjoberg and Smith demonstrate continuity with at least a part of sociology's heritage. From its beginnings, regardless of the varied sources of its legacy, North American sociology assumed that the purpose of theoretical understanding was to guide social reformation and to achieve "the good society."[7] Gradually, this "mission" came to be lost in a forest of empirical research, although it was to be emphasized again by Robert Lynd (1939) and C. Wright Mills (1956). Our volume attempts to recapture this concern.

In chapter 3 Gideon Sjoberg picks up two of the themes laid out in Collins's masterly overview of theory, selecting the issues of power and bureaucracy as central to the sociological endeavor. But he takes a somewhat more critical stance than Collins when he emphasizes the responsibility of sociologists not only to make their value commitments more explicit (answering Robert Lynd's seminal question, "Knowledge *for* what?" [1939]) but to set selective priorities concerning "Knowledge *about* what?" Acknowledging the vastly expanded power that the complex, bureaucratically organized institutions of state and economy, with their own dynamics and pathologies, have over our lives, he makes an ardent plea for sociologists to study these leviathans in order to bring them under greater democratic control and to make them more responsible to society. But he also hints at a theme that will become central to part 2 of this book, which examines the tendency for these forces to escape from the borders of the regulating nation-state to transnational zones beyond democratic control. Sjoberg also demonstrates, in his discussion of certain universal processes and potential pathologies of bureaucracy (such as hierarchy, blameability, secrecy, and the inverse relationship between power and responsibility), that the very "human" agents who are expected to execute the "will" of large-scale organizations do so according to some fairly universal, if perverse, principles of social behavior.

This theme becomes central to chapter 4 by Dorothy E. Smith. Her methodological contribution to a new type of ethnography goes well beyond the feminist lens that first alerted her to the interactional ground between large-scale organizations and their "agents" and "clients." Smith takes one of the legacies from early American sociological theory and shapes it to her new agenda. Her approach derives quite naturally from one strain of North America's sociological heritage: philosophical pragmatism. At the turn of the nineteenth century, New World philosophers such as William James (see [1906–7] 1945, [1909] 1975), Charles Peirce (see especially Hoopes 1991), John Dewey (e.g., 1910, 1939), and later George Herbert Mead (especially 1932) were creating perhaps the only truly indigenous American contribution to social thought. They came to question traditional positivist truisms and the transparency of "truth," and they explored the role that signs and language played in "creating" a commonly agreed upon *process* of knowing.[8]

Although Max Weber had paid lip service to *verstehen* as a method of penetrating the *meaning to the participant* of his or her social acts (see, e.g., Weber [1921–22] 1969), and Georg Simmel (1955) had laid out the basic metaphorical formula for investigating the embeddedness of social actors within a defining context of social networks, both insights were slow in becoming operationalized in sociological research. From the beginning, sociology distinguished between *objective* categories/ processual events and the *meanings* of such categories and occurrences to participants. While such questions of meaning and methods of observation and interpretation in the "social construction of reality" remain crucial, too few methodological breakthroughs and refinements have been achieved. Ethnomethodology, the logical outcome of concerns about the interpretations of "scientific" observers, would not be developed as an explicit method until the post–World War II period, despite W. I. Thomas's early acknowledgment that social actors' "definitions of the situation" (whether "true" or not) were very real in their consequences.[9]

It has been Dorothy E. Smith's contribution to explicate the ways in which contradictory but mutually affecting definitions held by bureaucrats and their clients often set in motion practices whose consequences may not be intended by either. In chapter 4 Smith places ethnographic methods at the core of sociology, but those close observations that all too often fail to yield insights into macroprocesses become, in her hands, a method for "unpacking" the larger social system. Although she first developed this method to explore how perceptions, definitions, concepts, and interactional patterns in contemporary North American society shape the fate of women—especially those with little power (and this continues to be her prime research preoccupation)—her method offers a powerful resolution to the twin methodological dilemmas that have been with sociology since its early years: namely, how to overcome the split between the "macro/objective" approach to institutions and the "micro/social psychological" interpretive approach to individual or small group behavior. Her method allows her to explore the complex processes through which these two levels intersect. But note how values enter into her research agenda: the purpose of a social science *mapping* of the everyday/everynight world in which most of us live in relation to powerful bureaucracies and institutions is to explain *how* the system works. Understanding, however, is prelude to reform, as in the great tradition of sociology from the time of Comte.

Smith's methods, among others in qualitative sociology, do have the capacity to unmask systematic interactional connections between individuals and their societal institutions. However, the detailed descriptive mapping of specific institutional arrangements often makes it difficult to generalize. (At the minimum, Canadian and U.S. institutions operate somewhat differently and on different subsets of clients with varying social distance from administrators.) For more nomothetic goals, sociologists have tended to place their faith in advancements in quantitative methods.

From its European beginnings, sociology's object of study was contested: Was its focus to be on common forms of sociation or on the composition, structure, and transformation of "society," understood as specific social formations differing and changing in time and space? To put it baldly, was sociology's mandate to search for universals of human social behavior, or was it to provide contextual diagnoses of its specific manifestations in time and place? We suggest that this has always been a false dichotomy. Nevertheless, this controversy persists and is linked to a second unresolved dilemma over the issue of "generalizations" in the social sciences, a dilemma that forges an inevitable connection between theory(ies) and method(s). Contrary to the usual distinction in sociological training, which tends to separate courses on theories from those on methods, the first section of this book argues implicitly against such a division. Sjoberg, Smith, and, in a somewhat different manner Levine and Wellman, all demonstrate the close connection between theoretical assumptions and methods.

Despite significant advances in historical and comparative analyses (discussed more fully by Arrighi in this volume), from its start American sociology also built strongly on the quantitative approaches initially developed in Europe, chiefly in French and British social surveys; this subfield is perhaps the most widely acknowledged contribution of North America to sociology.[10] Today, the existence of a wide variety of computer programs and of powerful computing facilities at universities, coupled with data from large-scale surveys (some of them periodically repeated on the same "panel"), as well as the availability of detailed census information both for small census areas and for individuals (through the Public Use Microdata Sample) have made it easier and easier to manipulate extremely large data sets in highly sophisticated ways. Although some of these quantitative studies have been criticized as mindless or at least atheoretical, many have yielded not only valuable descriptive precision but have been able to test specific alternative hypothesized propositions.[11]

A century of methodological progress has thus yielded ever more precise quantitative indicators and has refined ever more robust statistical techniques for exploring relationships among them and the dynamics of their change. But there may be a supreme irony in this progress. Many of the theories and conclusions of early "objective" sociology were based upon extremely fragmentary data, often ingeniously derived from nonsociological sources, and upon primitive methods of measurement and analysis. In contrast, we now have access to an almost unlimited supply of data and to powerful techniques for manipulating them. However, this inflation of data and refined statistical robustness comes just at the moment when we are losing confidence in our ability to *select* "scientifically" the most appropriate measures to answer specific questions and when our confidence that these categories and measures have stable and transparent meanings is being undermined not only by legitimate deconstructionist critiques but by real changes in the world. (And, as the chapters on race and ethnicity in part 3 of this book reveal, the categories are neither stable nor transparent.)

In general, the earlier gap between practitioners of participant observation and ethnographic methods, on the one hand, and specialists in quantitative/numerical analysis, on the other hand, has widened— yielding what Joel Levine, borrowing terminology from C. P. Snow ([1958] 1993), refers to as sociology's "two cultures." However, we should note that the recent critiques of sociology's positivist epistemologies, now coming relentlessly from the arenas of philosophy and cultural studies/literary criticism (usually subsumed under the gloss "postmodernism") are scarcely new. They have been with sociology almost from the start of the discipline. However, the proposed substitute methodologies (hermeneutics, deconstruction of texts[12] of *all* types [the world itself as "only" a text], and the so-called science of semiotics) have few rigorous methodologies that achieve a validity level as high as that claimed for positivist manipulations.

Thus, if Smith's essay grapples methodologically with the connections between macro and micro via her concept of the role that institutional texts play in explicating "relations of ruling," Joel Levine's contribution attempts to bridge the split between methods and theories. In chapter 5, Levine mounts a strong defense of mathematical modeling, arguing that judiciously employed quantitative methods are not merely parsimonious techniques for description or ways to test theories, but—and this is his most provocative statement—*are themselves theories*. According to Levine (in this volume), the current shifts from the verbal to the mathematical domains of theory "are being driven by two things: serious advances in what are called 'mathematical models' but [which] should [really] be called 'theory,' and the rapid decrease in the cost of data describing individuals and events." In his illustrations he demonstrates how intelligent mapping and modeling offer ways out of mindless numeracy. And he suggests a new approach to resolving the old nineteenth-century German debate on "scientism"

JANET L. ABU-LUGHOD

between nomothetic and idiographic approaches.[13] Levine distinguishes among three *different* strategies in mathematical modeling: the statistical, the deductive, and the inductive.

Although much of his chapter is devoted to demonstrating *how* models *are* theories, he also turns his attention to the opportunities that social scientists now have to make a real difference in the world because of new accessibility of incredibly large databases and of the enhanced computer power to mine them for significant knowledge. His chapter ends with a forceful plea that echoes themes first raised by Sjoberg: Knowledge about what (who runs the real world and how) and for what purpose (to make a difference).

One of the more promising inductive mathematical models singled out by Levine is network analysis, a field to which he has made significant contributions (see, e.g., Levine 1972). This theoretically rich and methodologically sophisticated statistical technique offers a way to pay systematic attention to the social embeddedness of individuals, thus operationalizing what in Georg Simmel's brilliant essay "The Web of Group Affiliations" remained only at the level of metaphor. Over the years, Barry Wellman, another pioneer in this field, has been mapping the social circles of residents of greater Toronto. His analysis of variations in the size, density, and range of social networks of subgroups with different social characteristics has allowed him to move beyond the specificities provided through the ethnographic study of bounded social groupings to generalizations that, when placed within a larger context of historical and comparative cases, do more than describe.

In chapter 6, Wellman not only summarizes some of his most important findings but raises new questions about social relations in the postmodern era (the new information age): namely, the potential effects of increases in the scale or extent of networks and the increasing fungibility of space on possibilities for social action and civic responsibility. Thus, by implication if not direct attention, he suggests the ways in which macrochanges in the globalizing world may be having unforeseen repercussions on the nature of social life and on motivations and capacities for economic and political action.

Quite unintentionally, prior frictions of space constituted significant barriers to complete social and political segregation, creating enforced but, of course, not conflict-free public arenas of interaction and struggle. Given the enhanced capacity today for more powerful groups to disassociate themselves from the common spaces of local politics within which such struggles were carried out, what will be the fate of the excluded and powerless? Wellman posits that the heightened possibilities for "choice" facilitated by the revolution in communications have ironically narrowed the public sphere in which spatially proximate but socially diverse citizens are forced to debate or struggle over issues. Rather, he suggests that, at least among his subjects in Toronto, there has been a retreat into privacy—into a social life based upon family, work, and interest affinities—that truncates involvement with larger issues. While these networks provide a certain amount of social support not anticipated by the earlier theorists of "urbanism as a way of life," they do not augur particularly well for diversity and democratic debate in the public arena. His conclusion is that many advances in communication technologies that *could have* expanded social participation in the public sphere have ironically facilitated a withdrawal from heterogeneous public space into private, highly encapsulated domestic space.[14]

But network theory and analysis also have potential for application to quite different sociological inquiries and have already begun to be employed to map the interconnections among collective units at scales well above the individual actors interviewed by Wellman (see, e.g., Blau and Schwartz 1984). Thus, the method is promising for mapping the interlocking directorates among national and transnational firms,[15] mapping core, semiperipheral, and peripheral positions of countries in the world system (Snyder and Kick 1979; Smith and White 1992), tracing commodity chains in international production and trade (Gereffi and Korzeniewicz 1990), and for explicating the mechanisms whereby cultural artifacts are disseminated via key distributional networks (see, e.g., the suggestions in Sklair 1991).

This brings us to part 2 of the volume, which looks more closely at such macrophenomena. However, whereas mathematical models may illuminate many particulars as well as lead to generalizations, a return to more verbal approaches is required to grasp the historical patterns of contemporary North American societies and their place in the world's evolving "network" of institutional actors.

Part 2: Appropriate Units of Analysis: The New Realities of Scale

The wider integration of the world (so-called globalization and transnationalization) has in recent decades significantly altered the older assumed relationships between states, firms, markets, and citizens. It is now a truism that economic networks of powerful transnational corporations have reduced the capacity of national political entities to regulate the behavior of these firms and to ensure their accountability. Furthermore, the relationship between the United States and Canada and the rest of the world system has been changing rapidly, as Western economies, including those of North America, have been undergoing basic restructuring in the international division of labor. In addition, transnational financial transactions have become so rapid and ephemeral that they can no longer be traced, much less regulated.

The last quarter of the twentieth century has witnessed changes in the world that are certainly as profound as those that constituted the focus of comparative historical studies during the late nineteenth century. Because of this, many of the assumed categories and units of analysis that had hitherto been powerful organizers of sociological analysis are in flux—fragmenting and recombining in ways that require rethinking of older concepts and approaches. The insulation of New World settlements from internationally generated flows of capital and labor was always overstated in sociology, although perhaps less so in Canada than in the United States.[16] Despite the continental origin of most of its "theory," the actual practice in North American sociology tended to focus on New World exceptionalism, with little recognition of the embeddedness of its history within a changing world system. Isolationism and a confidence in the New World's special privilege encouraged Americans to ignore the rest of the world, except insofar as that larger system created inconveniences (wars) or served as a source for cheap labor (immigrants). This insularity can no longer be defended intellectually.

In chapter 7 Giovanni Arrighi argues that conventional approaches of comparative historical analysis, which generally take "nation-states" as their prime unit of inquiry, are less and less suited to studying a globalizing world. Indeed, taking his cues from world-system theory, he contends, in agreement with the theory's originator and major proponent, Immanuel Wallerstein (see, e.g., 1974), that for some five hundred years at least and for all practical purposes, there has been only one legitimate unit of analysis—the world-system itself.[17] He thus questions whether the process of globalization is as new as many claim. However, he does suggest that its hierarchical arrangements have been undergoing deep transformations in the late twentieth century and argues that the study of the evolving world system must therefore be high on the agenda for the next century.

Some of the primary ways that change is taking place are those that reduce the autonomy of territorially bounded states and enhance the transnational powers of markets and firms in shaping and structuring economies and social life. This brings us back to a dilemma raised by Gideon Sjoberg in chapter 3: namely, how regulation and accountability can be achieved on a world scale when supranational bodies are weak or nonexistent and when they are increasingly not subject to democratic control. Can a "higher" moral ground be found?

Globalization, however, has often become a glossed oversimplification in contemporary sociological writings. While it is perhaps obvious that power, markets, and cultural artifacts are now increasingly "escaping" from the confines of given territorial units (to wit, those that make up the "state system" that was solidified in the nineteenth century and supplemented in the twentieth century by decolonization), this does not create a uniformly open or fungible arena. This paradox is the focus of chapter 8 by Saskia Sassen.

In her essay on the relationship between globalization and the twinned processes of deterritorialization and reterritorialization, Sassen uses the term "cracked casings"—a metaphor that to some extent can apply to all the topics in this book. Rejecting the simple diagnosis of the decline of the state and territoriality under the impact of an increasingly entailed global economy, she examines the far more complicated processes whereby states continue to play important roles in the international system and where corporations are not mere disembodied institutions, freed from spatial constraints, but have their own territorializing imperatives. However, she, too, emphasizes the lack of congruity between the scales of financial circulation and the scales of regulating institutions. Therefore, of the twin processes driving globalization—the movements of capital and labor—the former often evades state regulation and by its mobility contributes to the destabilization of national economies, whereas the latter poses real challenges to the integration of diverse populations within given nations (a topic addressed in part 3 of this book).

Harriet Friedmann has a somewhat different take on the subject of increasing scale and the ways it needs to be understood as influencing both sociology and social movements. In chapter 9 she identifies two serious lacunae in earlier sociology. The first was sociology's tendency to ignore, or at least consign to a separate "social" realm, all considerations of women and children as irrelevant to the politics and economy of the world, making the image of political economy a strangely truncated one. The second was sociology's tendency to separate humans from their "environment,"[18] an increasingly perilous separation, given the widespread and even global impacts of environmental changes.

Hers is a plea that we (by which she means all living entities and not just humans) now live in a single world environment. If we are not to destroy our common nest, we must learn to value it and to tend it responsibly. Among her values is a respect for diversity. (This plea constitutes a natural bridge to part 3 of the book, which explores the impact of the increased diversity of the populations inhabiting Canada and the United States, a diversity that is, in part at least, a result of the increased globalization of social life.)

The paradoxical need for global regulation under a system of ostensibly autonomous (but actually codependent) states raises issues concerning the role that social movements can play in bringing about change. Political efficacy had been one of the pillar assumptions of North American studies of society, and yet, never before has "self-determination" been so obvious a chimera. There is a growing disjunction between the scales at which political action can take place and the scales at which economic and social determinants operate. The world of local politics, civil society, and voluntary associations, idealized by Tocqueville and internalized in the complimentary self-images of North Americans, has been deeply undermined by the peripatetic nature of gigantic, transnational firms, by the unfettered flow of finance capital, and by a growing incommensurability between the powers of capital and labor, between "home" and "abroad."

Some of the pessimism that such a conclusion might engender, however, is mitigated by the recognition that social movements can be effective at various levels of scale: from globally organized Greens that operate in national politics, down to neighborhoods that block the siting of a garbage incinerator. Social movements may need to be mounted on a global level to address the interdependencies of countries and environments, but this need does not vitiate the value of social movements at much lower levels of scale: intranationally for more particularistic identities (e.g., the Civil Rights movement in the United States, the Quebec Independence movement in Canada), and even more locally. There is a need in sociology, therefore, to reconceptualize "new social movements," which, in the rebellious 1960s, appeared to constitute a fairly well defined field.

Chapter 10 by Pierre Hamel, Henri Lustiger-Thaler, and Louis Maheu looks at changes in the study of social movements required by recent developments. Theirs is an optimistic approach, suggesting that, despite the increase in globalization, the value of more local and particularistic social movements has certainly not vanished. First, they draw our attention to significant changes that have recently occurred within the United States and Canada that have made government policies more responsive to groups mobilizing around issues of inclusiveness. Referring to Ulrich Beck's conceptualization of a "new political culture," they stress that top-down decision making has been displaced by an administrative apparatus more receptive to engaging in "communicative" interaction with groups of citizens over decisions that will affect them. They point to the positive effects that involvement in social movements can have for experiential learning in civil society, and they stress that even when "miniature" social movements cannot directly achieve large political ends, participation enhances identities and builds solidarities in civil society.

Certainly, such solidarities are now being built around the issues of gender, race, and ethnicity. Even though one of the goals of an "old social movement" (the solidarity of the working class or proletariat) seems a long way away—in part because of persisting and newer fractures in social structures along lines of race, ethnicity, and gender—this is not to be mourned. Thus, even as markets are partially unified, albeit without global institutional accountability, nation-states are fragmented by those same global forces that have been moving populations with various cultural claims both within and between countries. These population movements are exacerbating preexisting cleavages within the United States and Canada and are generating new social movements and legal and social responses to proliferating racial and ethnic claims. It may be that, whereas some social movements of the 1960s have been pacified by their co-optation into the governmental apparatus,[19] other social movements have taken their place: both beyond the level of the nation-state, reaching into the global arena of ecology (see Friedmann for a strong argument of the need for this kind of movement), and within the nation-state, as identity politics associated with increased racial and ethnic diversity replaces more ostensibly ideological or class-based movements.

Part 3: The New Realities of Race/Ethnicity

Despite premature rumors of the decline of the state as a result of increased globalization, nation-states have certainly not lost their significance. Nation-states remain centrally connected to international or global forces not only because they are the chief actors in international political (and military) organizations, but because each state ultimately controls the movement of "others" into its territory. National laws determine who shall be allowed to enter and who shall be eligible for citizenship. Furthermore, national laws define and differentiate among subnational ethnic and racial categories that have increasingly come to be linked to special claims. Despite suggestions that cultural homogenization or syncretism will result from the generation of a "global culture," persisting heterogeneities are being internalized and even solidified within the territories of given states.

During the present era, both the United States and Canada have become the recipients of large numbers of immigrants, especially from noncognate cultural areas. But the two countries contrast sharply in their responses to this demographic diversification. This is what makes a comparison between Canada and the United States—societies assumed to be so similar in many other respects—an optic that refracts their deep differences and makes more visible the historically and culturally contingent nature of ethnic and racial categories. How the two countries are adapting to these new forms of diversity is deeply conditioned by historically specific social formations within them, social formations that evolved from very different origins and through nation-specific political institutions. This is where comparative historical analysis retains enormous strength, restoring significance to the national unit, despite the acknowledged reduced importance of the nation-state in other areas.

In chapter 11, Gilles Bourque and Jules Duchastel present a fascinating account of the evolution of multiculturalism in Canada, which originally approximated a neat tripartite division distinguished by law: the indigenous peoples (now called First Nations), the French Catholic settlers whose first arrival long predated the French Revolution, and the British Protestant settlers whose political hegemony followed from imperial rule. (Agrarian slavery, which played so formative a role in regionalism and racism within the United States and which has left so deep an imprint on an otherwise much transformed post–Civil War society, was absent from Canada, whose climate was unsuited to a plantation economy.) Of the three, the aboriginal populations, as in the United States, were simply marginalized, leaving a yet unresolved issue of incorporation.

In Canada, the settler groups that "counted" (recognized as coequal "founding peoples") were split along a cultural, rather than racial, divide: country of origin (France or Britain), language (French or English), and religion (Catholic or Protestant), and these cleavages were intensified by their differential regional distribution. The Constitution of 1867 that established the Canadian confederation was "a conservative compromise between the elites of the British colonies" who had been unable to resolve "the problem of a stable coexistence" between the French and English settlers. French Canadians have based their resistance to "assimilation" into the dominating Anglo-Saxon culture on their prior and equal claim to Canadian identity. In Canada, separatist movements, radical and unyielding de facto spatial fragmentation, bilingualism, and identity politics are now parts of the changing reality for which earlier models give poor guidance. Secession remains an object of contention and a perplexing possibility.

Today, however, Canada has become host to a large immigrant population of highly diverse origins (including "racial" minorities) and is struggling to devise a new institutional modus vivendi to cope with the potential fragmentation. Bourque and Duchastel trace the sequence of political and judicial solutions that have been put forth in parliamentary debates in Canada as that society has attempted to enlarge the identity rights of the three original communities and to extend certain linguistic and cultural rights to an open-ended set of other "minorities." And yet, as national and language groups have multiplied with the heightened "new" immigration, multicultural reality tries to find its resolution within the context of the bimodal cleavage of Canada's established European "nationalities."

The comparable bimodal cleavage within the United States, interestingly enough legally (and only partially) "resolved" in the same decade of the nineteenth century but in a quite different fashion by the Emancipation Proclamation and the Fourteenth Amendment, was along caste lines of race and conditions of previous servitude, which were also differentially inscribed on regional territories.[20] It turned on a distinction between "white" and "nonwhite," both concepts proving more ambiguous in reality and in law than the uses to which the distinction was put.

The creation of a social category called "white" has not been unproblematic. Given the enormous diversity of the Europeans who populated the United States, the bipolar "cultural" categories of the Canadian system were not an option in the United States; a different process of integration was the model. Although, as Roger Waldinger and Joel Perlmann point out in chapter 14, the Irish, the Jews, and the Italians may have been referred to as "races" during the nineteenth century, in the crucial "dichotomous sort" of persons into "white" or "nonwhite," they were eventually absorbed into the former category (see, e.g., Ignatiev 1995).[21] The assimilation theories of U.S. sociology presumed the coherence of a (white Protestant) cultural core that newcomers might modify but would not fundamentally challenge or break apart.

In this framework, nonwhites posed an anomaly, since the legacy of slavery and the resistance to assimilation meant that the cleavage was perpetuated and haunted by its origin in chattel slavery, exclusion from citizenship (and even full "humanity"), and, once these disabilities were legally removed by the Fourteenth Amendment, by gross and obdurate economic and political inequalities. The persistence of these inequalities, the legal and informal mechanisms whereby they have been perpetuated, and the functions white domination has served to preserve "white" superiority are the themes forcefully developed in Joe R. Feagin's chapter 12.[22]

Feagin focuses on the deep historic contradictions between a basically racist "white society" in the United States and a population that today is shifting toward a "nonwhite" majority. In line with earlier debates in the U.S. sociology of race, Feagin singles out the white-black line as crucial and assumes that the group on the most disadvantaged side of the line will remain those whose skin color is marked by the "badge of slavery" in earlier U.S. history. Instead, however, of concentrating on the shifting definitions of who is or is not a member of a minority group, he focuses on the mechanisms that have been used to maintain white dominance in the face of changing demographics. Indeed, one could hypothesize that what appear to have been "irrational" shifts in defining the racial identities of subordinate groups might be explained by strategies employed by the dominant group to enhance its power. The coming nonwhite majority in the United States poses for Feagin the basic dilemma of American pluralism. The anxieties of "white America" over the prospect of losing dominance by becoming a demographic minority may appear to parallel the anxieties of Anglo-Saxon Canada over the possible secession of Quebec or even the Maritime Provinces, but resolution must follow a different trajectory. Feagin calls for a making good on the promises of U.S. democracy by extending rights more universally and coming to terms with a truly multiracial and multicultural society.

In chapter 13, Tomás Almaguer and Moon-Kie Jung begin, as does Feagin, with the primary bimodal distinction between "whites" and "nonwhites," demonstrating how, over time, this was the presumed but contested template according to which U.S. law sought to incorporate (or more accurately, exclude) "others" in a social, economic, and political system of white domination. But the authors shift the focus of discussion from Feagin's treatment of the "powerful effects of the 'color line' to the 'color line' itself," with a highly nuanced and specific history of its origins and evolution. Beginning with the assumption that race is "fundamentally a sociohistoric construct," they trace the tortuous route in U.S. legislation and court decisions that classified and reclassified people by race, even in the face of mixture, diversity in origins, and a bewildered rejection of these definitions by, at the minimum, members of the third quasi racial-ethnic category, Latinos.

In the process, Almaguer and Jung contribute to a fundamental re-conceptualization of race and ethnicity, as these had been conceived in nineteenth-century continental and early twentieth-century North American theories. Sociology is now forced to "rethink" all forms of identity and the interactions among such a priori categories as race, class, gender, age, immigration status. These variables have generated increasingly overlapping and unclear unbounded "units," dependent upon socially generated or internalized meanings, and have required subanalyses in place of the master and privileged general categories of race and ethnicity. Also wide open is the question of possible future assimilation into a multicultural society.[23] If European immigrants were eventually "sorted into" the category of white, the sorting of others has been more problematic, especially as the "new" immigration that began after 1965 has brought populations to the United States from a variety of sending countries that do not "fit into" the dichotomies on which the system was based.

As Almaguer and Jung so clearly establish, the "one drop of blood" that presumably distinguished "white" from "black" shifted in practice, if not law, over the years. The slippage between genotype and phenotype was always there, as were shifts in the racial definitions of "Latinos" (i.e., Mexicans) after the areas of their original residence in the American West and Southwest were conquered from Mexico in the middle of the nineteenth century. They demonstrate how the racial categorization of Mexicans and their status as residents, guest workers, and "immigrants" shifted with political fortunes and economic demands. Their essay also explores how Asians, originally excluded by law from citizenship, although imported for their labor power, were gradually admitted to legal status and then to greater social equality.

There are two major challenges to the white/nonwhite sorting by "race." One has been the greater acceptance of persons of Asian origin and their elision toward the category of "white." The second has been the rapid growth (and concentration in only a limited number of major cities in a limited number of states) of the multiracial "ethnic" category of Hispanics (or Latinos, as they prefer to be called). A Census Bureau report released in the summer of 1998 indicated that, by 1997, close to 30 million U.S. residents (11 percent of the population) were classified as Hispanic, almost as many as were classified black.[24] Almaguer and Jung explain why Latinos have resisted U.S. racial classification, a resistance that may finally undermine the bimodal cleavage, despite attempts to redefine the race boundary between "whites" and "people of color." Clearly, the impact of these indeterminacies varies by region and city, and the future "fate" of immigrants from the Caribbean and especially from Mexico and their children remains to be studied.

Chapter 14 by Roger Waldinger and Joel Perlmann in some ways reinforces the argument of Feagin while expanding the purview to minority immigrants both in earlier times and today. They pose an important question about the capacity of American society to absorb immigrants from culturally different zones of the world, both in the nineteenth century and in the present. They begin by acknowledging that in the mid–nineteenth century Catholic Irish immigrants were viewed as a threat to "assimilation" and to the persistence of a U.S. culture in which white Protestants were the defining element, and that toward the turn of the century, Jews from Eastern Europe and Italians from Southern Europe were viewed with equal alarm. Even though those groups were all initially defined as "races," they were eventually assimilated and redefined as "white."

Waldinger and Perlmann compare the fates of these earlier groups with the prospects of the "new immigrants" who, in the aftermath of the Hart Celler Act of 1965, have introduced additional diversity into the racial and cultural stock of the nation. They demonstrate that the earlier fears of societal fission proved ungrounded in the long run, as U.S. culture absorbed and integrated the European immigrants of the late nineteenth and early twentieth century—if not in the first generation, then in the second and third, albeit with different trajectories of social acceptance and mobility. However, they are less sanguine about the ease with which the newest immigrants, especially those from Mexico and the Caribbean, can be absorbed, given structural changes in the global system and a restructured U.S. economy that no longer demands the unskilled brute labor that served as the starting point for earlier uneducated immigrants. In this restructured economy, opportunities are open primarily to those with high levels of education—characteristics the Mexican immigrants especially lack. One might add to this Feagin's sensitivity to the persistence of discrimination on the basis of skin color, which differentially affects the life chances of darker versus lighter Latinos.[25] The fates of their descendants are not necessarily predictable from the experience of either earlier immigrant waves or native African Americans.

Summing Up the New Agenda

It is our ardent hope that the new directions for sociological theory, methods, and substantive analysis laid out in the chapters of this book will constitute not so much answers to the questions raised, but guidelines to fruitful directions for sociology as we enter the next millennium. Sociology's second century, in that context, remains fraught with challenges, but offers new possibilities for understanding a changing world.

Notes

1. One of the outcomes of the North American Regional Conference was a deep recognition of how societies so close, and yet so different in many ways as the United States and Canada, come, quite naturally, to somewhat different preoccupations. Nowhere was this so evident as in our discussions of race and ethnicity. I believe that such recognitions were "part of the plot" when the ISA president Immanuel Wallerstein decided to stimulate the regional meetings.

2. Nor was the "New World" the only soil to which such ideas diffused; the influence of Durkheimian thought on Turkey, for example, or of political constitutionalism on the North African region suggests multiple paths through which European thought entered other quite different societies.

3. Called the "Green Bible" after the color of its cover.

4. Marx's name appears only seven times. The references are as follows, in their entirety: "Upon this point at least a Marxian simplification is nearer the truth than that of Jung" (77); "The orthodox Socialist appeals in unquestioning faith to the ponderous tomes of Marx" (343); "Karl Marx, accepting [sic] Ricardian economics, emphasized the misery and destitution resulting from the competitive process, and demanded the abolition of competition and the substitution therefor of the absolute control of a socialist [sic] state" (562); bibliographic entries for the "Manifesto of the Communist Party" (566) and chap. 15 of *Capital* (568); a passing reference to the fact that "a surprisingly large number [of the Wobblies] can quote extensively from Buckle's *History of Civilization* and from the writings of Marx" (912); and where Marx's name appears in the subtitle of a bibliographic entry to Moritz Kaufmann's 1879 book, *Utopias, or Schemes of Social Improvement: From Sir Thomas More to Karl Marx* (1,008). It should be remembered, however, that the Red Scare was sweeping over the United States in the wake of the October Revolution, which makes the neglect of Marx significant politically as well as intellectually.

5. Whereas feudalism was never the issue in the "open frontier" of North America, the institution of plantation slavery in the U.S. South was, even though the "transition-to-modernity" sociological literature paid scant attention to this. The "transition" from rural plantation slavery to capitalist "free labor" in cities has been remarkably undertheorized in U.S. sociology, perhaps because European theories had little to offer on this subject. The persistence of white domination in the United States, however, is inexplicable without a deeper understanding of this central institution (see chaps. by Almaguer and Feagin in this volume).

6. Harriet Friedmann (in this volume), however, points to significant blind spots in nineteenth-century approaches to political economy; namely, their relegation of women

and children to a "private" or "social" sphere considered irrelevant to either economics or politics, which reflected the values of the Victorian age. She suggests that rather than "always asking the right questions," sociology has until fairly recently *ignored* some pretty central ones.

7. Controversial from the start were assumptions about order and change, inexorability vs. agency. Contrast, for example, the blind evolution of Darwin with the social engineering of Comte. It must also be acknowledged that even among those who trusted in the efficacy of agency, the goals of recommended reforms were certainly not uncontested.

8. These philosophers/social scientists were the precursors of present-day literary critics who would naively "rediscover" it, drawing chiefly upon contemporary French theorists and calling themselves "postmodernists," which suggests that European ideas continue to influence American sociology, if only through the back door. But whereas postmodernist theory risks nihilism as a potential outcome, pragmatism, which yields interpretive and hermeneutic sociology, offers rich insights into the way the world works.

9. Perhaps the clearest statement of Thomas's position on the interaction between "objective reality" and "subjective consciousness" is found in the "Methodological Appendix" to W. I. Thomas and Florian Znaniecki's *The Polish Peasant in Europe and America* ([1918–20] 1927), although this has been conveniently reprinted in Janowitz (1966).

10. Quantitative methods also took on more indigenous forms in the New World. From the British social reformers had come the quantitative social survey, along with more ethnographic (anthropological) observational studies of poverty and "deviance." But in the new American context, these studies were at first directed almost exclusively to immigrant communities.

11. An examination of any issue of the *American Sociological Review* will reveal the discipline's strong preoccupation with secondary analysis of large data sets and a preference for regression analysis as a means of hypothesis testing.

12. But note Smith's identification of texts as key mechanisms in what she terms "ruling relations."

13. Following German philosophical practice, Max Weber had distinguished the social sciences from history, coming down squarely on the side of the former but actually practicing the latter, as he routinely used historical specificity in order to "extract" his "scientific" concepts. His avowed preference for nomothetics set back recognition of the importance of historical contexts for the sociology of knowledge and the study of culture-specific institutions. It was left to European-origin thinkers such as Vienna-born Karl Polanyi and Russian-born Pitirim Sorokin to keep alive this fertile and essential approach, an approach that would infuse the work of comparativists and, eventually, world-system scholars.

14. If his conclusions are correct, they may help to explain some of the evisceration in social movements described in chap. 10 by Hamel et al. However, as we shall suggest, the antisystemic movements of the 1960s have been transformed, in the 1990s, to identity politics, an issue raised in part 3 of this volume.

15. Indeed, I first came to admire Joel Levine's creativity when I read his 1972 article that mapped the network terrain of selected large American banks and corporations.

16. The proportion of capital flows from abroad during the nineteenth century that were used to develop Canada, the United States, and parts of Latin America was considerably higher than the international capital flows in today's world economy. Additionally,

because Canada remained politically linked to the British Commonwealth, it could never afford the illusion of isolationism.

17. The five-hundred-year thesis is found in Immanuel Wallerstein's *The Modern World System* (1974–89). But my work (Abu-Lughod 1989) demonstrates the existence of an earlier "world system" in the thirteenth century, and Frank and Gills (1993) argue for five thousand years of continuity.

18. While environmental factors were acknowledged in early conceptualizations of "ecology," especially in the work of Robert Park and the Chicago school, the actual practice focused on *analogies* between environmental and social systems rather than upon the relationship between them.

19. The election of a member of the Green Party to the unified German government is one case in point.

20. The "native" question had been solved by earlier decimation and internal exile, but was to resurface in the Oriental Exclusion laws of the 1880's, where the status of Asian immigrants was equated with that of native Americans who were ineligible for citizenship.

21. As Almaguer and Jung stress, this basic "sort" by race in the initial legal system of the United States had momentous consequences, because until the Fourteenth Amendment, *only whites* were eligible for citizenship, and, up to 1952, immigrants from Asia remained ineligible.

22. In addition to Feagin, I invited four African American sociologists from the United States to attend our North American conference and, if they chose, to contribute an essay on race. None was able to attend; it later turned out that our sessions conflicted with an important meeting of the Caucus of Black Sociologists. The lack of a contribution from these scholars remains a deep disappointment and constitutes a deficiency in this volume.

23. One of the symptoms of this in the United States is the recent debate over what categories the decennial census should employ to capture intersections of race and ethnicity that increasingly defy the earlier simplistic "sorts" into white and nonwhite, later modified to a fourfold division of biological "race," even later subdivided by Hispanic and non-Hispanic. The Census Bureau has had to make some decisions in preparation for the decennial census to be taken in the year 2000 on how to deal with persons of multiple racial and ethnic ancestry. For the time being, it has decided to retain the existing fourfold racial categories (white, black, Asian, and Native American) but to permit respondents to list more than one racial "ancestry"; the Hispanic/non-Hispanic categories remain as before. But the issue of Americans and their identification with racial and ethnic characterizations can be expected to perplex both census takers and social scientists well into the future.

24. Compare this figure with over 32 million who were classified as non-Hispanic black (then constituting 12.8% of the total population). However, the Census Bureau claims that the gap is narrowed when the 925,000 Hispanics who reported their race as black are subtracted from the black total. Of course, the undercount of Hispanics in the 1990 census was estimated at 5%.

25. I was particularly disappointed that our conference group did not include a scholar specializing in the status of Puerto Ricans. While not considered immigrants, Puerto Ricans have had experiences on the U.S. mainland that do not augur well for mobility of second- and third-generation Dominicans, Haitians, and Jamaicans—groups whose assimilation may take place in marginalized African-American inner-city areas.

References

Abu-Lughod, Janet. 1989. *Before European Hegemony*. New York: Oxford University Press.

Anderson, Perry. 1974. *Passages from Antiquity to Feudalism*. London: NLB, 1974.

Blau, Peter M., and Joseph Schwartz. 1984. *Crosscutting Social Circles: Testing a Macrostructural Theory of Intergroup Relations*. Orlando, Fla.: Academic Press.

Dewey, John. 1910. *How We Think*. Boston: D.C. Heath.

————. 1939. *Theory of Valuation*. Chicago: University of Chicago Press.

Frank, Andre Gunder, and Barry Gills, eds. 1993. *The World System: Five Hundred Years or Five Thousand?* London: Routledge.

Gereffi, G., and M. Korzeniewicz. 1990. "Commodity Chains and Footwear Exports in the Semiperiphery." Pp. 45–68 in *Semiperipheral States in the World-Economy*, edited by W. Martin. Westport, Conn.: Greenwood Press.

Hoopes, James, ed. 1991. *Peirce on Signs: Writings on Semiotics*. Chapel Hill: University of North Carolina Press.

Ignatiev, Noel. 1995. *How the Irish Became White*. New York: Routledge.

James, William. (1909) 1975. *The Meaning of Truth*. Cambridge, Mass.: Harvard University Press.

————. (1909) 1945. *Pragmatism: A New Name for Some Old Ways of Thinking*. New York: Longmans, Green.

Janowitz, Morris, ed. 1966. *W. I. Thomas on Social Organization and Social Personality*. Chicago: University of Chicago Press.

Levine, Joel. 1972. "The Spheres of Interest: A Methodological Inquiry into Banking and Industrial Networks." *American Sociological Review* 37 (February): 14–27.

Lynd, Robert S. 1939. *Knowledge for What? The Place of Social Sciences in American Culture*. Princeton, N.J.: Princeton University Press.

Mead, George Herbert. 1932. *The Philosophy of the Present*. Chicago: Open Court Publishing.

Mills, C. Wright. 1956. *The Power Elite*. New York: Oxford University Press.

Park, Robert E., and Ernest Burgess, eds. 1921. *Introduction to the Science of Sociology*. Chicago: University of Chicago Press.

Simmel, Georg. 1955. "The Web of Group Affiliations," translated by Reinhard Bendix. In *Conflict and the Web of Group-Affiliations*. New York: Free Press.

Sklair, L. 1991. *Sociology of the Global System*. Baltimore: Johns Hopkins University Press.

Smith, David A., and D. White. 1992. "Structure and Dynamics of the Global Economy: Network Analysis of International Trade, 1965–1980." *Social Forces* 70: 857–93.

Snow, C. P. (1959) 1993. *The Two Cultures, and A Second Look*. New York: The New American Library.

Snyder, D., and E. Kick. 1979. "Structural Position in the World System and Economic Growth, 1955–1970: A Multiple Network Analysis of Transnational Interaction." *American Journal of Sociology* 84: 1097–1126.

Thomas, William Isaac. 1920. "Social Personality: Organization of Attitudes." In *W. I. Thomas on Social Organization and Social Personality*, edited by Morris Janowitz, 11–36. Chicago: University of Chicago Press, 1966. This is a selection from the "Methodological Appendix." In *The Polish Peasant in Europe and America*, by W. I. Thomas and F. Znaniecki. New York: Alfred Knopf.

Wallerstein, Immanuel. 1974–89. *The Modern World-System*, 3 vols. Orlando, Fla.: Academic Books.

Weber, Max. (1921–22) 1969. "On the Concept of Sociology and the 'Meaning' of Social Conduct." In *Basic Concepts in Sociology by Max Weber*, edited and translated by H. P. Secher, 29–58. New York: Citadel Press, a convenient and clearly translated collection.

CHAPTER TWO

The European Sociological Tradition and Twenty-First-Century World Sociology

RANDALL COLLINS

What relevance do European sociological ideas of the nineteenth and early twentieth century have for the turn of the twenty-first? The leading roster of dead Germans (Marx, Engels, Weber, Simmel) and French (Durkheim and Mauss) is rounded out by Americans like George Herbert Mead, who were educated by sojourning in Europe. When one considers how much North American sociology descends from European refugees such as Coser, Gerth, Bendix, and Schutz, it appears that much of our intellectual tradition right down to Garfinkel and his pupils—or to C. Wright Mills and his radical offspring—is merely an expansion of a narrow community of Western European intellectuals. The purpose of this book might be construed as an effort to blow apart that German-French hegemony and to demonstrate its irrelevance to the world now coming over the horizon. If so, we need to start with the awareness that this is an autocritique, for there is none of us who was not profoundly formed by that tradition.

There are two aspects to the question: a sociology of knowledge or epistemological question, and a substantive question. Let me begin briefly with the former.

The Sociological Question of Knowledge

A tradition of analysis coinciding with the tradition at issue here has examined the ways in which ideas are produced by their social bases. We are playing the role of a latter-day Karl Mannheim (1940) when we ask: If the classic ideas of sociology come from the social conditions of 1840 to 1930, let us say, how can they be adequate to the world of 1990 to 2050? One can construct various answers, ranging from Mannheim's own focus on the organization of the intellectual community, to the various branches of today's sociology of scientific knowledge. While I do not intend here to retrace such well-trod ground, I do want to offer a metacommentary on a few favorite debating points.

In the intellectual world of the 1980s and 1990s, it has been fashionable to talk of disjunctures and to disavow universalism. A polemical contrast has been set up between the alleged imperialism of abstract reason and the liberating recognition of historicity and particularism. I call this a polemic because in the heat of argument the analysis does not go very deep and name-calling takes the place of careful consideration. Polemic turns a question into all-or-nothing. Either the world is completely subsumable into universal principles, or else everything is radically particular and unique. This could become a kind of epistemological nuclear war, in which the goal of one side is to blow the other off the face of the earth. If we can deescalate the argument, it should be apparent that the question is not a stark either/or. We cannot analyze particulars without abstract categories, and even what we think of as a particular name (e.g., "Canada in the nineteenth century") already contains a considerable amount of generalizing. Conversely, we never enter into a chain of argument about bare abstractions without indicating repeatedly, in the series of semiotic moves, examples on a lower level of abstraction of what we are talking about. There is a continuum of abstraction and particularity, and it is difficult to formulate pure endpoints in either direction. Ironically, when we polemicize about a stark contrast between the universal and the particular, we push quite far in the direction of a contrast among bare abstractions; we make an abstraction out of the concept of particularity (or historicity, or contextuality) in the very process of arguing for it.

There is little to be gained by playing in this epistemological labyrinth. I would prefer to treat the question more concretely. Here we have a set of European intellectuals from Marx to Mauss. Our question is how the conditions of European society that supported them could give rise to knowledge with a degree of universalism such that it could be applicable outside that time and place. Instead of treating this as a contest between European intellectuals and a blank space filled in with an unspecified but shining alternative, let us look at some of the non-European intellectual traditions of that time. Elsewhere (Collins 1998) I have provided a sociological analysis of contemporary intellectuals in Japan, China, and India. It is not possible to summarize this material here; suffice it to say that a sharp contrast between Western logocentrism and non-Western traditions of ideas does not hold up beyond the most elementary knowledge of non-European intellectual history. We should not expect to find a magic wand to wave over the twenty-first century by looking for non-European intellectual traditions.

The Expansion of Europe and the
Expanding Relevance of European Sociology

I have not yet made a stronger point: that the European tradition of sociology that comprises our own network of ancestors positively offers the best way to analyze the society coming over the horizon. We need not wash away all thinkers before 1950 and start afresh. In place of this negation, I want to present an argument adopted from Bruno Latour, the most interesting of today's social constructivist sociologists of science.

Latour's book on Louis Pasteur (*Les microbes*, 1984; English translation as *The Pasteurization of France*, 1988) shows how Pasteur constructed a laboratory setting in which he could control the anthrax bacillus that had been responsible for diseased cows. As a social constructivist, Latour does not want to say that Pasteur invented something that could intervene in nature, that could be taken from the theoretical science of the laboratory and then applied in the world. Instead, Latour argues, what Pasteur did was to expand the walls of the laboratory to encompass the farm. The barn became a sterilized laboratory, filled with the same kind of equipment that had formerly been confined to scientific experiments. Cows' milk was no longer what it had been in the state of "nature"; old nature no longer existed but was obliterated in the new practice of the world-encompassing laboratory. One could extend Latour's image to other areas of the scientific/technological transformation of the world. The wires that string from one house to another, going up and down inside our walls to come out at electric sockets, and the pieces of electronic equipment that surround us are not applications of scientific theory so much as they are extensions of equipment that used to be confined to the laboratories of a few scientists. Quite literally, the world that once existed only in the immediate vicinity of certain European scientists has now expanded around the globe. That Western technoscience works, in Polynesia or Brazil, does not have to be treated as an abstract epistemological question; it is an empirical, sensuously material, practical pattern of how far certain networks have expanded.

The analogy I wish to make is this. European sociologists from the era of Marx to Mauss built their sociology by analyzing several key transformations of the socioeconomic order around them. Those transformations have now spread around the world. Their sociology remains relevant, indeed indispensable, because their world is now pretty much everyone's world. I do not mean to suggest that nothing has changed. After all, there is a *significant* difference between a situation in which capitalism, bureaucracy, and a few other social patterns of this kind existed in the midst of a world that was predominately noncapitalist, nonbureaucratic, and so forth, and a world in which capitalism and bureaucracy have penetrated to a high degree almost everywhere. This hardly makes a theory of capitalism less relevant, even though it calls for revision in certain respects.

I seriously doubt that a historian, looking back from the vantage point of, say, 2300 A.D., will conclude that there was a sudden cutting point somewhere between 1960 and 2010 such that the sociology relevant to the type of society that existed before the rupture became radically out of date thereafter. There are much better grounds for saying that the period 1600–2200 (and perhaps even a wider swath of centuries) is all of a piece. What remains to be done is not to gird ourselves for epistemological doom, but to see what adjustments are needed to keep our theories current.

Four Dimensions of Macrosociological Modernity

Four lines of sociological theory from the classics to the present are central to understanding the future. These are our traditions of analyzing *capitalism, bureaucratization, mass mobilization,* and *state power.*

Capitalism

There can be little question about the continuing relevance of this line. Given that the topic is important, does our theoretical tradition have anything useful to say? I will confine myself to sociological studies of capitalism, not the views of orthodox economic theory. (Neither the followers of Adam Smith nor the neoclassical general equilibrium mathematicians contribute much to understanding real-world economic problems, especially to the macroeconomic question of long-term dynamics or the distributional question of what determines economic inequality.) The sociological tradition of studying economics as embedded in and mutually interacting with political and cultural structures, on the other hand, has always been focused on the right questions. Marx, Weber, Schumpeter, and Polanyi, whatever their shortcomings, always gave us models of economic change and economic stratification.

Their shortcomings are well known, and I will skip forward to present-day economic sociology, well represented by the Smelser and Swedberg *Handbook of Economic Sociology* (1994). We are in the midst of the network revolution, the movement to study economies not as idealized markets, where abstract quantities of supply meet demand, but as selective chains of connections among economic actors. The key insight seems to me to have been expressed most sharply by Harrison White (1981), namely, that profits are made by avoiding head to head competition; they result instead from producers finding niches for unique products (or unique combinations of price, quantity, and volume profitability) that have no competitors. There is a dynamic side to this niche-seeking process. Profitable niches attract competitors, and so there is a market-impelled drive toward continuous innovation, whether in product differentiation, productive and distribution processes, or financial devices. Niches in the capitalist market are therefore only temporary, and profits go to those who locate them first, reap their transient benefits, and then get out and into the next niche ahead of the competition. Networks are a key to this dynamic of transient niche finding, because the producers' advantage comes from being able to monitor one another and thereby to gauge where demand lies and where competition may be avoided. Notice the contrast with classical and neoclassical economics, which focus on an ideal-type of perfect competition that makes the existence of profit paradoxical. In network theory, capitalism is intrinsically stratified, because firms at the core of a network reap the greatest profits, followed by imitators next in the queue. Those firms at the periphery always arrive too late and must face the full press of profitless, open competition.

Orthodox economists and the popular ideology of politicians and new pundits manage to disguise this situation by combining an unrealistic free market model with a deus ex machina that they call "high tech." According to this apologia, it is lack of technical skills that handicaps the unfortunate, while technological innovation is the driving force justly rewarded by success. This is to substitute the tail for the dog. Technological innovation is driven by the process of seeking transient noncompetitive niches; it is capitalist profit seeking in network cores that generates "high tech." The rapid succession of changes in computer models in the 1990s shows the same wastefulness, and the same advertising hype, as the planned obsolescence of automobile style changes in the tailfin era. I am in accord with Baudrillard ([1968] 1996) on this point and would only add that what gets called "postmodern" is a continuation of the long-standing process of capitalism— although in the current era it is consumer goods rather than producer goods that are the most visible arenas for transient niche seeking.

The network theory of capitalism, formulated in the 1980s, is a break with what went before, although one that could only have come out of a distinctive sociological sensibility about the economy. Here the sociological classic that survives best is Marx, although we have had to jettison the part that attempts to derive socialism as the endpoint of a series of worsening capitalist crises. What survives best from the Marxian model is its focus upon stratifying processes and on the cyclical dynamics of production, profit, and employment. The world-system school has made most of the necessary modifications to adapt classic Marxian political economy to the global context. Journalistic opinion has recently caught up with the idea that the world economy is now in a postnational era. The sophistication of the world-system school has been its wider understanding that the context for all previous economic changes has always been larger world-system structures. The world-system school is admirably positioned to give the best insights available into the shapes of the future, as one can see from works of Chase-Dunn and others (e.g., Chase-Dunn 1989; Sanderson 1995), and more ominously in W. Warren Wagar's *A Short History of the Future* (1992).

The network revolution in analyzing the process of capitalism and world-system research on the global patterns of capitalist change might, respectively, provide the microeconomic and the macroeconomic components of a new paradigm. (I am using the terms "micro" and "macro" here in their connotations held among economists, not among sociologists.) The two levels are converging. We are coming to understand economic world systems as networks, as specific chains of connections. This enables researchers to specify comparatively the length and shape of the trading chains, anywhere in scale from early tribal economies to the wide commodity production chains that link Pakistan, Taiwan, and Los Angeles in today's transient niche-seeking fashion apparel industry. In short, we have a very good basis for understanding the capitalist economy of the twenty-first century.

Bureaucratization

This topic was discussed so much in the period before 1960 that most sociologists are tired of it. The fashion of ignoring what our field has learned about bureaucracy is a serious mistake because, as Gideon Sjoberg stresses (in this volume), this is the key to many problems of what we call the modern or postmodern era. Consider the upshot of the discussion as to whether bureaucracy constitutes an inescapable "iron cage." Alternatives to bureaucracy have been pointed out by researchers from the 1930s through the 1980s. They have noted the existence of informal groups inside formal organizations, the possibilities of self-governing professions as alternatives to hierarchic control, the fact that organizations facing task environments of high uncertainty often delegate initiative to decentralized task groups, and that fluid networks often transcend rigid organizational boundaries.

For two important reasons, these discoveries do not undermine the usefulness of bureaucratic theory. First, Weber's concept of bureaucracy is an ideal-type, paired with the contrasting ideal-type of patrimonial administration. Between these extremes is a continuum that runs from ideal hierarchic regimentation at one end to ideal delegation of responsibility through personalized connections at the other. Hence it should not be surprising that personalistic connections usually exist to one degree or another within a formal bureaucracy. The organizational types can be combined in various forms and proportions.

Second, the historical importance of Weber's contrast is to illuminate the struggle that broke down the archetypal "premodern" (in popular parlance, "feudal") institution, the patrimonial household, and largely replaced it with the more impersonal bureaucratic state. Patrimonial organization was a fusion of family, fortified dwelling place, and personal servitude, which constituted the political and economic unit of premodern social structure. Virtually all of the empirical discoveries of twentieth-century organizational researchers—informal groups, self-governing professions, decentralized control structures—are rather far up the continuum toward bureaucracy and away from the patrimonial household. A certain amount of patrimonial organization remains today, in family businesses and immigrant enclaves within the world economic core, but the vast majority of organizational alternatives today are merely small doses of personalistic/patrimonial features that keep bureaucracy just short of the extreme end of the continuum.[1]

The breakdown of the patrimonial household was historically momentous. It made possible the modern state, which monopolized organized force and supported it with a bureaucratic tax apparatus. The rise of state bureaucracy was an ideological watershed as well, because it destroyed the organizational basis of hereditary family rule and the aristocratic status group, replacing it with the organizational basis for the ideology of egalitarian and universalistic citizenship. The patrimonial/bureaucratic shift generated both the ideological resources and the material and organizational conditions for modern social movements to mobilize. The replacement of family servitude by the impersonal marketplace created the possibility for class conflict and, indeed, for most other movements aimed at social change through political pressure.

The feminist movement became organizationally possible when the patrimonial household shrank from being the center of the social world to constituting only a private component within a larger political arena. The several waves of feminist mobilization in the nineteenth and twentieth centuries can be explained by a series of partial changes that diminished, but did not eliminate, this remnant of patrimonial organization. One of the last vestiges of patrimonialism to erode was the shared economy of the household comprising full-time housewife and externally employed husband, who connected the household to the outer world. The shift of women from patrimonial households to the bureaucratized public arena reached a significant proportion in the 1960s and 1970s among educated, upper-middle-class women,[2] but the range of possible change in this respect for other social classes remains considerable for the future. In this area at least, the organizational struggle between patrimonialism and bureaucracy, which has been going on for at least five hundred years, is far from over.

Bureaucracy is an ambivalent phenomenon, because it is a strategy in the struggle for control. Bureaucracy is socially neutral, in the sense that it is a weapon that can be wielded on many sides and for many purposes. In the earlier period of the struggle to break out of the patrimonial household, the development of an administration of impersonal rights and formally stated obligations was regarded as liberating. Under the banner "the rule of law, not of persons," it was associated with slogans of justice, liberty, and universal personhood. Initially, kings used bureaucracy in their struggle to replace their recalcitrant aristocratic colleagues with an administration of nobodies. Bureaucracy creates new interest groups in place of those it displaced: Frederick the Great, mired in paperwork, famously declared, "I am the first servant of the state!"

Bureaucracy can be defined as organizational control achieved by explicit rules and regulations and by specifying responsibilities for action in written records. The organization replaces the individual by an abstract position, a slot in the machine as officially defined in documents on file. Analytically, these are the most important characteristics of bureaucracy, rather than the ancillary point of whether or not the organizational chart depicts a centralized chain of command. Programming of official actions by organizational members continues to expand today. The 1980s and 1990s—the very time when individual initiative and creativity have been touted—is a period in which bureaucratic controls have penetrated even more deeply, using newer forms of administrative planning and monitoring. Arlie Hochschild (1983) has shown how organizations like airlines expand work obligations into the intimacies of emotional labor or emotional impression management; Robin Leidner (1993) shows how today's service industries program even the content of talk. Although much of the organizational analysis around midcentury pointed to debureaucratization, currently there is a powerful countertrend to hyperbureaucratization.

The expansion of the educational system is another aspect of ongoing bureaucratization. Recall that the essence of bureaucracy is control by formal rules and documentation of all official action by written records. Students are moved through school according to the records they compile, graded according to their compliance with formally stated standards. We teachers like to think that grades, exams, course distribution, and all the rest have a substantive value, but whether they do or not, the critical factor that determines a student's fate is his or her record. All the personal letters of recommendation that we might add to the bare numbers on a student transcript do not break the bureaucratic paperwork mold, but simply supplement it. Education meshes with jobs because both are engaged in tracking careers by means of bureaucratic dossiers; the inflation of educational credentials, which stratifies career paths and feeds back into the demand for longer periods of schooling, is just one more aspect of hyperbureaucratization. Much of what postmodernists say about the self-undermining flux of meanings, when translated from the level of culture to the level of its organizational underpinnings, is a phenomenon of hyperbureaucratization.

The saga of patrimonialism and bureaucracy has been historically central to what we call modernity and postmodernity. Can we use these two organizational ideal-types to go beyond historical description? Do we have a dynamic theory that shows conditions and processes by which bureaucracy expands, and conversely, when, if ever, are there countertrends away from extreme bureaucracy?

In the past there have been attempts to expound such a theory in terms of the superior efficiency of bureaucracy, but this has been undermined by evidence that less bureaucratic forms are more efficient in certain task situations. Karl Mannheim (1940) put his finger on the main weakness of this way of explaining bureaucracy when he distinguished its dual aspects: the *formal* rationality of official procedures is often antithetical to the *substantive* rationality of actually getting things done to some real person's satisfaction.

The basic problem is that bureaucracy is a mode of control in the struggle for power. It can be used from above to control those below; it can be used by those below to constrain those above. Reinhard Bendix commented that democracy promotes bureaucracy. Successful movements for enhancing the rights of previously excluded groups institutionalize their victories by creating new laws and new agencies to enforce those laws. The labor movement created the administrative complexity of labor law in the same way that the civil rights movement created the apparatus of affirmative action (see Bourque and Duchastel, in this volume). General rules are necessarily impersonal and set the stage for a new round of struggle over the use of the rules. The conflict in recent years over "political correctness" is another round of an older struggle to combat informal group traditions by institutionalizing formal rules. But bureaucracy itself is also a mode of domination, and struggle over a rule-governed organization displaces attention from the original issue into further issues arising from the control process itself. Bureaucracy becomes oppressive in its own right, and movements to debureaucratize are generated periodically by the very success of movements to institutionalize other rights in formal regulations. The history of bureaucracy has been a dialectical one and seems likely to remain so into the future.

Mass Mobilization

A key Western trend of the period since about 1800 is increasing resource mobilization. The theoretical concept is fairly recent, but the underlying idea is older. Marx and Engels formulated the principle that political and ideological dominance goes to those who control the material means of action. They also noted that the distribution of such material means has shifted historically. Peasants were hamstrung by their dispersion and by a lack of organizational means for bringing their numbers into consolidated action, whereas factory workers were brought together by the very expansion of massive workplaces, which facilitated both organization and the development of a militant consciousness. This is the root of resource mobilization theory, formulated later with increasing generality by Dahrendorf (1959), McCarthy and Zald (1977), Tilly (1978, 1995), and others.

The generalized version of this theory has become detached from the specifics of Marx and Engels's predictions. The material conditions for mobilizing factory workers did increase for a century, but peaked and went into decline in the later twentieth century. If the factory system and the giant industrial corporation once helped to mobilize a labor movement, the decentralization of production made possible by later material conditions for transportation, communication, and automation has, to a considerable extent, demobilized the workers' movement. There is a theoretical point that transcends these specific historical transformations: the theory of movement mobilization is a set of variables, and it works just as well in explaining when movements fail as when they succeed.

A further point needs to be treated with theoretical care. More than one movement can be mobilized at a time, and in studying the outcome of mobilization we need to take account of how movements interact among themselves. The general trend throughout the twentieth century has been toward increasing the level of resources available throughout the population for movement mobilization: urbanization, transportation, education, the availability of communications media, the publicizing of techniques of previous movements. The result has been that a large number of different movements have mobilized. But high levels of mobilization do not guarantee ideological unity. Far from it. Marxists regarded class mobilization as the fundament that was bound to sweep all other considerations before it. Liberal democratizers and patriotic nationalists have similarly privileged their own movements. All of these have been upstaged by what they regarded as frivolous competition from movements as yet unthought of.

The so-called new social movements of the post-1950s do not have a generic unity on the ideological level, and any attempt to categorize them by their detachment from economic class interests does not take us very far. Their common denominator is not that they are idealistic harbingers of a postmaterialist society, but rather that they spring from a historically unprecedented situation of extremely high levels of resource mobilization in wealthy capitalist societies. High resource mobilization means that an extremely large number of different interests can be formulated in the public arena: women's rights but also father's rights; gay and lesbian movements, as well as skinheads and punk rockers; racial and ethnic movements bounded at a wide variety of cutting points; movements to condemn abortion as murder, for religious revival, for the protection of the environment, for escape from the federal government and the Internal Revenue Service, and so on. Since many sociologists who study social movements are also movement activists, we tend to adopt participants' categories and simplify the landscape to a contrast of "good guys" and "bad guys." There is an attempt to argue that all movements of the oppressed belong together in a

grand coalition, a rainbow coalition of gays, women, environmental-
ists, and workers. This is very shaky sociology. Violent conflicts among
Jews, blacks, and Korean-Americans are just one example of a pattern
that has many historical variants. Each group has its own view of what
constitutes oppression. From their own standpoints, right-wing tax
protesters or youth gangs challenging crackdowns on their favorite
music may all justify their militancy by their sense of injustice.

The expansion of resources for mobilization can promote the fragmentation of interests as much as the consolidation of interests. Can
we explain which happens when? An underlying issue is how many
interest groups potentially exist? We are tempted to regard certain la-
tent conflicts as more basic than others. But there are an infinite number of potential conflicts that can be mobilized. The conditions of the
late twentieth century suggest that these can go far beyond class and
gender. Ethnicity, far from being primordial, can be socially constructed in a large number of different ways, depending upon how
narrowly or widely participants draw their line, and there is no end to
the number of ethnic identities that might be mobilized in the future.
(See also the role of the state and laws in constructing such borders, as
described in the chapters by Almaguer and Jung and by Bourque and
Duchastel, in this volume.)

A more fruitful direction of analysis is suggested by Barry Barnes in
The Elements of Social Theory (1995): an interest group is constituted by
the very process of mobilizing it. It is the shape of the networks with
resources to meet in contested public arenas that creates the community of consciousness. At one time factories created a "movement" that
construed itself as "the working class," as opposed to earlier mobilized
categories such as "the cotters of Lichfield." In the same way, movements identifying themselves by the commitment to "right to life" or
"freedom of choice" did not latently exist all in themselves but were
shaped by a certain historical configuration of mobilizing conditions.
Among these conditions must be counted the mobilizing effects of
existing movements, including their enmities.

This is a more promising direction for theoretical development than
the essentialist effort to elevate certain interests as primordial. What
we need is a more refined theory of the overall process of mobilization,
explaining panoplies and cascades of movements rather than single
movements in isolation. We also need to avoid being hung up on the
ideological level, construing movements in terms of their own concepts
for seeing the world. Consciousness is not transcendent or fixed, but
is a transient product of social conditions. This is not to adopt the

postmodernist position, but instead to take a central phenomenon of postmodernist demoralization as one feature to be explained. Under certain conditions of resource mobilization, a chaotic array of movements are mobilized, resulting in further ideological efforts—so to speak, ideologies of the second order—to reduce the complexity by spanning fragmentary movements with ideologies of coalition. It is not impossible for grand coalitions to emerge at certain times in history, or at any rate the rise of the hegemony of one movement over others which successfully claims to speak in their name. Revolutions are occasions when the chaos of movements, unleashed by the breakdown of state control, is replaced at least temporarily by a movement organization that solidifies the situation by getting control over the state apparatus. Perhaps there are other ways in which the hegemonic simplification of movements comes about.

The theory of mass mobilization we need in order to understand present and future politics should answer two questions. First, what causes interests to be mobilized in the first place? And second, what determines the extent to which the entire array of mobilized movements is fragmented or consolidated? The earlier accomplishments of resource mobilization theory, from Marx and Engels through the present, have been to offer a fair answer to the first question. The second remains on the agenda.

State Power

It has taken longest to develop a satisfactory theory of state power. The classic Marxian approach subsumed the state as executive to the economy, the functionalist approach as head to the social body. Revolutions were treated as reflexes of economic or overly rapid social change. Weber made the state analytically independent, but most sociologists drew from this no more than a static classificatory scheme. A major accomplishment of historical sociologists of the later twentieth century has been a dynamic theory of state growth and state breakdown.

Consider the breakdown theory first. In the model developed by Skocpol (1979), Goldstone (1991), Mann (1986–93), and Tilly (1990, 1993), revolutions are not the result merely of the mobilization of movements at the bottom but are initiated by the breakdown of the apparatus of coercion at the top. The proximal causes are a fiscal crisis of the state and conflicts among officeholding and propertied elites over who is to pay for the state's budget deficit. In the long-range background, the state fiscal crisis is intensified by military spending, the largest component of state budgets. Still farther back in the chain of causes, as Skocpol has indicated, are geopolitical strains. Geopolitics, the external relations among states in potential or actual military confrontation, are therefore a key driving force of state change.

State breakdown theory meshes with the military-centered theory of state development. As Tilly, Mann, and others have shown, the military revolution over the centuries from 1500 to 1800 in Europe vastly increased the size and expense of the state apparatus. Armies grew much larger, became more heavily armed with gunpowder weapons, and furthermore were maintained at central state expense rather than mustered from the patrimonial followers of the paramount lord. State administrative bureaucracy grew in the military itself, as auxiliary branches to service the military and as an apparatus to raises taxes for military expense. This apparatus fought a long battle to destroy the resistance of patrimonial households (so-called feudalism) and, in the process, penetrated deeply into what was now becoming civil society. Because of geopolitical rivalries, no state could long avoid going down the path of military reform and experiencing its consequences. Struggle over the state's expanding military expenses promoted resistance and, in cases where fiscal strains and elite splits coincided with mass uprisings, led to the revolutions of the early modern period and to the concessions institutionalized in democratic power-sharing institutions. It is no exaggeration to say that the ramifications of the military revolution have affected every important aspect of the modern state. Even the peaceful aspects of state expansion, the provision of economic services and regulation and the larger activities of the welfare state, consisted in turning the organizational apparatus generated by the military revolution to new purposes under influence from the now-mobilized populace.

The story of this apparatus does not come to an end once some ideal-type modern state is in existence. The central dynamic of state breakdown and state growth continues to hinge on the relationships among state fiscal health or fiscal strain, struggles among elites (subdivided into the state administrators themselves and the dominant property class) over who is to make what concessions to meet fiscal problems, and the resource mobilization of the general population. Most major states at the beginning of the twenty-first century may not be heading for revolution, but they cannot escape moving along the continuum of problems set by the level of state budgetary strain, elite squabbling, and the background noise of popular movements. One of our analytical challenges is to extend this model from extreme situations to more normal ones, from the elevated crisis levels of state breakdown and revolution to chronic struggles along the moderate parts of the continuum.

Some Directions for the Future

Let me conclude by noting a way in which the fiscal-crisis-centered model of state dynamics meshes with the sociological theory of capitalism. I noted earlier that Marxian theory survives as an explanation for economic cycles in the world system (albeit jettisoning the old Marxian endpoint, the final transition to socialism). The downfall of the Soviet regimes in 1989–91 has allowed theories of capitalism to all but eclipse any interest in a theory of socialism. But it was the wrong strategy to look for a dynamic leading toward or away from socialism. By approaching the question from the vantage point of economic sociology, a theory of the appearance and disappearance of socialism comes much more directly from the theory of state power and state breakdown. The establishment of the major Communist regimes in 1917 and 1949 are among the classic cases for the theory of state breakdown and revolution. The breakdown of 1989–91, as I have argued (Collins 1995), should be seen in the same light—not so much an economic failure of socialism per se, but the result of fiscal strains of a Russian state (which happened to be Communist) locked in an untenable geopolitical situation, crippled by its military budgets, and undergoing internal dissolution of control at the top through the struggles of reformers and the privileged elite over how to solve the budgetary crisis. The contrast between Russia (the linchpin of the Soviet empire, including its Warsaw Pact satellites) and China shows the significance of contrasting geopolitical situations for whether Communist regimes undergo revolution. It is not the inferiority of socialism per se, or its intrinsic distastefulness to the populace, that caused the revolutions of 1989–91.

Let me draw out three theoretical consequences. There is no sociological reason to say that socialism is impossible, or that now that this unpleasant twentieth-century episode is over, we will have capitalism forever. Capitalism and socialism in many instances have been constructed on the rebound, in ideological revulsion against what went before a particular historical moment of state breakdown and revolution. It is not out of the realm of plausibility that there will be further rebounds in the future.

The second theoretical consequence is that revolutions continue to be possible: not because of future economic crises of capitalism (although I am not ruling this out), but because the main cause of revolutions was never the economy in the first place. It was always state-centered breakdowns, fiscal crises of the state driven to the sticking point by military costs; wars and paying for wars always raises the possibility of state breakdowns in the future. Ultimately revolutions cannot be ruled out because geopolitics cannot be ruled out.

The third point is the theoretical challenge that lies before us. World-system theory has been the most successful branch of economic sociology in developing a model of the long-term dynamics of capitalism. The weakness of world-system theory remains its attempt to derive all long-run state processes from economic processes. There is a connection, to be sure, since state fiscal problems are determined in part by the way in which a state is situated in relation to capitalist world markets. The Soviet Union and its empire fell, in part, because it was a state-socialist regime inside a capitalist world economy, and its military costs were driven by economic forces not under its own control. But this was only part of the situation. The world-system model plays into the state breakdown model, but there remain the geopolitical dynamics that have been the prime movers throughout the history of the state. The theoretical challenge is to integrate state theory and its military/geopolitical center of gravity with a world-system theory of capitalism.

The end result will not be exactly what Marx and Engels wanted, and certainly not what Durkheim hoped for. That is to say, I see no theory on the horizon that will satisfy our normative dreams for an end to oppression and conflict by showing how history will get us to a harmonious resting point. But I do think we will have a theory that satisfies the desire for theoretical comprehensiveness, that can show us how the dynamics of economy and state are connected as they wend their endlessly conflictual way.

Notes

1. But see the chapters in this volume by Dorothy E. Smith and Harriet Friedmann that advocate a somewhat different view.

2. And, we might note, for poor women caught in the meshes of the welfare system. Again, see the somewhat different views in Dorothy E. Smith's chapter (in this volume).

References

Barnes, Barry. 1995. *The Elements of Social Theory*. Princeton, N.J.: Princeton University Press.

Baudrillard, Jean. (1968) 1996. *The System of Objects*. London: Verso.

Chase-Dunn, Christopher. 1989. *Global Formation. Structures of the World-Economy.* Oxford: Blackwell.

Collins, Randall. 1995. "Prediction in Macrosociology: The Case of the Soviet Collapse." *American Journal of Sociology* 100: 1552–93.

———. 1998. *The Sociology of Philosophies: A Global Theory of Intellectual Change.* Cambridge, Mass.: Harvard University Press.

Dahrendorf, Ralf. 1959. *Class and Class Conflict in Industrial Society.* Stanford, Calif.: Stanford University Press.

Goldstone, Jack A. 1991. *Revolution and Rebellion in the Early Modern World.* Berkeley and Los Angeles: University of California Press.

Hochschild, Arlie. 1983. *The Managed Heart. Commercialization of Human Feeling.* Berkeley and Los Angeles: University of California Press.

Latour, Bruno. (1984) 1988. *The Pasteurization of France.* Cambridge, Mass.: Harvard University Press.

Leidner, Robin. 1993. *Fast Food, Fast Talk: Service Work and the Routinization of Everyday Life.* Berkeley and Los Angeles: University of California Press.

McCarthy, John D., and Mayer Zald. 1977. "Resource Mobilization and Social Movements." *American Journal of Sociology* 82: 1212–41.

Mann, Michael. 1986–93. *The Sources of Social Power,* 2 vols. New York: Cambridge University Press.

Mannheim, Karl. 1940. *Man and Society in an Age of Reconstruction.* New York: Harcourt.

Sanderson, Stephen K. 1995. *Social Transformations.* Oxford: Blackwell.

Skocpol, Theda. 1979. *States and Social Revolutions.* New York: Cambridge University Press.

Smelser, Neil J., and Richard Swedberg. 1994. *The Handbook of Economic Sociology.* Princeton, N.J.: Princeton University Press.

Tilly, Charles. 1978. *From Mobilization to Revolution.* Reading, Mass.: Addison-Wesley.

———. 1990. *Coercion, Capital, and European States,* A.D. *990–1990.* Oxford: Blackwell.

———. 1993. *European Revolutions, 1492–1992.* Oxford: Blackwell.

———. 1995. *Popular Contention in Great Britain, 1758–1834.* Cambridge, Mass.: Harvard University Press.

Wagar, W. Warren. 1992. *A Short History of the Future.* Chicago: University of Chicago Press.

White, Harrison C. 1981. "Where Do Markets Come From?" *American Journal of Sociology* 87: 517–47.

CHAPTER THREE

Some Observations on
Bureaucratic Capitalism:
Knowledge about What and Why?

GIDEON SJOBERG

My intention in this chapter is to revisit Robert Lynd's (1939) seminal question: Knowledge for what? However, for some years I have been persuaded that this query begs two other questions that are equally or perhaps even more profound: Knowledge about what? and What standard (or set of standards) should social scientists employ in evaluating such knowledge?

This brings me to focus on two serious lacunae in sociological analysis. The first is sociology's general failure to appreciate the role that large-scale organizations now play in shaping "bureaucratic capitalism." Thus sociologists fail to investigate the complex empirical processes by which such organizations establish their dominance. The second is a normative question, namely: How can these organizations be held morally and socially accountable for their activities, particularly if one wants to advance democratic ideals of social justice?

Both topics take on greater importance in the contemporary era, not only because these complex bureaucracies have expanded in scale and power but, paradoxically, because they have become both *closer* to the state and yet *freer* to move beyond the boundaries of the territorial units that formerly sought to regulate them. Thus, when we examine complex organizations, we must do more than focus on the power of the state. We must confront the reality that state control is nowadays intertwined and integrated with corporate power and control. It was not so long ago that one group of sociologists was imploring their colleagues to bring the state back in (Evans, Rueschemeyer, and Skocpol 1985). We must do the same for corporate organizations, for many of them, multinational in scope, are shaping not only the economic sector of societies but vital aspects of other social spheres as well.

Complex organizations (both corporate and state) are the engines

My extended conversations with Boyd Littrell, Elizabeth Gill, and Norma Williams have deeply influenced the contents of this essay. In addition, creative editing by Leonard Cain and Andrée F. Sjoberg has clarified my argument.

that run modern bureaucratic capitalism.[1] These organizations have made possible the worldwide development of contemporary capitalism, and they have done so in ways unimagined only a few decades ago. At the same time, these organizations play a central role in fostering inequality, injustice, and other social pathologies in modern life. Yet how many sociologists currently focus on bureaucratic (or organizational) domination?

My conceptual formulation seeks to reorient sociological analysis of large-scale, bureaucratic organizations by melding a neo-Weberian framework regarding organizations with the pragmatist theorizing of Mead and Dewey. Such a perspective seems essential not only to comprehend how these organizations shape the economy, the polity, and other social spheres (including family arrangements) but also to explore how human agents might be able to hold these organizations morally and socially accountable and, in the process, reshape them.

The problem of moral accountability brings to the fore the contentious history of the fact-value debate in sociology. The positivists or logical empiricists have insisted that the two realms are distinct, although in practice many logical empiricists have adhered to a version of utilitarianism.[2] The distinction between facts and values was developed in a somewhat different way by Weber and his adherents who have championed the need for value neutrality in social scientific activity.

A countervailing tradition exists within sociology, however. This is reflected in the writings of scholars whose theories differ considerably from one another. Durkheim, as recent commentators (e.g., Jones 1994) have stressed, interpreted his social facts within a moral framework. So, too, contemporary communitarians such as Robert Bellah (1983), Philip Selznick (1992), and Amitai Etzioni (1993) have challenged the fact-value distinction. We can also point to pragmatists such as John Dewey who, during his long and productive life, insisted that the moral and factual realms are bound together in complex ways.[3] Also, we can single out sociologists such as Dorothy Smith (1990; but see also Smith, in this volume), Sorokin and Lunden (1954), Gouldner (1970), Barrington Moore (1978) and C. Wright Mills (1959) who, in various ways, have perceived that moral standards are interconnected with empirical investigation. The relational logic that binds the moral and the empirical spheres is particularly pronounced in the study of power, as Steven Lukes (1974) has made eminently clear. All this is not to say that values (or morals) and empirical observations are the same. Rather, the two are bound together in ways that must be recognized and explored.

The Nature of Organizations and Agency

In engaging in a reanalysis of powerful large-scale organizations, I shall place my argument within the context of past and present scholarly debates before reconceptualizing the nature of organizations. For instance, it is significant that, although human agents and organizational structures have meaning only in relation to one another, neither can be reduced to the other. Contrary to the views of many sociologists, the processes by which organizational activities are constructed and the end product of these activities do not stand in a one-to-one relationship. With this framework in hand, we shall then be ready to consider, albeit briefly, the manner in which powerful organizations are structuring the nature of modern markets.

My emphasis will be on hierarchical power relationships, not upon those interconnections that emerge from networks that are basically horizontal (or social, as explored in Wellman's contribution to this book). True, bureaucratic organizations have contributed to modernity, but they have also fostered grave inequalities and injustices (what I shall call the process of "social triage"). This conclusion leads me back to the problem with which I began: namely, the accountability of these organizations within the framework of a robust set of democratic and moral ideals.

The Intellectual Background

Talcott Parsons (1937) was well aware of Weber's concern with capitalist bureaucracy. Although he continued to rely heavily upon many aspects of Weber's legacy, Parsons shunned Weber's concern with powerful organizations and chose instead to emphasize the role of associational groupings in the shaping of modern social orders. Far more than Parsons, Jürgen Habermas (1984, 1987) has been attuned to the problems posed by Weber's iron cage. In the process he has sought a way out of the relentless process of rationalization by emphasizing the lifeworld as a counterweight to the economic and administrative apparatus of the system in contemporary society. Although there is much to admire in Habermas's effort, he underestimates the pathologies associated with the organizational structure of modern capitalism.

As we turn to organizational theorists we find that they, too, seem ill equipped to examine the consequences of organizational domination. Whether one adopts the human relations approach or the orientations advanced by Chester Barnard, Philip Selznick, and the new institutionalists,[4] the focus is upon the virtues, rather than the failings, of modern organizational structures. Selznick (1992) is among the most sophisticated defenders of modern bureaucratic structures. He observes that these organizational forms are superior to earlier ones and, while recognizing some of their limitations, he reasons that they have built-in correctives based on their procedural rules. However, he glides over the social and moral inequities created by modern organizational forms.

The more critical theorists have not done much better in explicating bureaucratic capitalism. With rare exceptions, Marxists have shied away from a Weberian perspective on organizations; this holds even for the Weberian Marxists.[5] As for the postmodernists, we find that scholars such as Michel Foucault have cast an informative eye on prisons and mental hospitals. However, Foucault's conception of power as diffuse throughout the social fabric and his emphasis on localism lead him to question seriously the place of grand narratives in social analysis. For Foucault, selective features of the premodern era seem to be idealized (see Best and Kellner 1991); thus, reconstituting modernity becomes a flawed project.

In contrast to the postmodernists stand a number of management theorists—Peter Drucker, Tom Peters, and others—who, from somewhat diverse perspectives, provide both a rationale and a direction for large-scale organizational change.[6] One wing of management thinking even defines politics outside the realm of organizational analysis, viewing *any* political activity as a threat to organizational structures (Hardy and Clegg 1996).

In more general terms, this idealization of the free market model has contributed heavily to "state bashing."[7] It has also deflected attention away from the power of large corporations. Although a number of sociologists (Block 1996) have sought to counter the critiques of the state by supporters of the free market model, they have been far less willing to examine the corporate sector critically. It would be well to revisit the earlier writings on monopoly capitalism by Edward Chamberlain (1936) and Joan Robinson (1933), as well as earlier work on the role of managerial domination. The problems posed by some of these scholars—though not their solutions—merit reconsideration.[8]

The Power of Bureaucratic Organizations

To many, examining the role of bureaucratic organizations in the modern world may seem to be misplaced in a social order in which various forms of diversity are increasingly apparent. Without doubt, the increase in social and cultural diversity in the realms of gender, race and ethnicity, and life styles (including familial relationships) is calling forth changes in large-scale organizations that could potentially challenge the growth of centralized bureaucratic power. In a similar vein, a number of scholars are writing about fundamental changes in the nature of the organizations themselves, contending that these are becoming less hierarchical. Today, it seems rather fashionable to speak of post-Fordism and at times to fantasize about organizations as only a virtual reality. While it is true that we are witnessing ongoing decentralization in the form of outsourcing, flexible work arrangements, and so on, many of these patterns made possible by new technologies are reinforcing, not undermining, centralized control.

In addition, any analysis of bureaucratic capitalism must take into account the changing nature of the relationship between the corporate (or private) sector and the state (or public) sector. Although multinationals are not unprecedented, their influence and reach are qualitatively different than in the past. For instance, in recent decades, various financial markets have come to exist outside the range of regulation and control by nation-states. The corporate versus state relationship is further confounded by the push toward privatization, a pattern that varies within and among nation-states.

While state power has receded relative to corporate power, it has by no means disappeared. Despite the emergence of new political arrangements (such as the European Union), nation-states continue to provide the political stability upon which corporations depend. The state continues to define property rights and enforce contracts. It still holds a basic monopoly on the legitimation of violence, even though the reprivatization of some police functions has also been occurring. In effect, in most highly industrialized orders we find hybrid organizations that are a mix of the public and the private. Thus I tend to speak of corporate-state structures, all the while cognizant of the fact that, as we move toward the extremes, compelling distinctions between corporate and state structures become apparent.

Despite the aforementioned social trends and despite traditional social and cultural differences, I nevertheless persist in emphasizing the rise of bureaucratic power and control, for compelling reasons based on empirical data. To the extent that routinization and standardization are part and parcel of bureaucratic structures, one stands almost in awe of the manner in which modern complex social orders have come to be coordinated.

Even though we acknowledge a vast array of cultural differences, we can ill afford to downplay the standardization of activities within and across societies. In advanced industrial systems, food must be delivered and distributed daily if the urban sector is to survive; planes and trains generally run on time; and the provision of water and electricity is a standard bill of fare. In addition, consider the synchronization of radio and television programming and the generally standardized schedules adhered to by hospitals and schools. The rules and regulations are largely taken for granted, but any substantial rupture in them becomes newsworthy. What we discover is that life is ordered according to bureaucratic time and in such a fashion that divergent activities are linked together. Within this context, economic, political, and social sanctions are imposed upon those persons or groups who do not conform.

Along with the routinization and standardization of many strategic activities in advanced industrial-urban realms, a wave of mergers has appeared within the corporate domain, especially in the past few decades. This has resulted in increased economic, social, and political centralization. Consider the centralization of economic and social control in, for example, agribusiness, telecommunications, the financial sector, and in mining and oil industries. Although countervailing forces are at work, large and powerful corporations—within and across nation-states—have become the order of the day.

One consequence is that the elite sectors of the corporate-state apparatuses in cities such as Tokyo, Bangkok, Sydney, London, Buenos Aires, Berlin, and San Francisco, while differing in many cultural expressions, are more similar to one another than they are to the less privileged groups within their own societies (see Sassen 1991 and in this volume). Moreover, the managerial sectors within the private and the public realms interact with one another far more readily today than they did only a few decades ago.

Reconceptualizing Bureaucracy

We have arrived at the point where we can sketch out an alternative conception of bureaucracy. Although we begin with Weber, we depart considerably from him here. What can be preserved from Weber is his focus upon hierarchy, the division of labor, and efficiency.

Hierarchy, of course, is hardly unique to modern societies, but the manner in which hierarchy functions is. Hierarchical control is seen as essential for coordinating highly specialized personnel and their tasks and for coping with the political struggles that occur within the organizational field.

The division of labor into increasingly specialized units, both within and among organizations, has been dramatic. This specialization is readily apparent if one compares the offerings in course catalogues at large universities between 1950 and 1998. Yet the specialization of knowledge has developed within the context of hierarchical coordination and control.

And finally, the matter of efficiency is more complex than Weber acknowledged. We can follow Fligstein (1990) in recognizing that efficiency is socially constructed. However, it is constructed within definite boundaries. In defining efficiency, managers, especially in the private sphere, must meet two objectives: one is organizational maintenance and development; the other is the matter of "profits." Yet profits in modern organizations are constructed through complex accounting practices that are far removed from the manner profit and loss are determined in, say, households. Delaney (1992) has, in his research on bankruptcy, provided us with a glimpse of how assets and liabilities can, under particular circumstances, be constructed so as to further organizational power. It is not that these can be manipulated willy-nilly, since their manipulation occurs within a particular set of boundaries, but sociologists will need to pay far greater heed to accounting practices if they are to grasp both the nature of system enhancement and the meaning of "profitability." The discussion of efficiency suggests that we must modify Weber's conceptualization. In the process, we must more clearly comprehend the relationship between human agency and large-scale organizations.

The Question of Agency

Although Weber placed human actors at the center of his sociology, he relegated them to the background in his analysis of bureaucracy. To understand how organizations function we must comprehend the intersection of human agents and bureaucratic organizations.[9] With respect to the nature of human agency, the conceptions of George Herbert Mead and John Dewey are far superior to those of Weber. Mead (1934) talked not only about the social self but about the social mind (or what Dewey termed social intelligence); both the self and the mind are products of social interaction. Because of the social mind we can think about thinking, carry on conversations with ourselves, engage in complex social calculations, and sustain a social memory.

The reflectivity of human agents, especially as expressed through their social calculations, remains largely unexplored by sociologists. In the process of social interaction, human agents not only reason via formal rationality but also engage in classification (or typification), draw analogies, employ the dialectic (especially negation), and rely upon parts-whole logic. These modes of social calculation (or reasoning) make it possible to develop and sustain a variety of knowledge formations.

When we place active human agents within a formal organizational context, we find that they interpret and reinterpret rules (or norms). Yet concomitantly, they are unable to do so in the freewheeling manner suggested by sociologists such as Herbert Blumer (1969). One's position in the organizational hierarchy and in the web of the division of labor structures one's interactions with others and sets boundaries upon the kinds of interpretation that are possible (or even permissible), the kinds of information at one's disposal, and one's knowledge base in general.

The organizational structures affect the manner in which managers, in particular, reason. While "holism" may be out of favor today in many strands of sociology, it is alive and well among many managers. Like military generals, who have been known to sacrifice divisions so that the army could survive, corporate managers have been known to lop off parts of a system in order to create a more efficient and competitive whole. As the managers define the situation, the subunits become expendable in order that the organization can be seen to thrive. In turn, personnel who are downsized have little or no control over their fate. The parts-whole logic, which undergirds certain kinds of managerial decisions, seems to be poorly articulated by sociologists. This is a pity if one is to understand various kinds of organization decision making and their consequences.

Within bureaucratic organizations, in both the private and the public sectors, there are fewer rules for those on top than for those below. Moreover, persons in positions of authority and power delegate blameability under the guise of responsibility. Although persons within the lower reaches of organizations are able to create social space for themselves, they are far more constrained than those in positions of power. For Giddens (1984), organizations serve both to enable and to constrain social action. However, organizations are more enabling for those above than for those below. They are more constraining on those below than those above.

Once we acknowledge that human agents can and do reinterpret rules, we can more readily understand why secrecy systems emerge. However, we must be careful not to confuse secrecy with the formal versus informal distinction, because secrecy can be either formal (as with corporate or state secrets) or informal. Secrecy systems (or hidden arrangements) emerge for several reasons. Within organizations they arise as persons in the lower echelons seek to seal themselves off, to a modest degree, from manipulation by those in positions of authority and control. Managers, in turn, generate their own hidden arrangements in order to enhance their claim to a monopoly of vital information. Among organizations, secret arrangements arise because of real or perceived threats from other organizations within the organizational field. The negative economic, political, and moral consequences of such secret arrangements was illustrated, for example, in the savings and loan debacle of the 1980s in the United States.

Let us take stock of the implications of this argument. Once we recognize the role of human agents within organizational settings, two strategic patterns can be identified. First, although organizational structures cannot exist without human agents, organizations are not reducible to human agency. The normative order as well as the economic and political resources of organizations have a reality that is apart from any particular set of human agents. Second, if we take account of human agents in shaping organizational arrangements, we discover that the end product (or the "official reality") can be constructed by somewhat different sets of activities. I am now prepared to concretize my conception of organizations and human agency by detailing their implications for the construction of the market as well as resulting injustices.

Organizations and Markets

The nature of markets has, in recent decades, been of considerable interest to sociologists (see Smelser and Swedberg 1994). A number of sociologists have addressed questions relating to labor, as well as to financial, consumer, and industrial-firm markets and have challenged the taken-for-granted assumptions of economists regarding the nature of the market. Perhaps the greatest impact has been made by sociologists such as Mark Granovetter (1985) who emphasize the embeddedness of markets within institutions. Although the resultant theorizing and research on the interrelationships of social networks and markets represent a significant step forward, this approach neglects the role of bureaucratic organizations in shaping the market. It is increasingly imperative that we examine the processes by which powerful organizations shape the nature of supply and demand. We can offer some illustrative cases that lend credence to our assertions.

First, the data suggest that some decades ago the managers of General Motors (GM) set out, through the use of enormous financial and political power, to construct a market for automobiles. Specifically, GM, working in conjunction with Firestone and Standard Oil of California, took steps to buy up (and ultimately destroy) the rail systems that served cities such as Los Angeles. Much of this was accomplished without consumers' knowledge of how their demand for automobiles was being shaped (Feagin and Parker 1990).

Second, there is the case of tobacco products (Kluger 1997; Massing 1996). In the face of a large body of scientific data, cigarette companies persisted in denying that their products were harmful. Through aggressive advertising, as well as clandestine research efforts that sought to create a more addictive cigarette, these companies have structured the preferences of many consumers. Contrary to one of the sacred assumptions of many mainstream economists (or rational choice theorists such as James Coleman), preferences are indeed subject to manipulation. Although the moral (and social) accountability of these corporations has been called into question, their sheer size provides them with economic leverage (fines are unlikely to have any substantial impact), and their political leverage is well understood. Bigness counts.[10]

The third area is health care. During the 1980s Boyd Littrell (1989) conducted research on the health care market in Omaha. At that time hospitals were purchasing expensive medical equipment in an effort to retain their pool of physicians. After the equipment was purchased, the doctors came to have a stake in assuring that it would be utilized by their patients. Thus, the doctors were instrumental in creating certain consumer demands. Yet the medical equipment was paid for not only by increased patient fees but also by the depreciation allowances permitted by U.S. tax law.

The market for health care in Omaha and elsewhere has changed enormously in the 1990s as the health care system becomes based on managed care. Doctors, who at one time had been small-scale entrepreneurs, are now being outflanked by hospital mergers and insurance companies. Under this new arrangement, insurance companies, in collaboration with large-scale corporations or public-sector organizations, provide their members with a choice of selected health plans. Under these circumstances, the insurance companies can estimate (given the morbidity rates of the population in question) their potential costs. In addition, these companies can shape (within limits) the kinds of treatment and charges that are permissible by doctors in the HMOs with whom the insurance companies have contracted. This is accomplished through bureaucratic regulation of the market. In effect, insurance companies can project, with reasonable precision, both the supply and the demand curves with respect to health services. In the process they assure themselves of making a substantial profit.

A fourth case relates to the informal economy. Portes (1994) and his colleagues have done more than any others to systematize our knowledge in this realm. Nevertheless, Portes's analysis needs to be anchored within a larger organizational context, for there are at least two kinds of informal economy: that which is hidden from state (and large corporate) structures and that which is part of the corporate-state apparatus. In turn, both kinds of informal economy have legal, quasi-legal, and illegal dimensions. In the main, Portes's discussion is oriented to the economy that is hidden, particularly from state organizations. This economy, generally the province of the small-scale entrepreneurs, typically goes unreported.

Although of considerable import, this small-scale concealed sector may well pale in contrast to the informal economy that is part and parcel of the powerful corporate-state bureaucracy. The latter comes to public attention only during periods of social rupture, such as in the savings and loan scandals in the United States in the 1980s or the Mexican peso disaster of the 1990s.[11] What we must understand about the informal economy embedded within powerful organizations is that much of it is actually legal or quasi-legal, not simply illegal. We must take care to distinguish between rule avoidance and rule violation. Thus, corporations may engage in intraorganizational pricing in order to avoid the taxation systems of particular nation-states (see Braithwaite 1984). Yet these activities may be legitimated by standard (legal) accounting practices.

If it were possible to examine more fully the kinds of cases mentioned above, we would find that many aspects of the economy cannot be understood without placing them within the context of powerful organizational settings. Human agents engage in a complex range of activities within organizations that are characterized by hierarchy, an intricate web of specialization, and an emphasis on efficiency. Within large-scale (including multinational) corporations, blameability and secrecy emerge, and these processes tend to shape the manner in which economic markets are created and sustained. Sociologists will also find it advantageous to examine how multinationals at the core of the world system come to be related to the activities in other sectors of that system.[12]

The Consequences: Social Privilege and Social Triage

What are the social consequences of the corporate-state apparatus we have been describing? If we employ such a criterion as life expectancy we discover that, while bureaucratic capitalism has led to overall economic and social development, it has so far proved to be detrimental to the most disadvantaged sectors within and among nations. At the same time, the privileged sector has expanded not only within the developed world but also within developing nations. The "emerging markets" have created not only a source of cheap labor but also heightened consumer demand for many goods and services. Sociologists readily acknowledge the former but seldom address the latter. Yet the expanding privileged sector of developing nations seems to be a major market for goods and services produced by corporations based in the more developed world.[13]

One reason managers of corporate-state systems in, say, the United States can more or less ignore the truly disadvantaged is that emerging markets are expanding so rapidly. (Given this situation, we can perhaps understand why Keynesian economics has fallen on difficult times.) Global bureaucratic capitalism has resulted in enormous inequalities between the privileged and the truly disadvantaged. We must seek to understand the processes by which bureaucratic structures come to support and sustain privilege, as well as the processes by which social triage is produced.

The accumulation of capital does not occur within an organizational vacuum. Persons who attain privilege do so by relying on corporate-state organizations, and they sustain their advantages through a complex set of organizational rules (reinforced by police power). In a larger context we know that new billionaires are being created because corporate executives are able to award themselves handsome salaries and other perquisites with the approval of their corporate boards. Moreover, we have not grasped the broader implications of the U.S. savings and loan scandals or of the Mexican peso debacle. In both cases, persons in powerful positions in the corporate sectors, in collusion with actors in the state apparatus, made fortunes while taxpayers were called upon to foot the bill. In turn, the resultant fortunes have typically been protected from estate taxes and public inspection.

The assumption that one can sustain universalism within the context of bureaucratic hierarchy and control is seriously called into question. Take the case of the educational structures in the United States. Although these organizations are loosely coupled, a hierarchical system of power nonetheless exists. For instance, privileged families reside in those neighborhoods that provide their children access to advantaged school systems in which many learn to master standardized testing and to acquire the intellectual and social skills necessary for access to the top-ranking colleges and universities. In addition, some slots in the more elite private universities are reserved for the children of alumni. Despite the society's emphasis on merit in educational attainment, organizational arrangements exist that make the ideals unrealizable for most people.

In looking at the process of social triage we discover that persons can come to be defined as expendable by those with power and privilege. Recall that blameability is extended by the organizational leadership downward to persons who interact, often indirectly, with the corporate-state system. Consequently, people with the least knowledge of the system must interact with those organizational personnel who are the most constrained by the normative rules.

More profoundly, the most onerous burdens of the social order are carried by the least privileged sectors within and among social orders. The environmental realm dramatizes the manner in which the privileged sector exploits the most disadvantaged. A considerable body of data supports the assertion that the poor (especially racial and ethnic minorities) must bear the greatest burden with regard to toxic wastes or other litter produced by the more privileged sector. Then, too, the poor pay more for products and services or are excluded from them altogether.

Banking systems within the United States provide us with a glimpse of the manner in which the same organizational structure enhances privilege and generates social triage. The truly disadvantaged cannot afford to maintain bank accounts, and if and when they obtain loans, interest rates can be staggering. Persons with only modest incomes pay relatively more for the privilege of banking than do more advantaged customers. The flip side of this is that the more money one possesses, the more one profits from banking. For instance, large accounts reap higher interest rates. For banks it is more efficient to serve a few wealthy customers than a large number of persons with modest means.

Yet we must not underestimate the creativity of bureaucratic capitalism in benefiting from issues related to the most disadvantaged sectors. The rise of the prison-industrial complex is a compelling instance of this. Nils Christie (1993), a Norwegian criminologist, discusses the emergence of the prison-industrial system in the West and raises the issue of gulags, Western style. The prison-industrial complex in the United States serves two functions. It sweeps the "unwanted" (especially members of racial and ethnic minorities) off the streets, and it provides a stable market for producers of a rather wide range of goods and services. Given such potential benefits, one might reason that, from the vantage point of corporate-state structures, it would be more efficient to let most of the potential prison population die young.

The Moral Accountability of Organizations

This chapter can do little more than suggest new directions for sociological investigation on the question of moral (or social) accountability of organizations. There are several reasons why the significance of the moral accountability of bureaucratic organizations seems likely to intensify rather than lessen. Somewhat alongside the rise of large-scale bureaucratic organizations has been the spread of democratic ideals, although the two are by no means synonymous. One wing of democratic theory has emphasized fairness, social justice, and equity (even equality itself). In light of the widespread acceptance of these ideals, the privileged sector cannot evade the problem of political legitimacy. Moreover, we have reached a point in history when knowledge about highly sophisticated tools of destruction is being diffused among less advantaged groups within and among nations. This opens up the possibility of violence that could undermine the infrastructure on which the privileged members of bureaucratic organizations depend.

One of the gravest problems confronting bureaucratic capitalism is the environment (see Friedmann, in this volume). In examining the environment we would do well to follow the leads offered by Ulrich Beck (1995). Although he can be seriously faulted for glossing over social divisions (i.e., class) within and among nation-states and for downplaying the role of large-scale organizations, Beck nonetheless has provided us with a new perspective on the environment. As Beck contends, major environmental disasters can deeply affect all sections of a society. A large-scale disaster involving nuclear power, such as the one that occurred in 1986 at Chernobyl, could leave even the elite no place to hide. In these more extreme circumstances, the elite may well find that they have more in common with the disadvantaged than they ever realized. Within such a context, the meaning of social justice may come to be redefined. If we adopt a more global perspective than Beck does, and if we contemplate the possibility of China and India developing a consumer-based social order somewhat like that of the West, it is difficult to imagine that fundamental changes will not be required in the nature of production and consumption if the environment supporting capitalism is to be sustained.

Another facet of political (or democratic) accountability deserves to be considered. One pattern afoot in capitalist systems is an effort to insulate economic organizations from accountability. This has been brought into stark relief by the role of Moody's and of Standard and Poor's in evaluating the creditworthiness of organizations and nations. These private agencies shape fundamental economic policy, because the credit ratings they issue strongly affect the interest rates those units will be charged in future borrowings; no wonder that Moody's has come under some scrutiny for its role in the East Asia crisis (see Sender 1998). So, too, agencies such as the International Monetary Fund have been criticized for their role in the East Asian debacle (Sachs 1998). Indeed, the Wall Street–Treasury complex has been challenged by otherwise stalwart defenders of free trade and capitalism (e.g., Bhagwati 1998; see Krugman 1998), for these scholars perceive the need to regulate politically the flow of financial capital in order to manage a modern economic order effectively. The political (and moral) accountability of the powerful organizations that support and shape the course of modern capitalism is far from settled and is destined to become even more salient during periods of severe economic dislocation.

Under these circumstances, the moral dimension of social inquiry looms large. Most contemporary sociologists, except, say, the communitarians, fail to explicate the moral presuppositions that underlie their call for greater justice or equity. It is not uncommon for sociologists to adopt a moral orientation that is anchored in some form of utilitarian thought. With regard to large-scale organizations, it is frequently assumed that replacing the wrongdoer will correct organizational misdeeds. I am not suggesting that human agents are not responsible for particular ills, rather that some of the most severe problems inhere within the nature of organizational arrangements.

This reasoning is in keeping with my thesis that organizational structures possess a reality apart from any particular set of human agents, although organizations are subject to change by collective action. In actuality, some organizational arrangements have been judged to be morally unacceptable. After World War II, the victors deemed it necessary not only to hold individual Nazis responsible for their actions but also to dismantle elements of the Nazi organizational apparatus, such as the Gestapo. Likewise, because of internal and external moral demands, a number of the worst features of the apartheid system in South Africa have, to a considerable degree, been dissolved.

With the rise of large-scale multinational corporations whose structures transcend nation-state boundaries, there is an ever-increasing urgency to reconsider the moral accountability of organizational structures. In the face of these changes we must rethink the foundations of the question of how democracy can and should function. We stand in need of a minimal set of universal moral standards for evaluating both corporate and state organizations. (Let us not forget how brutal state power can be: e.g., the patterns of genocide in various parts of the world during the twentieth century.)

Historically, the advocates of a free market have typically championed the universality of utilitarianism and its biopsychological conception of human nature. In general, sociologists who have questioned the standards employed by utilitarianism have appealed to a moral system based on relativism or system maintenance or enhancement. Sociologists have typically ignored the emergence of an alternative moral orientation, one embedded in the human rights tradition that arose especially after World War II. A universal moral orientation grounded in human rights principles is far from being worked out, yet elements of it are in place (e.g., Sjoberg 1996).

A moral orientation based on the principle of human rights affords humankind with a foundation for justifying basic liberties, on the one hand, and for justification for the existence of a minimal set of social and economic rights, on the other. A minimal set of universal moral standards would make it possible for citizens of nation-states to lay claims against multinational corporations for violations against their citizenry; in addition, people worldwide could challenge the abuse of power by a particular state.

Conclusions and Implications

We must, in my view, examine the nature of modern bureaucratic capitalism. That we have been witness to the centralization of corporate power on an unprecedented scale can no longer be ignored. Modern economic life is embedded within the context of large-scale and powerful organizations. How these organizations shape the capitalist enterprise has not yet been properly investigated.[14]

But we must do more than interpret and analyze the nature of capitalism within these bureaucratic contexts; we must also consider ways in which bureaucratic organizations can be held morally accountable to those who live in what is said to be a democratic order. It is not enough to hold individuals accountable. An adequate moral theory, grounded in sociological principles, must also come to hold organizations accountable. Then, we shall be able to grapple with the matter of social justice, including the process of social triage, in a more adequate manner.

Still other challenges await sociologists. We will need to think about alternative futures in ways that are atypical of much current sociological research. Recently, sociologists from diverse intellectual anchorages have called for some kind of utopian reasoning (e.g., Bourdieu 1998; Giddens 1994; Wallerstein 1991). One utopian form might be constructed within the general confines of capitalism itself, another from the perspective of a system counter to what exists (Sjoberg and Cain 1971). I am not, of course, suggesting that sociologists abandon the empirical study of what exists, since any effective alternative must be predicated on our empirical and theoretical understanding of ongoing processes associated with bureaucratic capitalism. But without attention to a reconceptualization of desirable ends based upon moral standards and an evaluation of human potentials, an answer to the question, Knowledge for what? will continue to elude us.

Notes

1. Some general comments about sources are in order. I have approached bureaucratic capitalism from the perspective of organizations, economic sociology, and "organizational deviance." My conceptualization has also been shaped by such publications as the *Financial Times*, the *Economist*, the *Wall Street Journal*, and the *Far Eastern Economic Review*. It should be evident that I have relied on Weber's (1978) writings and on the critical responses to them. In addition, recent works on organizations and economic life have informed my reasoning, e.g., Harrison (1994), Barnet and Cavanagh (1994), Greider (1997), Kaysen (1996), Adams and Brock (1986), and Doremus et al. (1998). In addition to these more general surveys I have profited considerably from the contributions in McMichael (1994) on global agribusiness and from Bonanno and Constance (1996) on the global tuna industry. Another significant source for interpreting organizational and economic life is found in the research on organizational deviance, e.g. Braithwaite (1984), Calavita, Postell, and Tillman (1997), Shapiro (1984), and Vaughan (1983). Moreover, the data that have emerged from the scandals associated with Bank of Credit and Commerce International, or BCCI (Beaty and Gwynne 1993), and the Atlanta branch of Italy's government-owned Banca Nazionale del Lavoro (Mantius 1995) provide us with a much needed perspective on bureaucratic capitalism.

2. Utilitarianism has had a long and complex history in social thought. One might consider Adam Smith as representing one wing of utilitarian thought and Jeremy Bentham as representing another. It seems evident that classical economic reasoning, which has served to justify the free market model, has been founded on utilitarian reasoning. Today, utilitarianism finds expression in exchange theory and rational choice theory. For a good overview of recent rational choice theory, see Smelser (1992).

3. Elsewhere my colleagues and I (Sjoberg et al. 1997) have articulated John Dewey's

significance for sociology. His writings (1927, 1988) serve to complement the contributions of fellow pragmatist George Herbert Mead (1934). They are particularly meaningful in coming to terms with the "relational logic" between the moral and the empirical.

4. An overview of the traditional organizational literature (including works by Barnard and Selznick) can be found in Perrow (1979), whereas the contributors to Powell
and DiMaggio (1991) focus on the new institutionalism. For a consideration of the latter,
see also Brinton and Nee (1998).

5. Löwy (1966) surveys the Weberian Marxists from George Lukacs to members of
the Frankfort school; however, these scholars have not analyzed capitalism from the
vantage point of bureaucracy.

6. A useful scholarly assessment of managerial literature is available in Clegg, Hardy,
and Nord (1996), and a popular account of leading management gurus is set forth in
Micklethwait and Wooldridge (1996).

7. In my judgment, when the history of our era is written, it will become apparent
that scholarly endeavor in the West was heavily shaped by the reactions to the Soviet
model, particularly during the Cold War period. Thus, the proponents of the free market
model, such as Mises, Hayek, and Friedman, effectively employed the Soviet Union as
a counterorientation for advancing their theoretical analysis. The eventual collapse of
the Soviet system may lend support to their reasoning.

8. Since the time of Chamberlain (1936) and Robinson (1933), we find works by Marxists such as Baran and Sweezy (1966) and by liberal economists such as Galbraith (1967)
that should be consulted.

9. In analyzing the relationship between human agents and organizations I am building on earlier writings (Vaughan and Sjoberg 1984; Sjoberg et al. 1984).

10. The meaning and role of bigness awaits further clarification. For instance, the
centralization of corporate power in the United States seems to be aided and abetted by
the legal apparatus. Williamson (1996, 27) observes that "whereas the courts routinely
hear disputes over prices, delivery, quality, and the like in transactions between firms,
these same courts refuse to be drawn into identical disputes between divisions of a
single firm. In effect, hierarchy becomes its own court of ultimate appeal." Therefore,
the centralization of corporate power not only provides managers with greater control
over their external environment but also over their internal organizational environment.

11. Cameron and Aggarwal (1996) provide us with a good overview of the peso crisis.
However, these authors, as well as others I have read, generally fail to come to terms
with the larger organizational structures in which this crisis evolved. More attention
needs to be given to the role of fraud and corruption in these disasters and to the manner
that the bailout served not only organizational interests in Mexico but also those in the
United States.

12. Data suggest that economic crises—notably recessions—in sectors of the world
system may further the expansion of large-scale bureaucratic organizations that dominate the core of the world economy. Thus, U.S. and European corporations have been
on the march in East and Southeast Asia as they have sought to take over or merge with
the "ailing" organizational structures suffering from the recession that began in 1997
(see, e.g., Landers 1998; Walker 1998; Zachary 1998). Also, in areas such as Latin America
the process of privatization has made it possible for major corporations to extend their
reach.

13. What is especially intriguing is the place of the privileged sector—not the super-
rich but the highly privileged—in the expansion of capitalism in the latter part of the

twentieth century. I think the expansion of the privileged sector in developing countries has been a primary force in the growth of many corporations in the core of the world system. Thus, Citicorp has had its eye on the privileged sector of Indian society as users of credit cards (Barnet and Cavanagh 1994), since 10 percent of India's population yields a huge potential market. More generally in developing countries, markups on luxury items (clothing, cars, cellular phones, many computer items) are typically handsome. Certainly, one finds hints in the financial press (van der Post 1998) of the powerful place of luxury items in capitalist expansion. This line of reasoning harks back to Sombart (1967) and at least indirectly to Veblen (1953) and deserves full attention in an extended analysis of bureaucratic capitalism.

14. As I write, the gravest economic crisis since World War II appears to be unfolding, and with the resulting social ruptures new data will become available to those examining bureaucratic capitalism. Within the global context we could single out a number of informative case studies for investigation (including Japan), but, in my view, the Russian case stands out. Although the centralized planning model in the former Soviet Union was a failure, we also find that the substituted shock therapy is also likely to be judged a failure. Cohen (1998), a historian of renown, has observed that male life expectancy in Russia has declined to fifty-seven years of age, and he speaks of the "demodernization" of an industrial nation (see also Bohlen 1998; Wines 1998). Although there are complex reasons for the severe economic dislocations in Russia, one that receives insufficient attention is the role of multinational corporations.

References

Adams, Walter, and James W. Brock. 1986. *The Bigness Complex*. New York: Pantheon Books.

Baran, Paul A., and Paul M. Sweezy. 1966. *Monopoly Capital*. New York: Monthly Review Press.

Barnet, Richard J., and John Cavanagh. 1994. *Global Dreams: Imperial Corporations and the New World Order*. New York: Simon & Schuster.

Beaty, Jonathan, and S. C. Gwynne. 1993. *The Outlaw Bank: A Wild Ride into the Secret Heart of BCCI*. New York: Random House.

Beck, Ulrich. 1995. *Ecological Enlightenment*. Highlands, N.J.: Humanities Press.

Bellah, Robert N. 1983. "The Ethical Aims of Social Inquiry." In *Social Science as Moral Inquiry*, edited by Norma Haan, Robert N. Bellah, Paul Rabinow, and William M. Sullivan, 360–81. New York: Columbia University Press.

Best, Steven, and Douglas Kellner. 1991. *Postmodern Theory*. New York: Guilford Press.

Bhagwati, Jagdish. 1998. "The Capital Myth: The Difference between Trade in Widgets and Dollars." *Foreign Affairs* 77 (May/June): 7–12.

Block, Fred. 1996. *The Vampire State*. New York: New Press.

Blumer, Herbert. 1969. *Symbolic Interactionism*. Berkeley: University of California Press.

Bohlen, Celestine. 1998. "After Moscow's Binge, It's Hangover Time." *New York Times*, September 9, A1, A10.

Bonanno, Alessandro, and Douglas Constance. 1996. *Caught in the Net: The Global Tuna Industry, Environmentalism, and the State*. Lawrence: University Press of Kansas.

Bourdieu, Pierre. 1998. "A Reasoned Utopia and Economic Fatalism." *New Left Review* 227 (January/February): 125–30.

Braithwaite, John. 1984. *Corporate Crime in the Pharmaceutical Industry*. London: Routledge & Kegan Paul.

Brinton, Mary C., and Victor Nee, eds. 1998. *The New Institutionalism in Sociology*. New York: Russell Sage Foundation.

Calavita, Kitty, Henry N. Postell, and Robert H. Tillman. 1997. *Big Money Crime: Fraud and Politics in the Savings and Loan Crisis*. Berkeley and Los Angeles: University of California Press.

Cameron, Maxwell A., and Vinod K. Aggarwal. 1996. "Mexican Meltdown: States, Markets and Post-NAFTA Financial Turmoil." *Third World Quarterly* 17: 975–87.

Chamberlain, Edward. 1936. *The Theory of Monopolistic Competition*, 2d ed. Cambridge, Mass.: Harvard University Press.

Christie, Nils. 1993. *Crime Control as Industry: Towards GULAGS, Western Style?* New York: Routledge.

Clegg, Stewart R., Cynthia Hardy, and Walter Nord, eds. 1996. *Handbook of Organizational Studies*. London: Sage.

Cohen, Stephen F. 1998. "Why Call It Reform?" *Nation* 267 (September 7/14): 6–7.

Delaney, Kevin. 1992. *Strategic Bankruptcy*. Berkeley and Los Angeles: University of California Press.

Dewey, John. 1927. *The Public and Its Problems*. New York: Henry Holt.

———. 1988. *The Later Works, 1925–1953*. Vol. 13 of *The Complete Works of John Dewey*. Carbondale: Southern Illinois University Press.

Doremus, Paul N., William W. Keller, Louis W. Pauly, and Simon Reich. 1998. *The Myth of the Global Corporation*. Princeton, N.J.: Princeton University Press.

Etzioni, Amitai. 1993. *The Responsive Community: The Reinvention of American Society*. New York: Simon & Schuster.

Evans, Peter D., Dietrich Rueschemeyer, and Theda Skocpol, eds. 1985. *Bringing the State Back In*. Cambridge: Cambridge University Press.

Feagin, Joe R., and Robert Parker. 1990. *Building American Cities: The Urban Real Estate Game*, 2d ed. Englewood Cliffs, N.J.: Prentice-Hall.

Fligstein, Neil. 1990. *The Transformation of Corporate Control*. Cambridge, Mass.: Harvard University Press.

Galbraith, John Kenneth. 1967. *The New Industrial State*. Boston: Houghton Mifflin.

Giddens, Anthony. 1984. *The Constitution of Society*. Berkeley and Los Angeles: University of California Press.

———. 1994. *Beyond Left and Right*. Stanford, Calif.: Stanford University Press.

Gouldner, Alvin W. 1970. *The Coming Crisis of Western Sociology*. New York: Basic Books.

Granovetter, Mark. 1985. "Economic Action and Social Structure: The Problem of Embeddedness." *American Journal of Sociology* 91: 481–510.

Greider, William. 1997. *One World, Ready or Not: The Manic Logic of Global Capitalism*. New York: Simon & Schuster.

Habermas, Jürgen. 1984. *The Theory of Communicative Action: Reason and the Rationalization of Society*, vol. 1. Boston: Beacon Press.

———. 1987. *Lifeworld and System: A Critique of Functionalist Reason*. Vol. 2 of *The Theory of Communicative Action*. Boston: Beacon Press.

Hardy, Cynthia, and Stuart R. Clegg. 1996. "Some Dare Call It Power." In *Handbook of Organizational Studies*, edited by Stuart R. Clegg, Cynthia Hardy, and Walter Nord, 622–41. London: Sage.

Harrison, Bennett. 1994. *Lean and Mean: The Changing Landscape of Corporate Power in the Age of Flexibility*. New York: Basic Books.

Jones, Robert Alun. 1994. "The Positive Science of Ethics in France: German Influences on *De la division du travail social*." *Sociological Forum* 9: 37–58.

Kaysen, Carl, ed. 1996. *The American Corporation Today.* New York: Oxford University Press.

Kluger, Richard. 1997. *Ashes to Ashes: America's Hundred Year Cigarette War, the Public Health, and the Unabashed Triumph of Philip Morris.* New York: Vintage Press.

Krugman, Paul. 1998. "Saving Asia: It's Time to Get Radical." *Fortune* 138 (September 7): 75–80.

Landers, Peter. 1998. "Open the Gates." *Far Eastern Economic Review,* June 11, 52.

Littrell, W. Boyd. 1989. "New Technology, Bureaucracy, and the Social Construction of Medical Prices." *Journal of Applied Behavioral Science* 25: 249–70.

Löwy, Michael. 1996. "Figures of Weberian Marxism." *Theory and Society* 25: 431–46.

Lukes, Steven. 1974. *Power: A Radical View.* London: Macmillan.

Lynd, Robert S. 1939. *Knowledge for What?* Princeton, N.J.: Princeton University Press.

Mantius, Peter. 1995. *Shell Game.* New York: St. Martin's Press.

Massing, Michael. 1996. "How to Win the Tobacco War." *New York Review* 43 (July 11): 32–36.

McMichael, Philip, ed. 1994. *The Global Restructuring of Agro-Foods Systems.* Ithaca, N.Y.: Cornell University Press.

Mead, George Herbert. 1934. *Mind, Self, and Society.* Chicago: University of Chicago Press.

Micklethwait, John, and Adrian Wooldridge. 1996. *The Witch Doctors: Making Sense of the Management Gurus.* New York: Times Books.

Mills, C. Wright. 1959. *The Sociological Imagination.* New York: Oxford University Press.

Moore, Barrington, Jr. 1978. *Injustice: The Social Basis of Obedience and Revolt.* Armonk, N.Y.: M. E. Sharpe.

Parsons, Talcott. 1937. *The Structure of Social Action.* New York: McGraw-Hill.

Portes, Alejandro. 1994. "The Informal Economy and Its Paradoxes." In *The Handbook of Economic Sociology,* edited by Neil J. Smelser and Richard Swedberg, 426–49. Princeton, N.J.: Princeton University Press.

Powell, Walter W., and Paul J. DiMaggio, eds. 1991. *The New Institutionalism in Organizational Analysis.* Chicago: University of Chicago Press.

Robinson, Joan. 1933. *The Economics of Imperfect Competition.* London: Macmillan.

Sachs, Jeffrey. 1998. "The IMF and the Asian Flu." *American Prospect* no. 37 (March–April): 16–21.

Sassen, Saskia. 1991. *The Global City.* Princeton, N.J.: Princeton University Press.

Selznick, Philip. 1992. *The Moral Commonwealth.* Berkeley and Los Angeles: University of California Press.

Sender, Henny. 1998. "Moody's Blues." *Far Eastern Economic Review* (August 13): 10–13.

Shapiro, Susan. 1984. *Wayward Capitalists.* New Haven, Conn.: Yale University Press.

Sjoberg, Gideon. 1996. "The Human Rights Challenge to Communitarianism: Formal Organizations and Race and Ethnicity." In *Macro Socio-Economics,* edited by David Sciulli, 273–97. Armonk, N.Y.: M. E. Sharpe.

Sjoberg, Gideon, and Leonard D. Cain. 1971. "Negative Values, Countersystem Models, and the Analysis of Social Systems." In *Institutions and Social Exchange: The Sociologies of Talcott Parsons and George C. Homans,* edited by Herman Turk and Richard L. Simpson, 212–29. Indianapolis: Bobbs-Merrill.

Sjoberg, Gideon, Elizabeth Gill, Boyd Littrell, and Norma Williams. 1997. "The Reemergence of John Dewey and American Pragmatism." In *Studies in Symbolic Interaction,* edited by Norman Denzin. 21: 73–92. Greenwich, Conn.: JAI Press.

Sjoberg, Gideon, Ted R. Vaughan, and Norma Williams. 1984. "Bureaucracy as a Moral Issue." *Journal of Applied Behavioral Science* 20: 441–53.

Smelser, Neil J. 1992. "The Rational Choice Perspective: A Theoretical Assessment." *Rationality and Society* 4: 381–410.

Smelser, Neil J., and Richard Swedberg, eds. 1994. *The Handbook of Economic Sociology.* Princeton, N.J.: Princeton University Press.

Smith, Dorothy E. 1990. *The Conceptual Practices of Power.* Boston: Northeastern University Press.

Sombart, Werner. 1967. *Luxury and Capitalism.* Ann Arbor: University of Michigan Press.

Sorokin, Pitirim A., and Walter Lunden. 1954. *Power and Morality.* New York: Porter Sargaent.

van der Post, Lucia. 1998. "Life's Brittle Luxuries." *Financial Times* (July 18/19), Weekend Section.

Vaughan, Diane. 1983. *Controling Unlawful Organizational Behavior: Social Structure and Corporate Misconduct.* Chicago: University of Chicago Press.

Vaughan, Ted R., and Gideon Sjoberg. 1984. "The Individual and Bureaucracy: An Alternative Meadian Interpretation." *Journal of Applied Behavioral Science* 20: 57–69.

Veblen, Thorstein. 1953. *The Theory of the Leisure Class.* New York: Mentor.

Walker, Tony. 1998. "US Buys $8bn of Asian Business." *Financial Times,* June 15, 5.

Wallerstein, Immanuel. 1991. *Unthinking Social Science.* London: Polity Press.

Weber, Max. 1978. *Economy and Society,* edited by Guenther Roth and Claus Wittich. Berkeley: University of California Press.

Williamson, Oliver E. 1996. *The Mechanism of Governance.* New York: Oxford University Press.

Wines, Michael. 1998. "As Ruble Falls, Moscow Unravels Faster and Faster." *New York Times,* September 4, A4.

Zachary, G. Pascal. 1998. "Picking the Bones." *Wall Street Journal,* June 22, 1, 15.

CHAPTER FOUR

From Women's Standpoint to a Sociology for People

Dorothy E. Smith

I begin with what is becoming a central issue for me. It is a political issue. My method of inquiry working from the standpoint of women has led me to propose a sociology that takes the everyday/everynight world as its problematic. This world is the site of people's direct experiencing of the world, experiencing which is not of raw sensory data but is through and through socially organized.

Somewhere I acquired a habit that sociologists may take for granted, that of thinking beyond the local to its connectedness with relations beyond or elsewhere. I have begun to see that it is exceptional to have acquired an awareness that is the social analogue of being able at sunset to "see" the place I stand in on this globe turning away out of the sunlight and into the dark. Analogously I have learned to see where I am as embedded in social relations that do not begin and end with the scope of my daily activities: going to work, going shopping, sitting at the computer, looking up above my table to my photograph of the Bright Angel Canyon, which I once hiked from the north rim of the Grand Canyon to the Colorado River. I look at the labels in clothes on the rack in the store and know something of how clothes "made in" Guatemala, Honduras, Taiwan, China, Mexico have come to be there and about the conditions of their manufacture. I have seen the numbers of panhandlers on the streets near my apartment in Toronto grow steadily over the past ten years. I do not know exactly where they come from, but I know that there is a connection between their presence and the increasingly endemic high rates of unemployment. On the job at the institute where I work, I know how to trace the interlocking texts that articulate our work into the structure of the university and to organize it, and I use that knowledge.

When I hiked down the Grand Canyon, I was alone a lot of the way. I had a map, a very good map. I could locate where I was on the trail, what I could expect next, and how far I had to go. I had a pocket book that told me about the desert and desert hiking and what to look out for and how to act, and I took its advice (it was a hot day in June and a hot day in June is pretty hot at the bottom of the canyon). I want a sociology that will make maps for people so that we can grasp how to see where we are and how our lives are connected with those of others. I envisage such a sociology as aiming at making "maps" or explicating the relations and organizations articulated to people's own activities and as being directed as much for teaching as for advances in the discourse itself. I see that, in those areas in which we work at what is beginning to be called "institutional ethnography," we know how to make maps of the regions in which we are working, and I can teach those methods to people *as a skill* rather than as theory.

I have come recently to believe that people do not automatically acquire a way of seeing the local world that locates it in a map of how society is putting our lives together and that teaching people how their everyday/everynight living is embedded in and organized by social relations connecting them with the lives of multiple others at work elsewhere is itself a political practice. The project of teaching such a sociology relates to current issues of democratic process and the exposure of North American societies to a peculiar form of what might be called "class totalitarianism," a totalitarianism not of the state and not of terror, but of appropriation and management. As Herbert Schiller put it (1996, 1), "Today, a remarkable edifice of invisible control has been constructed, permitting the most far-reaching measures of social domination to escape significant public attention. This achievement is all the more startling when it is accompanied by the bold assertion, widely believed, that the overarching condition of American life is freedom, freedom that exists through the political realm and encompasses the full range of individual behavior."

The standpoint of "capital" is pervasive in contemporary public discourse. The latter is increasingly exclusive of alternative and particularly of progressive ways of thinking about the world (Blumenthal 1986; Messer-Davidow 1993). As members of an intelligentsia, our power to exercise public influence is diminishing. The increasing concentration of media ownership by a very small number of corporations is consequential both for the kinds of journalism that is practiced (e.g., a move away from investigative journalism) and for the exclusion of critical viewpoints and certain kinds of news (Bagdikian 1992; McChesney 1997; McManus 1994; Schiller 1996; Winter 1997). The mass media do not provide people with means of finding the connections between the actualities of our daily lives and what is going on in the economy or polity.

My proposal is not for an applied sociology, though the sociology

I am proposing could certainly be applied. Rather I am proposing a sociology that does not observe the divide between academic or scientific and applied sociology. Nor am I simply proposing a sociology that is popularly accessible. The research and investigations of such a sociology aim at making maps for people's uses, perhaps rather partial at this stage like the early maps of coastlines made by the Phoenician traders—partial but nonetheless workable. Making maps, explicating social relations, is technical business. Making tools for people to use or maps for them to read cannot be done in a language that is accessible to everyone. The technical work has to be done in order to explicate relations in ways that are ordinarily intelligible. It is only after we have found out how things are put together that we can make them visible to people whose lives are caught up in them. The business here is not to solve problems, but to unfold society from the standpoint of those who are living it and bringing it into being.

The sociology I practice or am learning to practice appreciates discourse as social relations or social organization. The poststructural-postmodern discovery of the subject constituted in discourse parallels the earlier sociological concept of role. Both formulate and abstract from forms of organization that are objectified in the sense of being detached from *particular* individuals and their relationships. New theories of the discursively constituted subject locate a positioning of the reader/writer/knower in particular ways in relation the objects of inquiry, both in terms of how they incorporate what people say and do into discursive texts and in the relations constructed within the texts themselves. There is therefore an issue of how these relations are organized and of the practices to which we become committed when we are positioned as knowers or inquirers within sociological discourse as it is.

Sociology's standard stylistic conventions constitute subject positions that locate the reader/inquirer outside the social world in which the text is read or written and where the positioned subject does her work, lives her life, and cares or does not care about the people she investigates. The people who bring the phenomena with which she is concerned into being disappear from view in nominalizations (or similar devices), grammatical forms that repress the presence of people as agents, replacing them with nouns or noun phrases constructed from activities. They are terms such as "meaning," "interests," "cognition," "information," "communication," "organization." They create for sociology a "layer" of discursive entities subsuming and displacing actual activities and actual people. They can be entered into sentences in which they may take on the syntactic capacity of agents as well as of objects.

Nominalizing enables statements to be made about general social processes without having to worry too much about what people are doing or think they are doing. Hence statements about the social are made as statements about relations among discursively constituted entities, quite uncertainly related to the world that people know as they are bringing it into being. Purely formal theoretical constructions predict to selected bits of actuality. Theories "select, i.e., abstract, according to their own criteria of relevance to theoretical problems" (Alexander 1995, 22). Insofar as people are present, they become the objects of investigation whose behavior is to be explained. In general, sociology's conceptual practices privilege sociological knowledge over people's own experience.

Women's Standpoint as a Sociological Point d'Appui

Working from women's standpoint as a method of inquiry has been an attempt to design a sociology with differently organized relations. Women's standpoint (as I have thought about it) is located in an historical trajectory in the history of capitalism in Western Europe. Capitalism is an organization of social relations mediated by an exchange of money and commodities independent of particularities of relationships among persons and connecting multiple sites of people's work and consumption. Correlative has been a development of extensive objectified relations and organizations that are mediated by texts and that I have come to call the "ruling relations," that is, relations that are an objectified specialization of consciousness and agency, technically elaborated and rationalized as discrete organizational forms. Examples include bureaucracy in Weber's account or Foucault's (1972) conception of discourse. These too are organized so as to be independent of particular individuals and particularized relationships and to govern local sites of people's activities without being reducible to them.

The dynamic trajectory of these relations has constituted regions of action increasingly separate from the local and particularized organization of the family-household. By the eighteenth century in Western Europe and North America, the domestic was emerging as a discrete sphere over against the spheres of business, politics, and the media. These latter were spheres of male activity and connected men at the national and even the international level. Women did not appear in them as authorized agents or speakers. Those subordinated by class and/or race were similarly excluded. While a media addressed to women was emerging, women only slowly emerged as writers themselves, and then they were writers primarily of the domestic.

This division between the domestic sphere and the spheres of men's activities in commerce and public affairs had been produced and reproduced throughout the institutional structure of Western capitalist societies. It was built into the ways in which women participated in the world of work outside the home, whether as teachers, secretaries and typists, or industrial workers. It was present in a women's media, in the ways in which women worked in other women's households, in the organization of trade unions, and in the worlds of universities, science, and politics. And this division is, of course, still very deeply embedded in contemporary institutional processes even though the women's movement has broken down the sharpness of the divide. (See Harriet Friedmann, in this volume, for a fuller discussion of how this divide was institutionalized in sociology.)

To begin in women's standpoint, then, is to begin on women's side of the divide that had been created in this historical trajectory. It means beginning in the everydayness of a work that is situated in a particular local site and in relation to particular others. It is done in the body and serves particular others as bodies. This is also where discourse and the ruling relations in general *happen* as something being done in time by particular people in the actual local settings of their bodily being within which the local practices that discard biography, personal considerations, and pragmatic preoccupations (Schutz 1962) are performed and the entry to the "reality" of scientific thought is engaged. It is work that organizes consciousness in relation to the fullness of what is there and that is always and inescapably in a particular time and place. From this standpoint, the extralocal, text-mediated, and objectified institutions—the ruling relations—come into view (Smith 1990a; 1990d; 1998).

Developing a sociological inquiry grounded in women's standpoint entails making a sociology that is in dialogue with the actualities of people's lives as they experience them. People are the experts of their own lives and local practices. Unlike sociologies that seek to generate a totalizing system, this sociology is always in the making. From different sites of women's experience, different social relations or different aspects of the same complex are brought into view and their organization explicated. As in Hans-Georg Gadamer's (1975) dialogic, such a sociology is always prepared to be changed by its encounter with others; indeed it must invite encounters with what it does not yet know how to think. Like a map, such a knowledge is always indexical in the sense that it is incomplete without the particularities of the terrain it indexes (Smith 1996, 1998). Such a sociology aims, like a map, at expanding rather than superseding people's knowledge of how the everyday/everynight world of their experience is organized by relations beyond their experience.

A Method of Inquiry

Central to this sociology for women is a method of inquiry. Rather than insisting that theories or concepts must be in place to govern research, its focus is the actualities of people's activities or practices and how they are coordinated or concerted. Hence it relies on the possibility of *investigation*, of finding out, of discovering. This is pretty much the move that Marx and Engels (1976) made in *The German Ideology* when they rejected beginning in imagination or in concepts and resolved instead to start with actual people and their activities under definite material conditions. The concerting of people's activities that constitutes this sociology's phenomenal domain is ongoing; it actually happens; it can be "observed," sometimes recorded, explored, and analyzed. Like ethnomethodology, a sociology from women's standpoint orients to people's practical activities in accomplishing order (Garfinkel 1967), but without prejudging that order is achieved or even aimed at. Unlike ethnomethodology, its primary focus is not with the competencies of individuals or with members' knowledge, but with something closer to what George Herbert Mead calls "the social act," that is, the ongoing concerting of actual activities in definite settings. This is what I mean by the social as the object of the sociologist's interest, expertise, and inquiry.

The coordinating of activities may be conceived and explored at multiple levels from the intimate tuning of copresent bodies in breastfeeding or sexual activity to the macrosocial relations explored by Marx in *Capital* and *The Theories of Surplus Value*.[1] The social relations that coordinate the activities of a multiplicity of people in a variety of local settings are both determinative of their situations and produced by their participation. The conjunction of local and extralocal organization is a special focus. Here are those interchanges between the local experience of individuals and the social relations that coordinate their activities with what lies beyond their experience: "Individuals always started, and always start, from themselves. Their relations are the relations of their real life. How does it happen that their relations assume an independent existence over against them? And that the forces of their own life overpower them?" (Marx and Engels 1973, 30).[2]

As Marx clearly saw, beginning with actual individuals and their activities means taking for granted that consciousness cannot be separated from them. It is always and only theirs. In Marx's time, the kinds of developments that I have called the ruling relations were only beginning the take-off—the results of which we live with today. How, therefore, consciousness may be objectified and still be inseparable from actual individuals was not something that he encountered as a matter of his own experience and observation. In our time, however, for many of us, these objectifications are integral to our working lives and not only as sociologists. The phenomena of large-scale organization, of bureaucracy, of professional organization, of administration, of academic, scientific, and technical discourses, of the discourses of the mass media, and so on, are forms of organizing knowledge, judgment, and will as external to particular individuals. I want to go further than this in pulling beliefs, concepts, theories, ideology, and so on into the same local and particular site as actual individuals live in. I discard the dual ontology, practice versus theory, and all the issues of how the latter affects the former. Rather I see that thinking, using concepts, working with theory, and so on are also people's actual practices, that they are done in actual settings where people are at work, or in conversation, or whatever. There is an actual moment when a concept is brought into play as a constituent of the sequence of action it coordinates. Theories, ideologies, concepts, and so on, are practices; they happen, they can be investigated.

Ruling Relations Revisited

"Ruling relations" as a concept is not strictly theoretical in that it is ostensive rather than analytic. It points to what became visible to me as I took up women's standpoint as a place to begin to work sociologically. The extralocal abstracted relations organizing multiple sites of people's activities in standardized ways could be seen as they too were (necessarily) people's local practices. Again, let me remind you that we are still talking about actual individuals, people coordinating their activities in particular local sites of their bodily being. The problem then is how to remain at that level and, at the same time, reach into relations and organization that coordinate people's activities extralocally and in generalized and generalizing forms.

In developing an account of the ruling relations as an objectification of processes of coordination of people's activities, I have traced over Marx's later thinking on the emergence of the economy. In a characteristic move, Marx (1973) does not take for granted the categories of political economy. Rather his method requires the social scientist to explore the social relations expressed or reflected in the categories. The "economy" does not exist a priori. It emerges historically as relations that have taken on an independent existence as a specialization and differentiation of what he calls "relations of dependency" among people. In analogous fashion I conceive of the social "relations of ruling" as objectified organization that emerge historically. Here is Marx's account of the emergence of the social relations of the economy:

> When we look at social relations which create an undeveloped system of exchange, of exchange values and of money, or which correspond to an undeveloped degree of these, then it is clear from the outset that the individuals in such a society, although their relations appear to be more personal, enter into connection with one another only as individuals imprisoned with a certain definition, as feudal lord and vassal, landlord and serf, etc., or as members of a caste etc. or as members of an estate etc. In the . . . developed system of exchange . . . the ties of personal dependence, of distinctions of blood, education, etc. are in fact exploded, ripped up. . . . So far from constituting the removal of a "state of dependence," these external relationships represent its disintegration into a general form, or better, they are the elaboration of the general basis of personal states of dependence. Here too individuals come into relation with one another only in a determined role. These material states of dependence, as opposed to the personal states, are also characterized by the fact that individuals are now controlled only by abstractions, whereas earlier they depended on one another. (Marx 1973, 164)

With the full development of the market as relations of exchange between people mediated by money and commodities, relations of dependence become differentiated and specialized as those relations we know as the economy. They come to have an autonomous status and dynamic.

I envisage the ruling relations and the historical trajectory of their development as an analogous process of differentiation and specialization. The ruling relations "extract" the coordination and concerting of people's everyday/everynight activities from relations between persons and subject them to specialized and often technical development as "organization," "communication," "information," "management," and the like. These relations are mediated by and based in texts and textual technologies, such as print, radio, television, and more recently electronics. The functions of "knowledge, judgment, and will" that Marx saw as wrested from the original "producer"—artisan or crafts-man—and transferred to capital, become built into a specialized com-plex of objectified forms of organization and relationship. Progres-sively, the individuated functions of knowing, judging, planning, and deciding are transferred to organization, ceasing to be capacities im-mediately of the individual. They are constituted as actual forms of concerting and concerted activities and can be investigated as such. "Objectivity," the focus of postmodernist critique, is only one form of objectification, though objectified organization relies extensively on text-mediated virtual realities (Smith 1990a). Forms of organization, such as the stock market, are objectified in the sense that they are not reducible to individuals or the actions of individuals and become, in-deed, the everyday/everynight condition, circumstance, means, and terrain of people's financial activities.

Texts and the Interchange between Micro and Macro

Beginning in the local settings of people's activities and relying on their experience in and of those activities seems to consign us to the limita-tions of the local and the particular, without possibility of generaliza-tion or of connecting with macrosocial relations. This has been the outcome for ethnomethodology, even when it has been deployed in the study of work organization or the interface of people and machines (Suchman 1987). Studies such as Deidre Boden's (1994) analyses of con-versations in the study of formal organization have not been able to go beyond exhibiting the organizational in the conversational. They have not been successful in escaping from the particularities of the conversational in ways that preserve the special merits of ethnomethod-ology's reliance on people's practical activities.

In my view, the solution to this problem is not to be found in a return to the nominalizations so strikingly characteristic of the study of large-scale organization and more recently of "institutions" (Scott 1996). Rather, it is to take advantage of the commitment of women's stand-point to remaining at the level of the embodied subject and to ask: Just how do we encounter the "expanding" social relations, whether of capital or of ruling, in which we are active?

We know how to respond in the case of capital. Economic relations "appear" in our everyday/everynight activities as money, whether cash, credit card, cheque, debit card, and so on. It is money that enters our activities into the expanded relations of exchange. Analogously it is the text as a material object that sutures the everyday/everynight site of our activities to the extralocal organization of the relations of ruling as it is "read" by particular people in the local settings of their activity at and during the time they are reading it.

The materiality of the text and its indefinite replicability creates a peculiar ground in which it can seem that language, thought, culture, and formal organization all have their own being outside lived time and the actualities of people's living other than as those actualities become objects of action or investigation from within the textual. But from the point of view of this method of inquiry, the textual mediation of these relations and forms of organization has the miraculous effect of creating a join between local and particular, and the generalizing and generalized organization of the relations of ruling, hence opening the latter to investigation in a new way.

Ruling relations are characterized by a capacity to realize the same forms, courses of action, relations, and so on, in the varieties and multiplicities of the local settings within which they operate and which they regulate. Indeed it is their capacity to reproduce standardized forms of control, management, communication, and so on, across multiple local sites and at different times that distinguishes them from other forms of organization or ruling. We could indeed read Weber's types of authority as analyses of the shifts from authority grounded in relations of personal dependence to the text-mediated organization of the offices of bureaucracy.

The textual bases that objectify knowledge, organization, and decision processes are essential to the ubiquity that characterizes these relations of ruling. They distinguish what individuals are in themselves from what they do organizationally, professionally, or as participants in a discourse. To investigate social relations and organization through their organizing texts, texts must be situated in the local courses or sequences of action in which they are read and come into play (note here that I am not distinguishing for these general purposes between printed texts, film, television, and the computer text). It is difficult for us to get away from accepting the text in the atemporal mode that it sets up for us. Texts contain their own internal sequences that are independent of the local sequences in which they are read (or written). But in fact all such reading is in and of a particular course of action and is integrally part of its organization. The notion of a course of action here is not meant to introduce a new entity but rather to set up an analytic device forcing the situating of a text in time and in action rather than treating it, as it is very generally treated in sociology, as a source of information about something other than itself.

Here then is located the hermeneutic moment, discovered now as a sequence of reading/interpretation or conversation that is a sequence embedded in an extended course—or multiple courses—of action. Interpretations are to be discovered, then, in the sociologist's analysis of how interpretations are done, focusing on how they are taken up into and organize what comes next. In the same way we can begin to explore the uses of concepts, theories, and so on, as standardized practices of interpreting and organizing texts that are learned and become standardized through people's participation in text-mediated discourses or other forms of organization.

When I read an interview giving an account of someone becoming mentally ill (Smith 1990c), I know how to go about interpreting the text to find in it what I know how to look for. The text, on the other hand, of the interview is itself organized to offer me what I need to find in order to make the reading it intends (Smith 1990b). The social (coordinative) character, is already there for me, as analyst, to find in practices of reading/interpretation or of writing to intend an interpretation. As sociologists we are not so much interested in idiosyncracies of reading/interpretation as in the standardized practices that enable the extralocality and objectification of these forms of social relations.

Take Gadamer's (1975) hermeneutic epistemology, which gives central place to conversations or dialogue in understanding. Imagine situating such conversations in their local settings among particular individuals and, I would emphasize, *in time*. The very notion of a tradition within which understandings emerge locates, from this point of view, a textual ground, though not necessarily through the technology of print. The people in conversation are at work. The conversation is informed by the reading and thinking that each conversant has done before their encounter. The text enters into the organization sequences of action. Each conversant is going on to write something, to teach perhaps, to tell someone else in some way. Being changed by the conversation is not, from this standpoint, a change in a mental state, "understanding," but a change in how each will carry on in what comes next. The focus shifts from securing the meaning of a proposition or, more loosely, what she said or of the text, to how it is "taken up" in "what comes next." The notion of making—bringing background assumptions into consciousness, a procedure that Garfinkel (1967) subjects to the critique of one of his "experiments"—puts things the wrong way around. This procedure is still stuck with the text itself as the container of meaning; it adopts a strategy of going around the textual ground or behind it to find out what it might mean to its readers. In contrast, the approach I'm recommending here does not look for context or background to eke out the *necessary* imperfections of the text. Rather, it investigates the ongoing world of activity into which the text is entered (how it is interpreted and what is brought to the interpretation) that brings it into an active relation with the sequences of action in which it is engaged. Following George Herbert Mead, language is understood as entering into, selecting, instructing, coordinating diverse consciousnesses in courses of social action rather than as carrying around packages of meaning that it deposits here and there like a cuckoo laying its eggs.

An Example of Institutional Ethnography

The research approach particularly associated with this sociology is called "institutional ethnography." It seeks to explore and explicate how the local settings of people's lives are coordinated by social relations not wholly visible to them. I thought it might be useful to concretize the differences between established kinds of analysis and how one might go about doing this kind of research by reflecting on how I might go about investigating a particular case. I mean it only to clarify what I have written above. I have chosen to work with this example, though I had alternatives, in part because I wanted to demonstrate that a sociology from women's standpoint offers a sociology for people. Hence the example is not specifically relevant to women.

I draw upon the work of Steven Vallas and John Beck (1996), who explore the transformation of work in changing technological and organizational settings. Their study participates in a discourse focused on the transformation of work in "postindustrial society." They take up the argument that large corporations are adopting new work arrangements enabling "flexible specialization" and minimizing hierarchy. Their study of four pulp and paper mills owned by a single multinational corporation aims at "assessing the validity of [these] post-Fordist claims" and opening "up for discussion aspects of workplace change that advocates of post-Fordism" have neglected (Vallas and Beck 1996, 340).

The authors observed work relations and interviewed workers and management at four plants where new technologies had been introduced. Their paper focuses on the different viewpoints of process engineers and older workers in this new setting. Before the introduction of new technologies, workers were directly involved in production and in overseeing machine-automated processes. Slight variations at one stage could have significant consequences "down the line." Workers learned on the job over time, gaining carefully guarded skills. In introducing new automated controls and "Total Quality Management" strategies, the corporation sought to achieve "greater stability in the operations and appreciable reductions in crew sizes" (Vallas and Beck 1996, 346). The latter strategy includes "Statistical Process Control," which interprets fluctuations in production outcomes to distinguish between random and systematic variations (Vallas and Beck 1996, 347). Operators now oversee and regulate processes at a distance through computerized controls. Process engineers are increasingly in command at the shop-floor level, and the experience-based knowledge of older operatives is discounted. One process engineer is reported as saying, "I'd rather have things that way [making an occasional error which can be corrected by putting in a new loop] than depend on a fifty-year-old man filling out control charts and applying complex rules by himself" (Vallas and Beck 1996, 350).

My purpose is not to criticize their study. On the contrary I find it very interesting and very thorough. Vallas and Beck's findings do not support the "flexibility" hypothesis, although this is not news, and they describe effectively the changes they do find. There is, however, an alternative, and that is to explore the social relations organizing the local settings of the shop floor and, in particular, how these social relations locate the process engineers and the workers whose knowledge the new computerized technologies supplant.

Here are some lines of exploration suggested by institutional ethnography. The approach used by Vallas and Beck treats the shop floor of the plant as a unit. It is influenced by management decisions to bring new technologies and new managerial strategies into the corporation and to make radical changes in the organization of work. There is no sense, however, that what has also been changed is the whole way in which shop-floor processes are hooked into the system of controls through which the corporation operates and how these links connect the shop floor to the stock exchange and the international markets that buy and sell capital. Statistical process controls are of special importance to multinational corporations engaged in similar industrial production in a number of local sites and are effective only if in fact production processes are highly standardized and strictly measurable from site to site.[3] Furthermore, statistical quality controls hook directly into the corporation's system of financial accounting that coordinates the different functions that constitute the corporation in relation to the value of its stock. There is an interlocking system of text-mediated management that ties the corporation's status on international capital markets with the work organization at the level of the shop floor in all its plants.

Accounting is not an exact science; it is the technical articulation of capital as a regime.[4] Accounting systems have built-in assumptions that become the enforceable practices of given jurisdictions, such as the New York or Tokyo Stock Exchanges. "'Organizing principles,' reflecting generalized national accounting conventions, mediate corporate employment, adjust strategies and the institutional configuration of that society" (Usui and Colignon 1996, 570). At the managerial level, accounting and other managerial technologies produce the texts of the virtual or hyperreality (Baudrillard 1994) in relation to which executives of large-scale capitalist organizations function.

They also are dimensions of the organization and reproduction of class. "In Germany and Japan, labor and capital are treated equally as factors of production. Labor is more a constant, rather than a variable for employers. In the United States, labor is a variable" (Usui and Colignon 1996, 370). Such differences, however, may be moderated as corporations from outside the United States adopt the accounting standards of the New York Stock Exchange. A 1993 editorial in the *Financial Times* spells out the implications of just such a move. German corporations have taken initiatives to participate in U.S.-designed capital markets. To do so, German corporations would be required to adopt the accounting practices of the New York Stock Exchange. The editorial speculates that such a change in accounting practices would likely endanger the "harmonious relations between management and workers within the company" that contribute to the "success of German industry." Accounting practices in the United States give labor costs greater weight in measuring profitability than do German companies, hence encouraging managers to give primacy to the reduction of labor costs in improving the visible profitability of their company and its standing in capital markets. Restructuring to advance a company's standing in capital markets has meant "the layoffs of tens of thousands of workers" (Usui and Colignon 1996, 551) from major industrial corporations in the United States. It is only now that such patterns are beginning to be reported from Germany.

An institutional ethnography would begin at the shop floor, as Vallas and Beck do, but be concerned with how the social relations of the financial markets enter into the changing work organization at the shop-floor level. The regulatory functions of the formalized record-keeping procedures would be explored, including how their texts are produced, where the worked-up texts go, and how they are read at various transitions points in the organization. Differences of views and experience would provide different points of entry into the objectified coordination of corporation and financial markets. The different pulp mills would cease to be seen as discrete entities belonging to a single company; their coordination within a single financial entity would begin to emerge as well as the complex intersections of their functioning within the dynamic of global financial markets.

A "Modest" Proposal for New Institutional Ethnographies

Institutional ethnography knits together an ethnography of work organization with analyses of the textual as an organization of the local, including the text-born concepts of the interpretive armamentarium of the speech genre (Bakhtin 1986) of that region. These are the generally neglected aspects of sociological ethnographies, perhaps mainly because sociologists have not known what to do with them.[5] But they are the work processes (and, of course, they are work) that produce organization within the ruling relations.

Texts regulate. They do not *program* the local settings of action. Textual technologies make possible a standardization of the language or image that enters and plays a part in courses of action across multiple sites of a text's "reading." Textual technologies play their part not only in pulp and paper mills, but, for example, in the fashion business where they coordinate women's images of their own and other women's appearance with the markets in clothing and cosmetics (Smith 1990b).

I do not envisage one colossal study, but rather the piecing together of representations and analyses of institutional processes from the different positions they define. Alison Griffith, Ann Manicom, and I (Griffith 1984, 1995; Griffith and Smith 1987, 1990a, 1990b; Manicom 1988, 1995) have done something very like this in studies that explore the work that mothers do in relation to their children's schooling and how it contributes to the work of the elementary school teacher in the classroom. Ellen Pence (1996) has used institutional ethnography to explore critically the interrelations of police, district attorneys, courts, probation officers, social workers, and so on, in relation to protecting women from abuse by their partners.[6]

Nor do I envisage relevant studies as originating only with those who have chosen to work with this approach. Saskia Sassen's (1991) investigation of "the global city," which explores the intersection of international financial organization with the regional geographies of major cities, is entirely congenial, as is the work she has projected in her essay in this volume. Such studies do not perpetuate the older and now largely aborted project of a scientific sociology but are engaged on a piece-by-piece extending of our knowledge of how the world we live in is being put together. To my mind, this is the most pressing agenda for sociology in the coming century. Institutional ethnography is a powerful tool to address this vast lacuna by linking micro- and macroanalyses from the standpoint of people.

Notes

1. See Rubin's (1973) explication of Marx's theory in terms of social relations.
2. The passage is presented in the complete version, but has been translated differently.
3. Among other things, some kinds of problems of costs may only take on significance when they can be identified in multiple sites, and that is only possible if the production processes themselves are highly standardized and their conformity to the measurable can be guaranteed.
4. I have read an account of the accounting system of a collective farm in the former Soviet Union that is based on Marxist economic theory. There, the accounting procedures connected the shop floor—cows, barns, milk production, dairy workers, and so on—with the centralized bureaucracy.
5. Latour and Woolgar's *Laboratory Life* (1986) and Lynch's (1985) study of a laboratory are rare exceptions. Neither, however, do the work of following up on the relational sequences that the texts coordinate.
6. There is other work, some completed and some ongoing. A useful representative collection is found in Campbell and Manicom (1995).

References

Alexander, Jeffrey C. 1995. *Fin de Siècle Social Theory: Relativism, Reduction, and the Problems of Reason.* London: Verso.
Bagdikian, Ben H. 1992. *The Media Monopoly.* Boston: Beacon Press.
Bakhtin, Mikhail M. 1986. *Speech Genres and Other Late Essays.* Austin: University of Texas Press.
Baudrillard, Jean. 1994. *Simulacra and Simulation,* translated by S. F. Glaser. Ann Arbor: University of Michigan Press.
Boden, Deirdre. 1994. *The Business of Talk: Organizations in Action.* Cambridge: Polity Press.
Blumenthal, Sidney. 1986. *The Rise of the Counter-Establishment: From Conservative Ideology to Political Power.* New York: Times Books.

Campbell, Marie, and Ann Manicom, eds. 1995. *Knowledge, Experience, and Ruling Relations: Studies in the Social Organization of Knowledge.* Toronto: University of Toronto Press.

De Montigny, Gerald A. J. 1995. *Social Working: An Ethnography of Front-Line Practice.* Toronto: University of Toronto Press.

Foucault, Michel. 1972. *The Archaeology of Knowledge,* translated by A. M. Sheridan Smith. London: Tavistock Publications.

Gadamer, Hans-Georg. 1975. *Truth and Method.* London: Sheed & Ward.

Garfinkel, Harold. 1967. *Studies in Ethnomethodology.* Englewood Cliffs, N.J.: Prentice-Hall.

Griffith, Alison. 1984. "Ideology, Education, and Single Parent Families: The Normative Ordering of Families through Schooling." PhD thesis. University of Toronto, Department of Education.

———. 1995. "Mothering, Schooling and Children's Development." In *Knowledge, Experience, and Ruling Relations: Studies in the Social Organization of Knowledge,* edited by Marie Campbell and Ann Manicom, 108–22. Toronto: University of Toronto Press.

Griffith, Alison, and Dorothy E. Smith. 1987. "Constructing Cultural Knowledge: Mothering as Discourse." In *Women and Education: A Canadian Perspective,* edited by Jane Gaskell and Arlene McLaren, 87–103. Calgary: Detselig.

———. 1990a. "Coordinating the Uncoordinated: How Mothers Manage the School Day." In *Perspectives on Social Problems,* vol. 2. Edited by Gale Miller and James Holstein, 25–43. Greenwich, Conn.: JAI Press.

———. 1990b. "What Did You Do Today, Dear? Women's Educational Work in the Family." In *Perspectives on Social Problems,* vol. 2. Edited by Gale Miller and James Holstein, 3–24. Greenwich, Conn.: JAI Press.

Latour, Bruno, and Steve Woolgar. 1986. *Laboratory Life: The Construction of Scientific Facts.* Princeton, N.J.: Princeton University Press.

Lynch, Michael. 1985. *Art and Artifact in Laboratory Science.* London: Routledge & Kegan Paul.

McChesney, Robert W. 1997. *Corporate Media and the Threat to Democracy.* New York: Seven Stories Press.

McManus, John H. 1994. *Market-Driven Journalism: Let the Citizen Beware?* Thousand Oaks, Calif.: Sage.

Manicom, Ann. 1988. "Constituting Class Relations: The Social Organization of Teachers' Work." PhD thesis. University of Toronto, Department of Education.

———. "What's Health Got to Do with It? Class, Gender and Teachers' Work." In *Knowledge, Experience, and Ruling Relations: Studies in the Social Organization of Knowledge,* edited by Marie Campbell and Ann Manicom. Toronto: University of Toronto Press.

Marx, Karl. 1973. *Grundrisse: Introduction to the Critique of Political Economy,* translated by Martin Nicolaus. New York: Random House.

Marx, Karl, and Frederick Engels. 1973. *Feuerbach: Opposition of the Materialist and Idealist Outlooks.* London: Lawrence & Wishart.

———. 1976. *The German Ideology.* Moscow: Progress Publishers.

Mead, George Herbert. 1947. *Mind, Self and Society: From the Perspective of a Social Behaviorist,* edited by Charles W. Morris. Chicago: University of Chicago Press.

Messer-Davidow, Ellen. 1993. "Manufacturing the Liberal Attack on Liberalized Education." *Social Text* 36 (fall): 40–79.

Pence, Ellen. 1996. "Safety for Battered Women in a Textually-Mediated Legal System." Ph.D. dissertation. University of Toronto.

Rubin, Iakov Izrailevich. 1973. *Essays on Marx's Theory of Value*. Montréal: Black Rose Books.

Sassen, Saskia. 1991. *The Global City: New York, London, Tokyo*. Princeton, N.J.: Princeton University Press.

Schiller, Herbert I. 1996. *Information Inequality: The Deepening Social Crisis in America*. New York: Routledge.

Schutz, Alfred. 1962. "On Multiple Realities." In *Collected Papers*, 1: 207–59. The Hague: Martinus Nijhoff.

Scott, W. Richard. 1995. *Institutions and Organizations*. Thousand Oaks, Calif.: Sage.

Smith, Dorothy E. 1987. *The Everyday World as Problematic: A Feminist Sociology*. Toronto: University of Toronto Press.

———. 1990a. *The Conceptual Practices of Power: A Feminist Sociology of Knowledge*. Toronto: University of Toronto Press.

———. 1990b. "Femininity as Discourse." In *Texts, Facts, and Femininity*. New York: Routledge.

———. 1990c. "K Is Mentally Ill: The Anatomy of a Factual Account." In *Text, Facts, and Femininity*. New York: Routledge.

———. 1990d. *Texts, Facts, and Femininity: Exploring the Relations of Ruling*. New York: Routledge.

———. 1996. "Telling the Truth after Postmodernism." *Studies in Symbolic Interaction* 19 (3): 171–202.

———. 1998. *Writing the Social: Critique, Theory and Investigations*. Toronto: University of Toronto Press.

Suchman, Lucy A. 1987. *Plans and Situated Actions: The Problem of Human Machine Communication*. Cambridge: Cambridge University Press.

Usui, Chikako, and Richard A. Colignan. 1996. "Corporate Restructuring: Converging World Pattern or Societally Specific Embeddedness?" *Sociological Quarterly* 37 (4): 551–78.

Vallas, Steven P., and John P. Beck. 1996. "The Transformation of Work Revisited: The Limits of Flexibility in American Manufacturing." *Social Problems* 43 (3): 339–61.

Winter, James. 1997. *Democracy's Oxygen: How Corporations Control the New*. Montréal: Black Rose Books.

CHAPTER FIVE

We Can Count, but
What Do the Numbers Mean?

JOEL H. LEVINE

Professor Abu-Lughod's suggested title carries double content. It is, on the surface, a question about the direction in which quantitative work in sociology will move at the beginning of the new millennium. It is also an invitation to discuss the tension in sociology that characterizes the end of the present millennium, the tension between "numbers" and . . . , and what? Like C. P. Snow, in *The Two Cultures and the Scientific Revolution* (1959), I am not sure what label to use for the other side. There are the numbers people, and there are those who are defined by their contrast to the numbers people.

I raise the matter of this tension here, at the beginning, in order to make my key point clear: *meaning lies in numbers.* More precisely, meaning lies in the equations when those equations are closely related to data. In sociology it will be more true than for some of the natural sciences that meaning will lie in the equations.

Would that sociology could be easier. Would that pure mind, rhetoric, and verbal exchange could steer a true course through obstacles that are difficult to penetrate by data, by numbers, and by method. But it is not so. In the words of Émile Durkheim's *Rules of Sociological Method*, written at the beginning of the century now coming to an end:

> In the present state of the discipline we do not really know the nature of the principal social institutions, such as the state or the family. . . . Yet it suffices to glance through the works of sociology to see how . . . it is believed that one is capable, in a few pages or a few sentences, of penetrating to the inmost essence of the most complex phenomena. This means that such theories express, not the facts, which could not be so swiftly fathomed, but the preconceptions of the author before he began his research. (Durkheim [1901] 1982, 38)

In our era, at the end of this century, there is a balance between the quantitative and verbal communities. Much of the quantitative work is concerned with description, significance testing, and extrapolation. But the balance is shifting as both concept formation and theory are becoming quantitative. That which is grandly and vaguely called "sociological meaning" is shifting into the quantitative domain and that which is even more grandly and more vaguely called "sociological theory" is also shifting into the quantitative domain. The shifts are being driven by two things: serious advances in what are called "mathematical models" but should actually be called "theory," and a rapid decrease in the cost of data describing individuals and events.

Mathematical Models

To understand the advances in models it is necessary, first, to understand that the quantitative community recognizes, within itself, at least three different strategies, each of which appropriates the word "model" to a different purpose. There is first, and best known, the statistical strategy embedded in the canon of our statistical methods classes. Second, there is the deductive strategy, strongly represented in game theory, decision theory, and aspects of rational actor theory. And third, there is the inductive strategy, which features the inductive modeling strongly represented in network analysis and stratification models.

All three strategies use the word "model." Within the first, the statistical strategy, "model" refers to equations, like the linear equation and the Gaussian distribution. In Carl Sagan's words, science is skepticism, and in our discipline the statistical "doubting" of description with significance testing is the strongest barrier among the fragile defenses that separate sociology from prescientific speculation and from absorption by ideological agendas. For detecting the presence of relations and for defining criteria of reasonable doubt the statistical disciplines are an intellectual and practical triumph.

By contrast, in both inductive and deductive models, a model *is* theory. The distinction between statistical models and theoretical models is a matter of degree. It lies in the extreme detail with which a theoretical model is compared to data. Outside certain areas of biology, it was never intended that the line and the Gaussian distribution (of the statistical strategy) be interpreted precisely, in all their detail, as theoretical models. However, as theory, every part of a theoretical model has meaning.

Let me illustrate by translating the linear equation and the Gaussian distribution into words *as if* they were theoretical models. To see the difference between one use of a model and the other, begin simply, as if you were once again a bright undergraduate. Take a group of undergraduates, preferably undergraduates with experience in natural science, and show these undergraduates the scatter diagram supporting one of sociology's "big" reliable correlations. Show them something like the correlation between the social economic status of a son and the social economic status of his father. Then talk about these data using the word "line" in your description, and watch the undergraduate reaction: they see no line in the scatter diagram of these data and, in detail, they are right. Even with strong correlations such as "$r = .4$," which are strong by professional standards, and even with extremely strong correlations such as "$r = .8$," which are rare, there is no line in these scatter diagrams. It takes statistics to find the correlation in such data and to verify its presence. There is absolutely a positive correlation between the status of the father and the status of the son, absolutely. But a *line?* No.

This level of scrutiny becomes appropriate only when you use statistical models as if they were theories. Perhaps fifty years ago, sociologists might have believed that they could hack their way through the underbrush of large data bases, piece by piece, accumulating "variance explained." They would assemble more complicated models, piece by piece: 15 percent of the variance explained by one independent variable, 10 percent more explained by another, 10 percent more by a third, gradually eliminating uncertainty. And then, presumably, the predictions of sociology would approach certainty as "explanation" approached 100 percent. That has not happened, of course. It was a misreading of these models that led to the expectation, among some, that it might. And it would be a mistake to become discouraged because it has not.

What would it mean if the line and the bivariate normal distribution were interpreted as theoretical models? What would it mean if social mobility, status of son compared to status of father, were normally distributed? As theory, the details of these models are alive with meaning; every symbol has meaning for the scientist. Even the x in a linear equation is a hypothesis. To write x is to say that there is a "space" in which people move. Usually, and surely with the bivariate normal, to write x is to hypothesize that the space in which people move is one-dimensional. That is meaning—probably not valid meaning for social mobility—but that is meaning expressed in an equation.

The detail of the Gaussian equation, interpreted as theory, says more. In detail, the equation is a hypothesis about which events are most frequent (those for which the status of the son is equal to the status of the father) and a hypothesis about the rate at which frequencies decrease as a function of the distance between father and son. It says,

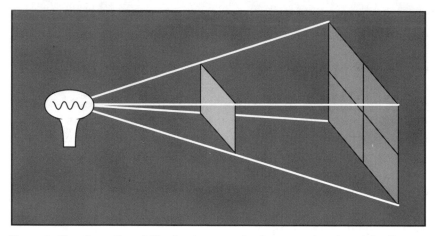

Figure 1. The attenuation of illumination per unit of area as a function of the distance from the source.

specifically, that the frequencies decrease as a negative exponential function of the square of the distance between them.

Those are numbers and equations (the exponential and the value of the exponent) that have meaning about nothing less than the "nature" of social space, or they would have that meaning if the statements were valid as theory. To see the meaning invested in the exponent "2," consider the inverse square laws of physical space. In physical space the "2" of the inverse square laws goes hand in hand with the "nature" of physical space. The easiest physical example is the attenuation of light (see fig. 1).

The light illuminating a unit square one unit from the source diffuses to illuminate four unit squares at a distance of two units from the source. Therefore it is reasonable to expect that the illumination on a single square will diminish in proportion to the inverse *square* of the distance. "Reasonable" is not enough, of course. It has to be checked. But the point is that the number 2 in the inverse square laws is rich with meaning. The number is a statement about the dimensionality of the space (three dimensions) and about the process of diffusion. The Gaussian equation, with its inverse exponential squared distance "law," would be a theoretical statement about social space—if it were correct.

That is the translation if you use the normal distribution literally, as a social model. Social space, it says, exists. Social space, it says, is one-dimensional. And social mobility, it says, scatters or diffuses as a function of the square of the distance. If you mean these things literally, as theory, then the whole package—the equation, the meaning, the interpretations, and the theory—are in jeopardy when the equation is compared to the data.

Fortunately, it fails. I say fortunately because if it were a good fit we would have to live with the meaning. It fails, but not because it is not very good at explaining variance. The line and the Gaussian are actually very good at explaining variance, but they make systematic errors that show that some part or all of the package is wrong. It fails because it systematically predicts that too few people will move, fewer people than are actually found to move when the model is compared to the data. Therefore, all or part of the package—social space, one-dimensionality, squared distance—is wrong (see Levine 1972, 1978, 1993).[1]

That is what makes a model a theory. But as I suggested, this is not the end of the story. The current state of the saga of quantitative methods in sociology is that some of the models have begun to work. The disputes continue among those of us who work with log-linear models, and with crossings models, and with special interaction effects. The meanings of the equations we write have changed. And the models have begun to work—for some cases and for some data. Some of the current theoretical models work well enough to exhaust the information in the data (Levine, 1990a, 1990b, 1993).

In some cases, with some occupational data and with some social network data, here is what we now know, at least tentatively:

Fix number 1. The Gaussian model, if it were correct, would mean that social space was one-dimensional, at least for the occupational data and the network data to which it applied. That is unlikely. It is reasonable to expect one dimension, status, to dominate the pattern of social distance, but it would be surprising if that one dimension were sufficient. Changing the symbol from "x" to an "$\bar{X}$"—from a single coordinate to coordinates in two or more dimensions, works better.

Fix number 2. The Gaussian model, if it were correct in two or more dimensions, would include a hypothesis about geometry. Never mind the meaning of "Euclidean geometry" as geometry is taught in mathematics. For us, in our science, the meaning of the phrase "Euclidean geometry" is a hypothesis about the combined effect of differences in two or more dimensions. It predicts that the strength of the combination of two dimensions will be predicted, first by computing the squares of the two differences, second by adding the two squares together, and third by taking the square root of the result. (That is the Pythagorean theorem, translated as theory). The Euclidean model is a

Figure 2a   Figure 2b

Figures 2a and 2b. Two back-to-back exponential decay functions of distance: 2a shows back-to-back negative exponential functions of the squared distance, and 2b shows back-to-back negative exponential functions of simple distance.

truly bizarre model of the combined effect of differences in two or more dimensions. It is all the more bizarre because it actually works—in physical space. Imagine the experience of intellectual triumph that must have accompanied that discovery twenty-five hundred years ago.

It would also be bizarre if differences in two or more dimensions combined this way in our own science. Imagine comparing my social economic status to someone else's by computing the square of the difference between our years of education as well as the square of the difference between our incomes, by adding the two squares together, and then by taking the square root of the result. Possible, but not obvious. An alternative would be simply to add the differences in the separate claims to status, predicting that the strength of the combination will be found by adding the individual components—no squares, no square roots. Translated back to the math, that means hypothesizing a city block metric, not a Euclidean metric, for social space. And that model works better (see Torgerson [1958, 251–4] referring to Attneave [1950] and Coombs [1964, 202–6] referring to Landahl [1945]).

Fix number 3. The Gaussian model uses squared distance in the equation, and it predicts too few people "staying" in the status of origin. Changing the number in the exponent from 2 to 1, from squared distance to simple distance without the square, creates a different prediction. It changes the shape of the curves from the shape in figure 2a to the shape in figure 2b.

Simple distance predicts greater immobility (at the center) relative to other events (off center). If it works, then the explanation of this power, 1, is a theoretical problem, a *real* theoretical problem. It suggests, too, that we have to understand something about the diffusion of information in social networks. For mobility it may mean that job searches are, somehow, only one- or two-dimensional, even though the occupational system itself is more than two-dimensional. Whatever the explanation, the result, the 1 referring to the first power of distance, is a statement about social process that has to be explained, because it works—better.

Fix number 4. And finally, the clincher: Join these fixes in one equation and you have a hypothesis that fits the data well enough, in some cases, to exhaust the information present in the data. The statement about the fit is restricted: With *some* problems in social mobility and with *some* work in social networks, the models match the data as well as it would be matched by going back to the source and replicating the data (Levine 1985).

Implications

So what? Why should sociology at large be changed by advances in stratification and networks?[2] In part, of course, because stratification and networks are central to the discipline. And in part, because the mathematics of these models offers simplicity. The mathematics is simpler than verbal gymnastics and no more difficult than the mathematics of contemporaneous statistical models used for policy and forecasting.

More important, sociology at large is affected because when one area undergoes serious change consequences are felt broadly. It is already the case that in some areas of stratification, the language of theory is mathematics. Words can attach intuition to the equations. Words can help communicate. But the first language of theory is, in some areas, mathematics—not English, not French, not German, but mathematics. Question: Is social space, is *social organization* divided and partitioned into classes or is it, by contrast, "continuous" (stratified but undivided)? Question: Is ownership of the means of production critical to social status? The primary language for such research is mathematics. In this area of discussion, debate is wasted unless the arguments are put in falsifiable form, as models, and tested in detail against the data.[3]

Data

At least two areas of the discipline are changing: models are one, the cost of data is another. The cost of data is not just bookkeeping, whether it costs $10, $100, or $1,000 per subject. More than that, cost insinuates itself into the way we think. In principle, at least, sociology is about relations among people and relations among social facts. But sociometric data that describe relations among people in real world organizations are far more expensive than survey data that describe personal attributes of a random sample of individuals.

In social psychology and network analysis, much of the research uses small groups. Much of the research uses small networks, often face-to-face groups and often set pieces, like the venerable bank wiring room data first analyzed in the early 1930s by George Homans. Why would anyone want to analyze the data recording petty battles of obscure individuals in odd work groups, children's camps, and college dormitories? I do not think anyone cares about these things per se. They were a means to an end that lay, in part, with the need to understand the compelling events during the 1930s as fascism grew in Europe. Social psychologists asked: What were the bases of democracy? What were the prerequisites of acceptable human organization? What tendencies led to authoritarianism?

Even in the 1930s it was never clear that small groups were the right experimental animal for questions raised by the larger society, but it was worth a try. Other psychologists and sociologists, responding to the same moral urgency, created works like *The Authoritarian Personality* (Adorno 1950) that looked into the human mind. Other sociologists created studies like *Union Democracy* (Lipset, Trow, and Coleman 1956) that examined labor unions as organizations created for laudable purpose that had, nevertheless, moved in some cases toward authoritarianism. And some social psychologists looked at small groups, like summer camps and school classrooms that seemed capable, in some cases, of ending up like Golding's *Lord of the Flies* (1962). Perhaps what ailed these small groups was the "model" for what ailed the larger world.

And in any case, whether small groups were the best experimental animal or not, it would have been difficult, at that time, to use anything larger. The data were just too expensive. It took the resources of the Harvard Business School and a promising graduate student, George Homans, to collect data for the fourteen men of the bank wiring room. And almost to this day, two generations later, there is still a premium on detailed sociometric data—data that record who does what to whom, in detail, and in time series, for real world groups, large or small.

Now, sixty-five years later, our options are different. Models, discussed earlier, are changing the nature of theory, and the Web is changing our access to data. Today on-line databases present any scholar, indeed anyone, a report of who does what to whom on a world scale.

We have hundreds of paid observers called reporters. That is what they call themselves, but we know they are working for us: toiling in the interest of our science, collecting the data on who does what to whom and on the nature of the relation—daily, on a large scale, with multiple observations. Newspaper abstracts update the daily activities of our subjects. Citation indices give us access to the developing structure of science, literature, and politics. On-line intelligence reports connect events and their players on a world scale. Library indices and search engines connect world problems, international organizations, lobbyists, politicians, intellectuals, and business.

Consider the arithmetic of these new data bases. A master index of world biographies contains about 6 million entries. Six million is an upper bound on the population that "counts" and it includes massive double counting. If the president of the United States has a biography in *Who's Who in America* and in *Who's Who in the East*—or *in Washington*, or *in Politics*, or in any other register—all of these are counted as separate entries among the total of 6 million. Eliminating duplications pares the number of people who "count" down from 6 million to a considerably smaller number. And, at the risk of offending a few million poets, baseball players, and movie stars whose lives are included among the 6 million biographies, I am willing to omit them from the total as well.

This leaves perhaps a million people, perhaps a hundred thousand, as the number of people who appear in these archives, about 1 million to 100,000 people who "act" on either a world scale or local stages. This is not a large number by today's technical standards.

These data, including both the Web itself and the larger array of electronic archives, may be viewed as the new experimental animal awaiting adoption by our discipline—if we dare. No need for sociologists to pull someone aside for an interview and ask "How do you feel about so-and-so?" All we need to do is to *read*—as the major players signal who is in, who is out. Or, when signals fail, all we need do is to read the budgets to see who is supporting whom or to check the movement of armies to see who is the ally of whom or to check the casualty reports and body counts for definitive evidence of negative affect.

The Result

I suggest that these two taken together—better theory and data on a new scale—*can* or *must* change the discipline. When I say these *can* change the discipline I mean to suggest that there is an opportunity, now, to do sociology as our predecessors might have wished to do it from the beginning. Parts of our statistical methodology, parts of our mainline methods of data collection were, in their time, brilliant adaptations to the limits of the time. Formerly, as a practical matter, it was difficult to study detail except in small populations. It was necessary to study large populations by aggregating people into categories; this allowed us to work around methodological problems and data problems that no longer constrain us so heavily.

When I say these changes "must" change the discipline, the challenge is this: Good science requires jeopardy. Sociology can go a long way by collecting data, analyzing them, classifying them, comparing them, contrasting them—and then presenting the result to professional audiences. But good science must take chances. It must look at people and issues that are important, using real names and making predictions. It must say things that matter to people outside the science. It must make statements in full public view. And here is the risky part: It must take the chance of being wrong on matters of significance, also in full public view.

If we were to make a foolish statement about Hasulak and Taylor (two denizens of the bank wiring room), few people outside the profession would even catch the reference, much less the foolishness of the statement. There is little risk with such experimental animals. By contrast, if we were to make a statement about institution building and coalitions in Russia, or in Central Africa, or Yugoslavia, there would be jeopardy. If the statement were foolish, then there would be obvious pressure to reformulate the theories behind the statement. If the statement were prescient, then the larger world would take note. Getting our discipline out into the real world is critical to the health of the discipline. Better theory, better data, and the computing power to handle them make it possible to move our discipline closer to the real world. The health of the discipline requires that we seize the opportunity and the jeopardy.

Notes

1. The effect is similar to the finding in the pioneering work by Blumen, Kogan, and McCarthy (1955), as discussed in greater detail than here in Levine (1985).

2. This discussion is condensed from Levine (1993). The argument with respect to stratification is presented at length in chap. 10, "Real Social Distance." The argument with respect to networks is presented in chap. 8, "Friends and Relations."

3. The implications of these changes in sociology are condensed from the discussion in Levine (1993).

References

Adorno, T. W., et al. 1950. *The Authoritarian Personality.* Publication no. 3 in the American Jewish Committee Social Studies Series. New York: Harper.

Attneave, F. 1950. "Dimensions of Similarity." *American Journal of Psychology* 63: 516–56.

Blumen, Isadore, Marvin Kogan, and Philip J. McCarthy. 1955. *The Industrial Mobility of Labor as a Probability Process.* Cornell Studies in Industrial and Labor Relations, vol. 4. Ithaca, N.Y.: Cornell University Press.

Coombs, Clyde. 1964. *A Theory of Data.* New York: Wiley & Sons.

Durkheim, Émile. (1901) 1982. *The Rules of the Sociological Method,* translated by Halls. New York: Free Press.

Golding, William G. 1962. *Lord of the Flies.* New York: Coward-McCann.

Landahl, H. D. 1945. "Neural Mechanisms for the Concepts of Difference and Similarity." *Bulletin of Mathematical Biophysics* 7: 83–88.

Levine, Joel H. 1972. "A Two Parameter Model of Interaction in Father-Son Status Mobility." *Behavioral Science* (September): 455–65.

———. 1978. "Comparing Models of Mobility." *American Sociological Review* 43 (February): 118–21.

———. 1990a. "Friends and Relations: A Comparison of Positive and Negative Sociometric Forms." *Connections* (1990).

———. 1990b. "Measuring Occupational Stratification Using Log-Linear Distance Models." In *Social Mobility and Social Structure,* edited by Ronald L. Breiger, 208–24. New York: Cambridge University Press.

———. 1993. *Exceptions Are the Rule: Inquiries on Method in the Social Sciences: A Critique of Sociological Methodology, with Structuralist Solutions.* Boulder, Colo.: Westview Press.

Levine, Joel H., and John Spadaro. 1988. "Occupational Mobility: A Structural Model of Intragenerational Mobility in Time Series." In *Social Structures,* edited by Barry Wellman and Stephen Berkowitz, 452–75. New York: Cambridge University Press.

Lipset, Seymour Martin, Martin Trow, and James S. Coleman. 1956. *Union Democracy.* Glencoe, Ill.: Free Press.

Snow, C. P. 1959. *The Two Cultures and the Scientific Revolution.* Rede Lecture. Cambridge: Cambridge University Press.

Torgerson, Warren S. 1958. *Theory and Methods of Scaling.* New York: Wiley & Sons.

CHAPTER SIX

From Little Boxes to Loosely Bounded Networks: The Privatization and Domestication of Community

BARRY WELLMAN

Life Is a Network

It became clear to me growing up in New York City in the 1950s that gangs as corporate entities did not exist. It was impossible to draw up a membership list. It was as futile to try to learn the borders of each gang's turf as it is to draw a map showing precise ethnic boundaries in Eastern Europe (Magocsi and Matthews 1993). My New York consisted of unbounded networks of friends and of friends of friends. When a fight was coming up, groups of friends would call each other and come together to be a gang for that night. On another night, when other friends would call, some of the same teens would become members of another gang. Much of organized crime operates in the same way, be it a Colombian or Chinese drug cartel, the Cosa Nostra, or the Moscow mafia (1993). So do communities and, in practice, many organizations (Burt 1992).

My New York childhood prepared me for my life's work: analyzing how communities, organizations, cities, and societies are organized as networks. When I arrived at graduate school, sociology was full of concern about the supposed loss of community in newly developing suburbs and "decaying" inner cities. Indeed, politicians and pundits continue to assert this, although cyberspace has now replaced suburbia as a community destroyer in their rhetoric.

Fortunately, social network analysis was also in the air at Harvard in the 1960s. The essence of social network analysis is that it does not assume that the world is always composed of normatively guided individuals aggregated into bounded groups. Rather, it starts with a set of *nodes* (which could be persons, organizations, states, etc.) and a set of

Research for this chapter has been supported by Communication and Information Technology Ontario and the Social Science and Humanities Research Council of Canada. Janet Abu-Lughod, Beverly Wellman, and Sharon Zukin made comments on an earlier draft that have been most helpful. The Centre for Urban and Community Studies, University of Toronto, has been a supportive home.

ties that connect some or all of these nodes. Social network analysis conceives of social structure as the patterned organization of these network members and their relationships. Social network analysts work at describing underlying patterns of social structure and explaining the impact of such patterns on behavior and attitudes (Wellman 1988). Hence the network approach allows analysts to go looking for social relationships that transcend groups. Indeed, a group is really a special form of a social network that is *densely knit* (most nodes are directly connected) and *tightly bounded* (most relations stay within the same subset of nodes).

The social network approach provides ways for analysts to think about social relationships that are neither groups nor isolated dyads. Instead of an either/or distinction between group membership and social isolation, researchers can bring to bear in their analysis a set of structural variables, such as the density and clustering of a network, how tightly it is bounded, and whether it is diversified or constricted in its size and heterogeneity, how narrowly specialized or broadly multiplex are its relationships, and how indirect connections and positions in social networks affect behavior. For example, the fact that person A and person B interact may have to be interpreted in the light of the relationship of person B to person C. Thus thinking about relationships in social networks rather than in groups can allow analysts to take into account the contexts within which relationships operate.

Although all studies have to start somewhere with some populations, many social network analyses do not treat formal group boundaries as truly social boundaries, be they departments in organizations or officially designated neighborhoods in cities. Instead they trace the social relationships of those they are studying, wherever these relationships go and whomever they are with. Only then do network analysts look to see if such relationships actually cross formal group boundaries. In this way, formal boundaries become important analytic variables rather than a priori analytic constraints. Just as a local area network is only one kind of a computer network, a group is only one kind of a social network. More precisely, a group is a social network whose ties are tightly bounded within a delimited set and are so densely knit that almost all network members are directly linked with each other. To be sure, there are densely knit and tightly bounded work groups and community groups. Yet there are other kinds of work and community networks whose relationships are sparsely knit with only a minority of members of the workplace or community directly connected with each other. These relationships tend to reach out in many directions like an expanding spider's web rather than curling back on themselves into a densely knit tangle.

For example, people who hang out together—at work, in a café, or on an Internet discussion group—can be studied as either a group or a social network. Those who study them as a group assume that they know the membership and boundaries of the group. They might ask how important each group is to its members, how the group is governed and makes decisions, and how the group controls members. Yet in all but laboratory situations researchers will be faced with the real-world problem that members are entering and leaving a group over time. By contrast, those who study such entities as social networks can treat their membership and boundaries as open questions. For example, frequent participation in a friendship circle might be treated as the basis for membership but so might be the indirect connections (and resource flows) that friends provide to others outside the circle. The pattern of relationships becomes a research question rather than a given (see Wellman [1988, 1997] for further discussion).

Once you adopt this perspective, it is clear that communities, organizations, and world systems are social networks, and that many communities, organizations and political systems are not the dense, bounded groups that politicians and organizational executives insist they are (see Bourque and Duchastel in this volume; see also Taub et al. 1977). Analysts have shown whoever cared to look that life is full of networks. Tools such as UCINet (Borgatti, Everett, and Freeman, 1999) have made it almost as easy to play with networks as it is for SPSS users to play with surveys of individuals. Although network analysts have often done *sheer* documentation—demonstrating the existence of networks—much of their research has been more than *mere* documentation. It has shown social scientists ways to shift away from thinking of social structure as nested in little boxes and away from seeing relationships as the product of internalized norms.

The social network approach does not preclude finding that communities are urban villages where everyone knows each other and provides abundant, broadly based support, that is, what Tönnies ([1887] 1955) called *Gemeinschaft*. Nor does it preclude discovering that organizations really function as Weberian hierarchical bureaucracies. But the social network approach allows the discovery of other forms of community, perhaps sparsely knit and spatially dispersed, and other forms of organization, perhaps loosely coupled or virtual (Weick 1976). Indeed, it was through using the social network approach that analysts discovered that community had not disappeared. Rather it had moved out of its traditional neighborhood base as the constraints of space weakened. Contemporary Western communities rarely are tightly bounded, densely knit groups of broadly based ties. They usually are loosely bounded, sparsely knit, ramifying networks of specialized ties (Wellman 1993). Hence analysts should find community wherever it exists: in neighborhoods, in family solidarities, or in networks that reach farther out and include many friends and acquaintances (Wellman 1979; Wellman and Leighton 1979; Fischer 1982).

In this chapter, I discuss the nature of contemporary communities and the implications of their nature for the privatization, specialization and loose coupling of community and organizations. I do this in the form of seven propositions about the network nature of contemporary community. Where examples are called for, I draw upon our research group's thirty years of experience in studying community and organizational networks in Toronto.

Proposition 1: Community Ties Are Narrow, Specialized Relationships, not Broadly Supportive.

Both scholars and the public have traditionally thought of communities as composed of broadly based relationships in which each community member felt securely able to obtain a wide variety of help. In Toronto we have studied *personal communities*, social networks defined from the standpoints of the egos at their centers. We have found that most ties are specialized, with active personal community members usually supplying only a few dimensions of social support. For example, those network members who provide small services or emotional aid rarely provide large services, companionship, or financial aid (Wellman, Carrington, and Hall 1988; Wellman and Wortley 1989, 1990). Parents and adult children provide the widest range of support, although they rarely supply sociable companionship. Accessible ties— people living or working nearby or otherwise with frequent in-person or telecommunications contact—provide important goods and services (Wellman and Wortley 1990). The strength of ties is important, with socially close, voluntary and multiple-role ties providing high levels of support. Yet Granovetter (1973, 1982) has cogently argued the importance of weak ties for linking sparsely knit communities and providing people with a wider range of information.

This means that people must maintain differentiated portfolios of ties to obtain a wide variety of resources. They can no longer assume that any or all of their relationships will help them, no matter what is the problem. In market terms, they must shop at specialized boutiques for needed resources instead of casually dropping in at a general store. They search for support in relationships that they work hard to maintain. We need to know the consequences for people having such insecure sources of supply.

Proposition 2: People Are not Wrapped up in Traditional Densely Knit, Tightly Bounded Communities but Are Floating in Sparsely Knit, Loosely Bounded, Frequently Changing Networks.

Scholars and the public have traditionally seen communities as densely knit solidarities. Such communities tend to have tight boundaries so that relationships largely stay within the solidarities. Dense-knit and tight boundaries make it easy for communities to control their members and to coordinate their behavior, whether this be supplying aid to those in distress or punishing those who transgress.

In reality, personal communities are usually sparsely knit and loosely bounded. For example, the 0.33 density that we found in two Toronto studies means that only one-third of a person's active community members have active ties with each other. Moreover, these networks become even more sparsely knit as people age and their networks get more complex: mean network density declined from 0.33 to 0.13 over a decade (Wellman et al. 1997). Variation in the composition and structure of these community networks is more complex than the traditional Tönniesian dichotomy of communal versus contractual organization (Wellman and Potter 1999).

The complex and specialized nature of personal communities means that these are fragmented networks. People must actively maintain each supportive relationship rather than relying on solitary communities to do their maintenance work. Thus the kinship system does not supply much social support—extended kin rarely are supportive—but a more restricted set of ties with parents, children, and siblings. The fragmentation, specialization, and low density suggest that tie characteristics may be more important than network characteristics in the provision of social support. Yet the characteristics of community networks do have some effect, with the size, heterogeneity, and density of networks related to the kinds of resources that flow through them (Frank and Wellman 1998; Wellman and Gulia 1999b). Emergent properties are alive and well and living in Toronto.

The population of community networks is not stable. Only 28 percent of Torontonians' intimate ties were still intimate a decade later.

Thirty-six percent of the once-intimate ties became less active over a decade, while the rest became very weak or disappeared altogether. Although kinship is more stable, only 34 percent of intimate kinship ties remained intimate a decade later while another 28 percent continued as active, but not intimate, relationships (Wellman et al. 1997). It is not that people's communities are disintegrating, but that they are in flux. Rather than being locked into one social circle, each person has about a thousand ties that spread across changing, fragmented communities to connect them to the diverse resources of multiple social arenas (Kochen 1989). Indeed Stanley Milgram's (1967) and Harrison White's (1970) observations that the entire world is linked by paths of five or fewer indirect ties provide the basis for a recent movie, *Six Degrees of Separation* (Guare 1990, 1993). With sparsely knit, fragmentary, loosely bounded communities, it is possible to reach many people through even shorter paths. One consequence is that people must actively search their far-flung ties in unbounded networks to deal with their affairs instead of having to depend on the goodwill of a single, bounded community.

Proposition 3: Communities Have Moved Out of Neighborhoods to Become Dispersed Networks that Continue to Be Supportive and Sociable.

As well as contemporary communities being fragmented, sparsely knit, and loosely bounded, they are no longer local groupings of neighbors and kin. The residents of developed societies usually know few neighbors, and most members of their personal communities live outside their neighborhoods (Wellman 1990, 1992b). People easily maintain far-flung relationships by telecommunications (with telephones recently being joined by faxes, electronic mail, and the Web) and transportation (based on cars, expressways, buses, trains, and airplanes). In Toronto, being within an hour's drive or the local telephone zone is more important than being within a neighborhood's walking distance as the boundary for where face-to-face contact and social support start decreasing. A large minority of relationships extend even farther than the metropolitan area. This lack of local ties and the presence of community members living elsewhere weakens local commitment and encourages people to leave their neighborhoods when conditions are bad rather than staying to improve things.

This is not to say that communities have totally cut their domestic roots. Even the most spatially liberated person cannot avoid neighbors.

Local relationships are necessary for domestic safety, controlling actual land use, and quickly getting goods and services, as Jane Jacobs (1961) pointed out for contemporary North America, Vicente Espinoza (1992, 1999) for impoverished Chileans, and Charles Tilly (1973) for preindustrial Europe. But most neighborly relations have become voluntary relations, similar to friendship ties with the added bonus of quick access. It is only the less mobile minority who are committed to their neighborhoods by necessity: children, those who stay home to raise children, the elderly, and the infirm. Indeed, when we interviewed Torontonians about their ties, only those women who were full-time homemakers and child rearers had many involuntary ties with members of their personal communities. Their neighbors (and fellow full-time child rearers) were like coworkers: people they did not necessarily like but depended on to share the tasks of raising children (Wellman 1985).

In saying that communities are not as local as they used to be, we need to avoid committing the pastoralist fallacy of thinking our cities and suburbs are inferior to the villages or pestilent cities of yore, with their disease, crime, and insecurity. Moreover, preindustrial communities may never have been as locally bounded as tradition has maintained. As Levine's chapter points out, the initial frame of reference may seriously affect the subsequent analysis. Whenever scholars have looked for nonlocal ties, they have found far-ranging networks. For example, radioactive analyses of obsidian have found Neolithic spear points and choppers more than one thousand miles from their origin (Dixon, Cann, and Renfrew 1968). In historic times, Emmanuel LeRoy Ladurie (1975) has used Inquisition data to describe the far-flung relationships of Pyrenean villagers. The male shepherds were always moving about, following the flocks or going off to war. So were the soldiers in *The Return of Martin Guerre* (Davis 1983), returning to their villages from distant medieval wars. The wanderings continue: Ladurie's *The Beggar and the Professor* (1997) shows, in his biographies of the sixteenth-century Swiss family Platter, that men made long journeys around Europe (eastern as well as western), with fluid networks and much social and spatial mobility. The Platter women moved less frequently: when they got married and when their households changed cities.

Consider the unlikely comparison of the communities of eighteenth-century Latvia and twentieth-century Toronto (Wetherell, Plakans, and Wellman 1994). By contrast to the mythical kinship-ridden past, the rural Latvian community did not have enough kin to construct the kinds of social networks that exist today. As these farmers did not appear to have had many friends living beyond the local area, it seems that half the myth was true. Although their networks were much more local than late-twentieth-century Torontonians, they had only small clusters of kin at their core. Nor does nonlocalism seem to be a phenomenon of our postindustrial age. Kenneth Scherzer's (1992) study of mid-nineteenth-century New York City reveals that many wedding guests came from outside the neighborhood, often from other counties or states.

Proposition 4: Private Intimacy Has Replaced Public Sociability.

Rather than operating out of public neighborhood spaces, contemporary communities usually operate within private homes. Yet until well into this century, men customarily gathered in communal, quasi-public milieus, such as pubs, cafés, parks, and village greens. More accessible than private homes, such places drew their clienteles from fluid networks of regular habitués (Roche 1981). Men could drop into such places to talk and to escape domestic boredom. The high density of the city meant that they were likely to find others to talk with there. This density, combined with the permeability of the public spaces, provided men with chance encounters with friends of their friends and gave them opportunities to form new bonds. Although the men generally went out to enjoy themselves, they also used these public communities to organize politically, to accomplish collective tasks, and to deal with larger organizations. For example, in colonial New England, "neighbors assumed not only the right but the duty to supervise one another's lives" (Wall 1990).

This public community was largely a man's game. For example, in eighteenth-century Paris, a woman who went alone to a wineshop risked being mistaken for a prostitute (Garrioch 1986). Although some women always operated in public, and some respectable public spaces often existed for many women (church groups, clubs, etc.), in general, community for men was much more public than was community for women (Tristan [1840] 1980; Ryan 1990; Cohn 1996; Hansen 1997). And men's public communities operated largely independently of women's private communities.

Community for men as well as for women has now moved inside, into private homes. The separation of work from residential localities means that coworkers are more apt to commute from different neighborhoods and no longer come home from work in solidary, sociable groups. While men now spend more time at home, the feminization of paid work means that women spend less time there. Husbands and wives are in no mood to go out together after their weary trip home from work. In any event, zoning regulations and development patterns in North America cause commercial areas to be far from home. Domestic pursuits dominate, with husbands and wives spending evenings and weekends together instead of the men going off to pubs and street corners (for more details, see Wellman [1992a]). Workaholics bring their computer disks home; couch potatoes rent videos.

Rather than being accessible to others in public places, people now overcome their isolation by getting together in each other's homes or by the private media of the telephone and electronic mail. Most members of Torontonians' personal communities do not live nearby but at a median distance of nine miles apart (Wellman et al. 1988). Yet the easy accessibility of local relationships makes them continue to be significant. Although neighbors (living within one mile) comprise only 22 percent of the Torontonians' active ties, these neighbors engage in fully 42 percent of all interactions with active network members (Wellman 1996).

Thus the neoconservative privatization of Western societies, the withering of collective public services for general well-being, is reflected in the movement indoors of community life. Even in Toronto, the safest North American metropolis, 36 percent of the residents feel somewhat unsafe walking alone in their neighborhoods at nights. Yet the usual flight to safety—driving one's car or staying home and using the telephone or e-mail—offers little opportunity for enriching, diversifying contact en route. Cars leave garages as sealed units, opened only on reaching the other's home; telephones and modems stay indoors, sustaining only closed duets.

Where North Americans a generation ago often spent Saturday night going out for a movie and pizza, they now invite a few friends over to their homes to watch videos and order a pizza to be delivered. People watch videos at home an average of thirty times per year but go out for entertainment only three or four times a year (Film Canada 1990; Strike 1990). As Toronto social critic Marshall McLuhan observed (1973), North Americans go out to be private in streets where no one greets each other, but they stay in to be public, that is, to meet their friends and relatives.

Public spaces have become residual places to pass through or to shop in. Rather than participating in clubs or organizations, when they do go out, North Americans tend to go out alone, in couples or in small, informal groups (Putnam 1995). North American church attendance has declined, and Canadian movie attendance declined from eighteen times per year in 1952 to three times per year in 1993. The public community of the pub in the long-running television show *Cheers* was appealing because it is so rare. In reality, the 1989 Canadian National Alcohol Survey showed that only 10 percent of adult Canadians go to a pub as often as once a week, with men attending somewhat more frequently than women. Suburban shopping malls have become residual agoras—for consumption purposes only, but not for discussions. Their cafés mock the name, deliberately using tiny tables and uncomfortable chairs to discourage lingering sociability. There is little possibility for casual contact or for the expansion of networks.

As community has become private, people continue to feel responsible for their relatively strong relationships but not for the many acquaintances and strangers with whom they rub shoulders but to whom they feel no connection. Private contact with familiar friends and relatives has replaced public gregariousness, so that people pass each other unsmiling on streets. This privatization may be responsible for the lack of informal help for strangers who are in trouble in public spaces (Latané and Darley 1976). One consequence of this privatization of community in a world of strangers is that people feel that they lack friends even when their personal communities are abundantly supportive (Lofland 1973).

Proposition 5: Communities Have Become Domesticated.

Home is now the base for relationships that are more voluntary and selective than the public communities of the past. Personal communities now contain high proportions of people who enjoy each other and low proportions of people who are forced to interact with each other because they are juxtaposed in the same neighborhood, kinship group, organization, or workplace (Feld 1981). Friends and relatives get together as small sets of singles or couples, but rarely as communal groups (Wellman 1992a). This voluntary selectivity means that personal communities have become homogeneous networks of people with similar attitudes and lifestyles.

Where public communities were essentially men's worlds, home-based personal communities now bring husbands and wives together. Men's communities are tucked away in homes just as women's communities usually have been. As community has moved into the home, homes have become less private. Previous generations had confined visitors to ground-floor parlors and dining rooms, but visiting community members now roam all floors. They watch movies in elaborate home theaters; they soak in multiperson hot tubs.

In their domestic headquarters, Toronto couples jointly operate their networks (Wellman and Wellman 1992), a far different scene from the segregated networks that Elizabeth Bott (1957) described in 1950s England. To a great extent it is the household that exchanges support rather than the person: for example, our research shows in-laws to be as supportive as blood relatives (Wellman and Wortley 1989). By contrast to the specialized support that community members exchange, spouses supply each other with almost all types of social support (Wellman and Wellman 1992). Hence unmarried adults obtain much less social support domestically and do not have access to the networks (and their resources) that accompany spouses.

In the current situation, married women dominate the practice of community in their households. Women have historically been the "kin keepers" of Western society: mothers and sisters keep relatives connected for themselves, their husbands and their children. They continue to be the preeminent suppliers of emotional support in community networks as well as the major suppliers of domestic services to households (Wellman 1992a; Wright 1989). With the privatization and domestication of community, community keeping has become an extension of kin keeping, with both linked to domestic management. No longer do husbands and wives have many separate friendships. As men now usually stay home during their leisure time, the informal ties of their wives form the basis for relations between married couples. Wives define the nature of friendship and help maintain many of their husbands' friendships. Women bear more than the "double load" of domestic work and paid work; their "triple load" includes *net*work.

Thus the privatization and domestication of relationships have transformed the nature of community. As Dorothy Smith (in this volume) emphasizes, women's everyday practices have become the personal community's norm. Because communities interact in private homes, they are more likely to focus on household concerns, and they provide less opportunity for casual encounters with friends of friends. Women's ties, which dominate personal communities, provide important support for dealing with domestic work. Community members help with daily hassles and crises; neighbors mind each other's children; sisters and friends provide emotional support for child, husband, and elder care. Because women are the community keepers and are pressed for time caring for homes and doing paid work, men have become even more cut off from male friendship groups (Wellman 1992a). North American men rarely use their community ties to accomplish collective projects of work, politics, or leisure. Their relationships have largely become sociable ties, either as part of the relationship between two married couples or as disconnected relations with a few male "buddies."

This domestication helps explain the contemporary intellectual shift to seeing community and friendship as something that women do better than men. Just as husbands and wives are more involved with each other at home, the focus of couples and male friends is on private, domestic relations. Men's community ties have come to be defined as women's have been: relations of emotional support, companionship, and domestic aid (Canary and Emmers-Sommer 1997). The nature and success of community are now being defined in domestic, women's terms. Concurrently, the growing dominance of the service sector in the economy means that the manipulation of people and ideas has acquired more cultural importance than the industrial and resource-extraction sectors' manipulation of material goods.

With developed economies having more managers and professionals than blue-collar workers, many workplaces share the emphasis on social relationships that women have traditionally practiced at home. Some workplaces contain intense emotional relationships (Kornblum 1974; Coupland 1995; Hochschild 1997). For example, coworker ties at one Toronto software firm are supported by a sports gym, a masseuse, and private rooms for quick romantic encounters. Most of the workers' lives revolve around the firm. This is an unusual situation. Most of the Torontonians we studied are usually eager to go home after work, leaving their work stresses and coworkers behind (see also Halle 1984).

The material comfort of most North Americans means that they no longer need to rely on maintaining good relations with community members to get the necessities for material survival. The goods and services that community members exchange are usually matters of convenience, rarely of necessity, and hardly ever of life and death. Community ties have become ends in themselves, to be enjoyed in their own right and used for emotional adjustment in a society that puts a premium on feeling good about oneself and others. This resonates with the contemporary feminist celebration of women as more qualified in the socioemotional skills that are the basis of contemporary communities—and the downgrading of the allegedly masculine qualities of instrumentalism and materialism. Community is no longer about men fixing a car together; it is about couples chatting about domestic problems.

Contemporary discussions of community often reverse the traditional sexist discourse that has seen women as inadequate men. Men are now seen as unable to sustain meaningful community relationships, especially when such relationships are defined only in terms of socioemotional support. This socioemotional definition has almost totally replaced the traditional definition of community as also including instrumental aid. Patriarchal arguments for male superiority in getting things done are being replaced by celebrations of female superiority in knitting together emotionally-supportive networks (Bly 1990). As self-styled "feminist author" Maggie Scarf (1987) said on the Oprah Winfrey television show, "Men just don't have friends the way women have friends. Men just don't like to make themselves vulnerable to other men."

Proposition 6: Political, Economic, and Social Milieus Affect the Nature of Communities.

Although the assertion that women have greater capacity for community has raised much consciousness, it is an idea that is time bound, culture bound, and empirically unsound. It ignores the thousands of years during which men's bonds largely defined community in public discourse. By reducing the definition of community to socioemotional support, it assumes that the world at large is as materially comfortable as it is for most North Americans.

In less comfortable parts of the world, community members do more for each other than being privately sociable and emotionally supportive. Consider how Eastern Europeans use friends for economic, political, and social survival (Sik and Wellman 1999); Greek men argue and plan projects in cafés; poor Chileans help neighbors survive and find jobs for kin (Espinoza 1992, 1999); and Hungarians help each other build new homes (Sik 1988; Sik and Wellman 1999). Even in more affluent Britain, people value getting services and information from community members as much as they value getting esteem and affection (Argyle 1990). To put matters more broadly, communities do not function in isolation but within the context of political, economic, and social milieus that affect their composition, structure, and operations. The nature of different societies strongly affects the opportunities and insecurities with which individuals and households must deal, the supportive resources they seek, and the ways in which markets, institutions, and networks structure access to these resources.

Communities are not just ways in which people spend some of their leisure time but key mechanisms by which people and households get resources. Yet most North American research has ignored the broader implications of community ties and looked only at "social support," the effects of community ties on maintaining physical and mental health. A broader view would see community as an essential component of society. For example, as French Revolutionaries proclaimed, "fraternity" (i.e., community) is one of five principal ways by which people gain access to resources:

1. *Market exchanges* (as purchases, barter, or informal exchanges). Seeing this as the only means of access to resources is in line with the neoconservative belief in the loss of community. [*Liberty*]

2. *Institutional distributions* (by the state or other bureaucracies as citizenship rights, organizational benefits or charitable aid). Such access to resources is in line with those who have traditionally seen society as a moral community writ large, as in the ongoing American debate as to whether health care is a community obligation or a market decision. However, the use of the term "community" to describe such institutional distributions can be a subterfuge for bureaucratic privilege, as was the case in socialist Eastern Europe. [*Equality*]

3. *Community exchanges.* If informal, interpersonal access to resources occurs within neighborhood or kinship solidarities, then they fit models of traditional community. If the exchanges are less bounded (and hence less normatively enforceable), then they fit the ramified community networks that have been described here. [*Fraternity*]

4. *Coercive appropriations* (predatory behavior by interpersonal or institutional bullies, i.e., robbery or expropriation). Involuntary appropriations usually occur under the legitimating guise of imbalanced market exchanges or state extractions for unequal institutional distributions (as in governments forcing farmers to sell produce to urbanites at low prices [Tilly 1975]). More extreme instances of the loss of community are common in societies where institutional and communal mechanisms of social control have broken down, such as in Bosnia or Rwanda. [*Robbery*]

5. *Self-provisioning* (making and growing things in one's household). Self-provisioning is used even in market societies (see Pahl's [1984] discussion of growing food in England) and in socialist-institutional

ones (see Sik's [1988] discussion of Hungarian home building). Such self-provisioning rests on an infrastructure of market and community exchanges that provide advice, skills, and materials. [*Yeomanry*]

Although all types of resource access can be found in all societies, market exchanges are especially characteristic of Western societies, while institutional distributions are characteristic of centrally planned statist societies, and community exchanges are characteristic of Third World societies with weak states and few formal organizations (see also Abu-Lughod, Collins, and Sjoberg in this volume; Wolf 1966). While personal communities are important in Western, statist, and Third World societies, communities are differently composed, structured, and used in each type of society. For example, the insecurities of members of Western societies largely come from physical and emotional stresses in their personal lives and social relations. Hence people seek support from community members for emotional problems, homemaking chores, and domestic crises, and they look to markets and institutions to deal with their economic and political problems.

The comparatively low importance of economic and political concerns in Western societies distinguishes the communities in them from those in societies which are less economically or politically secure. Most Westerners rely on market exchanges for almost all of their production and much of their consumption. In most Western countries, institutional benefits such as schooling and medical care are abundantly available as citizenship rights. Westerners do not pay as much attention as do the inhabitants of statist societies (such as the former East European socialist states) to having community members who can make and fix things or who have connections to strategic institutional circles (Sik and Wellman 1999). To make another contrast, because Westerners rarely have urgent cares about daily survival, they can manage domestic resources with less apprehension than thirdworlders living on the space margins.

Proposition 7: Cyberspace Supports "Glocalized" Communities.

It is a direct progression to go from talking about personal communities linked by phones, planes, and cars to talking about virtual communities linked by computer-mediated communication media such as electronic mail and videoconferencing. After all, a computer network is a social network when it connects people and organizations. Although hopes and fears are exaggerated, computer-mediated communication will affect work and community. As in community, there is a move away from densely knit, tightly bounded work groups (in offices and factories) to more loosely coupled organizations, with shifting roles, collaborations, and reporting structures. The experiences of workers in tightly bounded, densely knit, open-office fishbowls are similar to those in traditional village communities. Yet many workers and recreational E-mail users move among a variety of situations and social networks. They function in loosely bounded, sparsely knit, multiple, fragmented networks, switching among a diversified set of relationships to accomplish their tasks (for more details, see Garton and Wellman [1995], Wellman et al. [1997], Wellman [1997], and Wellman and Gulia [1999*a*]).

Although scholars once feared that computer-mediated communication could not sustain subtle, ambiguous, or intimate conversations, research has shown that almost everything that can be done offline is being done online. Computer networks seem especially suitable for supporting weak (as well as strong) ties, expanding the size of people's active networks, forming direct ties with friends of friends, and fostering ties based on shared interests rather than on similar demographic characteristics (Parks and Roberts 1998). This is part of the continuing sociological shift from social organization based on "ascription" (what one is born into) to "achievement" (what one becomes). As a *New Yorker* cartoon put it, "On the Internet, nobody knows you're a dog" (Steiney 1993).

Some scholars have been fascinated with virtual communities that function almost entirely online (e.g., Rheingold 1993). Such communities can be as densely knit and all-consuming as traditional urban villages. Yet, although virtual communities are imageable, in fact most people make only partial commitments to online relationships. They may interact online in specialized communities, such as a "listserve" that is devoted to BMW cars. Or their online interactions may be interwoven with in-person and telephone interactions. Two persons living or working nearby might use the Internet to arrange a meeting (Haythornthwaite and Wellman 1998; Salaff et al. 1996), or two persons living apart may sustain a relationship online until their rare in-person meeting. It is still an unresolved question if such online relationships add new ties to one's existing personal network, maintain and expand the frequency and purview of existing ties, or substitute weaker online ties for more robust face-to-face ties (Kraut et al., 1998).

The Loosely Coupled World

With the Internet able to leap large oceans at a single bound, there is the possibility that community and work will become "glocalized." On the one hand, the cost of maintaining a computer-mediated relationship will be almost as low across the ocean as it is across the state. Moreover, the ability of media such as the Web or the Internet to store and forward communication will lessen the constraints of community or organizational members functioning on the same schedule. On the other hand, these same media can keep virtual communers and teleworkers bound to their home desktops for work and play, an extreme form of localization. In such situations, loosely coupled global networks will intersect with tightly bounded, densely knit domestic networks. Family members will see even more of each other around the home. Although men have done few domestic chores until now, such involvement in cyberspace may lead to new domestic divisions of labor. Doing the laundry may become a rest stop on the information highway.

Malvina Reynolds (1960) sang more than a generation ago in a sarcastic description of American suburbia and society:

> Little boxes made of ticky-tacky;
> Little boxes, little boxes, little boxes;
> All the same.

Yet such little boxes were the way sociologists thought of the world then and probably the way much of the world was: bounded work and residential units hierarchically linked in cities and regions, workplaces, and organizations. I suspect that the world is now more loosely coupled, whether it be through personal community networks, management by matrix, or virtual organizations. Time and space matter less; people work and commune with multiple others, switching frequently between roles and tasks, opportunities and constraints. Advances in communication and transportation have facilitated this transformation from hierarchical boxes to loosely coupled networks. This transformation has accompanied changes from the micro to the macro levels, from the proliferation of paid work for women to the almost seamless functioning of the world financial and production systems. The result is that people no longer know to which few units they belong, whether in their community or on the job. They need to cope with multidimensional networking in a loosely coupled world.

References

Argyle, Michael. 1990. "An Exploration of the Effects of Different Relationships on Health, Mental Health and Happiness." Paper presented to the International Conference on Personal Relationships, Oxford, July.

Bly, Robert. 1990. *Iron John: A Book about Men.* Reading, Mass.: Addison-Wesley.

Borgatti, Stephen, Martin Everett, and Linton Freeman. 1999. *UCINet 5.* Natick, Mass.: Analytic Technologies.

Bott, Elizabeth. 1957. *Family and Social Network.* London: Tavistock.

Burt, Ronald. 1992. *Structural Holes.* Chicago: University of Chicago Press.

Canary, Daniel, and Tara Emmers-Sommer. 1997. *Sex and Gender Differences in Personal Relationships.* New York: Guilford Press.

Cohn Jr., Samuel K. 1996. *Women in the Streets: Essays on Sex and Power in Renaissance Italy.* Baltimore: Johns Hopkins University Press.

Coupland, Doug. 1995. *Microserfs.* New York: HarperCollins.

Davis, Natalie Zemon. 1983. *The Return of Martin Guerre.* Cambridge, Mass.: Harvard University Press.

Dixon, J. E., J. R. Cann, and Colin Renfrew. 1968. "Obsidian and the Origins of Trade." *Scientific American* 218 (March): 38–46.

Espinoza, Vicente. 1992. "Networks of Informal Economy: Work and Community among Santiago's Urban Poor." Ph.D. thesis. University of Toronto, Department of Sociology.

———. 1999. "Social Networks among the Urban Poor: Inequality and Integration in a Latin American City." In *Networks in the Global Village,* edited by Barry Wellman, 147–84. Boulder, Colo.: Westview Press.

Feld, Scott. 1981. "The Focused Organization of Social Ties." *American Journal of Sociology* 86:1015–35.

Film Canada. 1990. *Film Canada Yearbook.* Toronto: Telefilm Canada.

Fischer, Claude. 1982. *To Dwell among Friends.* Berkeley: University of California Press.

Frank, Kenneth, and Barry Wellman. 1998. "Sources of Social Capital in Ties and Networks: A Multilevel Analysis of Social Support in Personal Communities." Paper presented to the Conference on Social Networks and Social Capital. Duke University, October.

Garrioch, David. 1986. *Neighbourhood and Community in Paris, 1740–1790.* Cambridge: Cambridge University Press.

Garton, Laura, and Barry Wellman. 1995. "Social Impacts of Electronic Mail in Organizations: A Review of the Research Literature." *Communication Yearbook* 18:434–53.

Granovetter, Mark. 1973. "The Strength of Weak Ties." *American Journal of Sociology* 78:1360–80.

———. 1982. "The Strength of Weak Ties: A Network Theory Revisited." In *Social Structure and Network Analysis,* edited by Peter Marsden and Nan Lin, 105–30. Beverly Hills, Calif.: Sage.

Guare, John. 1990. *Six Degrees of Separation.* New York: Random House. (On film, *Six Degrees of Separation.* 1993. Fred Schepisi, director; John Guare, screenplay. MGM/UA. Santa Monica, Calif.)

Halle, David. 1984. *America's Working Man.* Chicago: University of Chicago Press.

Hansen, Karen. 1997. "Rediscovering the Social: Visiting Practices in Antebellum New England and the Limits of the Public/Private Dichotomy." In *Public and Private in*

Thought and Practice: Perspectives on a Grand Dichotomy, edited by Jeff Weintraub and Krishan Kumar, 268–302. Chicago: University of Chicago Press.

Haythornthwaite, Caroline, and Barry Wellman. 1998. "Work, Friendship and Media Use in a Networked Organization." *Journal of the American Society for Information Systems* 49 (12): 1101–14.

Hochschild, Arlie. 1997. *The Time Bind.* New York: Henry Holt.

Jacobs, Jane. 1961. *The Death and Life of Great American Cities.* New York: Random House.

Kochen, Manfred, ed. 1989. *The Small World.* Norwood, N.J.: Ablex.

Kornblum, William. 1974. *Blue Collar Community.* Chicago: University of Chicago Press.

Kraut, Robert, et al. 1998. "The Internet Paradox: A Social Technology that Reduces Social Involvement and Psychological Well-Being." *American Psychologist* 53 (9): 1017–31.

Latané, Bibb, and John Darley. 1976. *Help in a Crisis: Bystander Response to an Emergency.* Morristown, N.J.: General Learning Press.

Lofland, Lyn. 1973. *A World of Strangers.* New York: Basic Books.

LeRoy Ladurie, Emmanuel. (1975) 1978. *Montaillou.* New York: George Braziller.

———. 1997. *The Beggar and the Professor.* Chicago: University of Chicago Press.

Magocsi, Paul Robert, and Geoffrey Matthews. 1993. *Historical Atlas of East Central Europe.* Toronto: University of Toronto Press.

McLuhan, Marshall. 1973. "Liturgy and the Media." *The Critic* (February): 15–23.

Milgram, Stanley. 1967. "The Small-World Problem." *Psychology Today* 1: 62–67.

Pahl, Raymond. 1984. *Divisions of Labour.* Oxford: Blackwell.

Parks, Malcolm, and Lynne Roberts. 1998. "Making 'MOOsic': The Development of Personal Relationships on Line and a Comparison to Their Off-Line Counterparts." *Journal of Social and Personal Relationships* 15 (4): 517–37.

Putnam, Robert. 1995. "Bowling Alone: America's Declining Social Capital." *Journal of Democracy* 6 (1): 65–78.

Reynolds, Malvina. 1960. "Little Boxes." New York: Schroeder Music.

Rheingold, Howard. 1993. *The Virtual Community: Homesteading on the Electronic Frontier.* Reading, Mass.: Addison-Wesley.

Roche, Daniel. 1981. *The People of Paris: An Essay in Popular Culture in the 18th Century.* Berkeley: University of California Press.

Ryan, Mary. 1990. *Women in Public: Between Banners and Ballots, 1825–1880.* Baltimore: Johns Hopkins University Press.

Salaff, Janet, Dimitrina Dimitrova, Deborah Hardwick, Katherine Hoski, and Susan Branderth. 1996. "Teleworking Potential: Evaluating Corporate Jobs." *Report to Bell Canada.*

Scarf, Maggie. 1987. *Intimate Partners: Patterns in Love and Marriage.* New York: Random House.

Scherzer, Kenneth. 1992. *The Unbounded Community: Neighborhood Life and Social Structure in New York City, 1830–1875.* Durham, N.C.: Duke University Press.

Sik, Endre. 1988. "Reciprocal Exchange of Labour in Hungary." In *On Work,* edited by Raymond Pahl, 527–47. Oxford: Basil Blackwell.

Sik, Endre, and Barry Wellman. 1999. "Network Capital in Capitalist, Communist and Post-Communist Countries: The Case of Hungary." In *Networks in the Global Village,* edited by Barry Wellman, 225–54. Boulder, Colo.: Westview Press.

Steiney, Peter. 1993. "On the Internet, No One Knows You're a Dog." [cartoon]. *The New Yorker,* July 5.

Strike, Carol. 1990. "The Film Industry in Canada." In *Canadian Social Trends,* edited by Craig McKie and Keith Thompson, 255–57. Toronto: Thompson Educational Publishing.

Taub, Richard, George Surgeon, Sara Lindholm, Phyllis Betts Otti, and Amy Bridges. 1977. "Urban Voluntary Associations: Locality Based and Externally Induced." *American Journal of Sociology* 83:425–42.

Tilly, Charles. 1973. "Do Communities Act?" *Sociological Inquiry* 43:209–40.

———. 1975. "Food Supply and Public Order in Modern Europe." In *The Formation of National States in Western Europe,* edited by Charles Tilly, 380–455. Princeton, N.J.: Princeton University Press.

Tönnies, Ferdinand. (1887) 1955. *Community and Organization (Gemeinschaft und Gesellschaft).* London: Routledge & Kegan Paul.

Tristan, Flora. (1840) 1980. *Flora Tristan's London Journal.* London: George Prior.

Wall, Helena. 1990. *Fierce Communion: Family and Community in North America.* Cambridge, Mass.: Harvard University Press.

Weick, Karl. 1976. "Educational Organizations as Loosely Coupled Systems." *Administrative Science Quarterly* 21:1–19.

Wellman, Barry. 1979. "The Community Question." *American Journal of Sociology* 84:1201–31.

———. 1985. "Domestic Work, Paid Work and Net Work." In *Understanding Personal Relationships,* edited by Steve Duck and Daniel Perlman, 159–91. London: Sage.

———. 1988. "Structural Analysis: From Method and Metaphor to Theory and Substance." In *Social Structures: A Network Approach,* edited by Barry Wellman and S. D. Berkowitz, 19–61. Cambridge: Cambridge University Press.

———. 1990. "The Place of Kinfolk in Community Networks." *Marriage and Family Review* 15:195–228.

———. 1992a. "Men in Networks: Private Communities, Domestic Friendships." In *Men's Friendships,* edited by Peter Nardi, 74–114. Newbury Park, Calif.: Sage.

———. 1992b. "Which Types of Ties and Networks Give What Kinds of Social Support?" In *Advances in Group Processes,* edited by Edward Lawler, Barry Markovsky, Cecilia Ridgeway, and Henry Walker, 207–35. Greenwich, Conn.: JAI Press.

———. 1993. "An Egocentric Network Tale." *Social Networks* 15:423–36.

———. 1996. "Are Personal Communities Local? A Dumptarian Reconsideration." *Social Networks* 18:347–54.

———. 1997. "An Electronic Group Is Virtually a Social Network." In *Culture of the Internet,* edited by Sara Kiesler, 179–205. Mahwah, N.J.: Lawrence Erlbaum.

Wellman, Barry, Peter Carrington, and Alan Hall. 1988. "Networks as Personal Communities." In *Social Structures: A Network Approach,* edited by Barry Wellman and S. D. Berkowitz, 130–84. Cambridge: Cambridge University Press.

Wellman, Barry, and Milena Gulia. 1999a. "Net Surfers Don't Ride Alone: Virtual Community as Community." In *Networks in the Global Village,* edited by Barry Wellman, 331–66. Boulder, Colo.: Westview Press.

———. 1999b. "The Network Basis of Social Support: A Network Is More than the Sum of Its Ties." In *Networks in the Global Village,* edited by Barry Wellman, 83–118. Boulder, Colo.: Westview Press.

Wellman, Barry, and Barry Leighton. 1979. "Networks, Neighborhoods and Communities." *Urban Affairs Quarterly* 14:363–90.

Wellman, Barry, and Stephanie Potter. 1999. "The Elements of Personal Communities." In *Networks in the Global Village,* edited by Barry Wellman, 49–82. Boulder, Colo.: Westview Press.

Wellman, Barry, Renita Wong, David Tindall, and Nancy Nazer. 1997. "A Decade of Network Change: Turnover, Mobility and Stability." *Social Networks* 19:27–51.

Wellman, Barry, and Scot Wortley. 1990. "Brothers' Keepers: Situating Kinship Relations in Broader Networks of Social Support." *Sociological Perspectives* 32:273–306.

———. 1990. "Different Strokes from Different Folks: Community Ties and Social Support." *American Journal of Sociology* 96:558–88.

Wellman, Beverly, and Barry Wellman. 1992. "Domestic Affairs and Network Relations." *Journal of Social and Personal Relationships* 9:385–409.

Wetherell, Charles, Andrejs Plakans, and Barry Wellman. 1994. "Social Networks, Kinship and Community in Eastern Europe." *Journal of Interdisciplinary History* 24 (spring): 639–63.

White, Harrison. 1970. "Search Parameters for the Small World Problem." *Social Forces* 49:259–64.

Wolf, Eric. 1966. "Kinship, Friendship and Patron-Client Relations." In *The Social Anthropology of Complex Societies*, edited by Michael Banton, 1–22. London: Tavistock.

Wright, Paul. 1989. "Gender Differences in Adults' Same- and Cross-Gender Friendships." In *Older Adult Friendship*, edited by Rebecca Adams and Rosemary Blieszner, 197–221. Newbury Park, Calif.: Sage.

PART TWO

The New Realities of Scale

CHAPTER SEVEN

Globalization and Historical Macrosociology

Giovanni Arrighi

Globalization and Its Contents

History continually makes untidy the neat conceptual frameworks and theoretical speculations with which we endeavor to understand the past and forecast the future of the world we live in. In our attempt to cope with the "chaos of existential judgments" (Max Weber's phrase) engendered by events and processes that challenge our understanding of the world, we tend to deny or exaggerate the novelty of what is actually happening. Denial leads to changes in the familiar meaning of words. Exaggeration leads to the coinage of new words of uncertain meaning. Either way, to quote John Ruggie (1994, 553), "Times of change are also times of confusion."

Some twenty to thirty years ago, the main source of confusion in the study of the global political economy was the persistent use of the term "imperialism" to designate tendencies that, in key respects, were antithetical to the tendencies that had been the object of classical theories of imperialism, both liberal and Marxist. In a critique of this anachronistic use of the term, I underscored how the establishment of U.S. hegemony after the Second World War had dissolved the very *explanandum* of classical theories of imperialism, namely, the tendency for intercapitalist competition to translate into open and generalized warfare. The growing tendency for processes of capital accumulation to become organized in multinational corporations undermined the separate and mutually exclusive character of nation-states on which classical theories of imperialism had been premised. Far from leading advanced capitalist states toward open and generalized warfare, this tendency could be expected to lead them toward what John Hobson, the liberal founder of theories of imperialism, had called "experimental and progressive federation" (Arrighi 1978, esp. 148).

Twenty years after this was written, the term imperialism has, for all practical purposes, disappeared from social scientific discourse, and the problem is no longer one of a theory that has lost its *explanandum*.

Rather, it is the problem of an ill-defined *explanandum* ("globalization") in search of theories able to make sense of whatever is brought to our attention by the use of this term. Given the uncertain meaning of the term, the search must begin with an inventory of the processes that go under the name of globalization and that actually deserve our attention.

The most widely recognized among these processes is the one I had used in my epistemological critique of theories of imperialism: the growing number and variety of corporations that organize their profit-making activities across state boundaries. The idea that the emergence of a system of multinational corporations undermines the power of states—not just of the smaller and weaker states that never had much power to begin with, but of the larger and stronger states as well—has been around ever since Charles Kindleberger (1969, chap. 6) declared that this emergence meant that the nation-state was "just about through as an economic unit." It was only some two decades later, however, that this idea was recycled, along with other ideas, under the new name "globalization."

What happened in those twenty years is that the expanding system of multinational corporations had set off two other processes that acquired a momentum of their own and gave credence to the idea that there is only one, indivisible, global market economy. One process is what came to be known as "financial globalization." The other is the revival of neoutilitarian doctrines of the minimalist state.

In the wake of the Great Depression and the Second World War, financial markets became nationally segmented and publicly regulated. The expression "financial globalization" came into use to denote the process of reintegration of these markets into a single, largely unregulated global market. As a result of this reintegration and deregulation, global *private* finance—"high finance," as it was known in the nineteenth century—"like a phoenix risen from the ashes . . . took flight and soared to new heights of power and influence in the affairs of nations" (Cohen 1996, 268).

This resurrection of global high finance was accompanied by the parallel resurrection of long discredited doctrines of the self-regulating market—what Karl Polanyi (1957, chaps. 12–13) had aptly called "the liberal creed." As the creed spread, vigorous attempts by governments to regulate the production and distribution of world money subsided, thereby adding new momentum to the deregulation and global reintegration of financial markets. The financial system that emerged as a result of this double resurrection was, in fact, no more "global" than the preceding Bretton Woods system. The term "globalization" was thus introduced primarily to denote "a shift from one global system (hierarchically organized and largely controlled politically by the United States) to another system that was more decentralized and coordinated through the market, making the financial conditions of capitalism far more volatile and far more unstable" (Harvey 1995, 8).

David Harvey confesses that, in his more cynical moments, he finds himself wondering whether "the financial press . . . conned us all . . . into believing in 'globalization' as something new when it was nothing more than a promotional gimmick to make the best of a necessary adjustment in the system of international finance" (1995, 8). Gimmick or not, the idea of globalization was intertwined from the start with the idea of intense interstate competition for increasingly volatile capital and a consequent tighter subordination of most states (the United States included) to the dictates of private capitalist agencies. Globalization may be a misleading term with which to denote the shift from a global financial system controlled by a hierarchy of governmental agencies headed by the United States to an equally global financial system in which governments have little control over their finances and compete fiercely with one another for the favor and assistance of privately controlled capital. But whether or not we want to retain the term, we can hardly hope to make sense of what has been going on in the world over the last twenty years or so without paying close attention to the shift itself.

The attention is all the more justified in view of the fact that the shift has been associated with two other epoch-making events: the sudden demise of the Soviet Union as one of two global military superpowers and the more gradual but still extraordinarily rapid rise of East Asia as an industrial and financial powerhouse of global significance. Taken jointly, the two events provide additional evidence to support the view that the sources of wealth, status, and power in the contemporary world are undergoing some fundamental changes.

On the one hand, the sudden collapse of the Soviet Union has demonstrated beyond reasonable doubt what was already implicit in the far more gradual and limited disempowerment of the United States in the financial sphere; namely, how vulnerable even the largest military-industrial complexes in world history had become to the forces of global economic integration. On the other hand, in spite of recent setbacks, the extraordinary economic expansion of East Asia has demonstrated that the forces of global integration do not necessarily disempower states. But the states that have experienced the greatest empowerment do not fit the predominant image of nation-states. Some are city-states—one sovereign (Singapore) and one semisovereign (Hong Kong). Others are semisovereign military protectorates of the United States—Japan, South Korea, and Taiwan, as Bruce Cumings (1997) has characterized all of them. And all are of no global military significance and far removed from the traditional power centers of the Western world.

Again, globalization may be a misnomer for whatever is going on. But the sea change that the use of the term purports to signify seriously challenges established ways of thinking about the world.

Historical Macrosociology Meets Globalization

In the same period that globalization transformed the world, North American macrosociology was itself transformed by the emergence of two new schools of thought: one organized primarily in the Comparative and Historical Sociology (CHS) Section of the American Sociological Association (ASA), the other in the Political Economy of the World-System (PEWS) Section of the ASA. Both schools aimed at mobilizing historical knowledge toward the solution of macrosociological problems. But they diverged radically in the way they defined their fields of study.

Under the slogan "Bringing the State Back In," CHS scholarship typically took states as its privileged unit of analysis and proceeded to analyze them in search of generalizations about common properties and principles of variation among instances across space and time. In contrast, PEWS scholarship typically took *systems* of states encompassed by a single division of labor as its privileged unit of analysis and proceeded to analyze them in search of generalizations about interdependencies among a system's components and principles of variation among systemic conditions across space and time. Quite a few individuals crossed the methodological divide. By and large, however, the mainstreams of the two historical macrosociologies developed in almost complete isolation from one another and without much awareness of the fact that different problems required different units of analysis.

At first sight it might appear that globalization has challenged CHS more fundamentally than PEWS macrosociology. Is not globalization dissolving the coherence and independence of states, on which CHS macrosociology is premised? And is globalization not bringing to everyone's attention the transnational interconnectedness of processes of state formation and capital accumulation on which PEWS macrosociology is premised? Understandably, PEWS scholars have not been shy in making claims of this kind (in addition to the quote below, see Friedmann 1996, 319):

> Today the phrases "world-economy," "world-market," and even "world-system" are commonplace, appearing in the sound-bites of politicians, media commentators, and unemployed workers alike. But few know that the most important source for these phrases lies with work started by sociologists in the early 1970s. . . . Not only did these [world-systems sociologists] perceive the global nature of economic networks 20 years before such networks entered popular discourse, but they also saw that many of these networks extend back at least 500 years. Over this time, the peoples of the globe became linked into one integrated unit: the modern "world-system." (Chase-Dunn and Grimes, 1995, 387–88)

Just as understandably, CHS scholars have been more reluctant to acknowledge the problems that globalization poses for their privileged unit of analysis. In revisiting the field of the comparative analysis of social revolutions fifteen years after the publication of her highly influential study on the subject, Theda Skocpol (1994) does not even mention globalization as creating (or not creating) problems for the state-centered method of analysis of which she has been among the most forceful advocates. Peter Evans, another prominent CHS scholar, does confront the revival of neoutilitarian theories of the minimalist state, but only to reiterate the centrality of the state in economic development and in macrosociological analysis (Evans 1995; Kohli et al. 1995).

Both kinds of claims—that globalization has demonstrated the validity of PEWS macrosociology or that it has not undermined the validity of CHS macrosociology—are in many ways justified. Nevertheless, neither claim has gone unchallenged from within the school in which it has been made. Far from welcoming the popularity of world-system terminology, Immanuel Wallerstein has warned his fellow PEWS macrosociologists that this semantic appropriation "for other, indeed opposite purposes [than those of world-systems analysis] . . . can cause serious confusion in the general scholarly public, and even worse, may lead to confusion on our own part, thus undermining our ability to pursue the tasks we have set ourselves" (1998, 108). Charles Tilly, for his part, has warned his fellow CHS macrosociologists that globalization poses a serious threat to their privileged method of analysis, because "the system of distinct, bounded sovereign states that long served as its implicit warrant is rapidly disintegrating" (1995b, 3–4).

More important, as a recent exchange between Tilly and Wallerstein shows (Symposium 1995), each variant of historical macrosociology has its own blind spots and bright lights in recognizing globalization as a macrosociological problem worthy of attention. In the article that prompted the exchange, Tilly defines globalization as "an increase in the geographical range of locally consequential social interactions, especially when that increase stretches a significant proportion of all interactions across international or intercontinental limits" (Tilly 1995a, 1–2). He suggests that over the last millennium, at least three waves of political and economic globalization did just that: first, in the thirteenth century, when the formation of the Mongol empire created the conditions for the emergence of the Afroeurasian world trading system (analyzed in great detail in Abu-Lughod 1989); second, in the sixteenth century, "when European commercial and military expansion connected the Indian Ocean with the Caribbean through a dense web of exchange and domination"; third, in the nineteenth century, "when a rush for empire put four-fifths of the world's land area under the dominion of European peoples" (Tilly 1995a, 1).

Tilly then goes on to list nine items that seem to him to provide strong circumstantial evidence that we may be in the midst of a new wave of globalization. In his subsequent discussion of the effects of this new wave on workers' rights, he contrasts the present wave's impact on state capacities with that of the previous wave. In the midst of the nineteenth-century wave, that is from about 1850, states (in fact, European and other Western states on which Tilly's contentions are based) acquired enhanced means of influencing technological innovation, employment, investment, and supplies of money by acting more vigorously to monitor and control the accumulation, movement, and transfer of capital, goods, persons, and ideas within and across national frontiers. In the present wave, by contrast, states are losing the capacity to monitor and control such stocks and flows, and therefore to pursue effective social policies. "Multinational corporations, international banking syndicates, and large criminal organizations are engineering some of these changes, but so are multinational compacts such as the European Community" (Tilly 1995a, 14).

In his response, Wallerstein claims to have no major disagreement with the overall picture drawn by Tilly, except on two related issues. First, he rejects the idea that "the origin of the decline of the strong state is the rise of the 'powerful supranational organizations,' not least of which are the transnational corporations" (Wallerstein 1995, 24). In his view, powerful supranational organizations such as the International Monetary Fund exist because there are powerful states that support them. More important,

> Transnational corporations are maintaining today the same structural stance vis-à-vis the states as did all their global predecessors, from the Fuggers to the Dutch East India Company to nineteenth-century Manchester manufacturers. They both need the states and fight the states. They need the states to guarantee their global attempts at monopolization and hence high profit levels, as well as to help limit the demands of the workers. They fight the states insofar as the states act as protectors of antiquated interests or are overresponsive to workers' pressures. I see nothing fundamentally different in this regard in 1994 from 1894, 1794, or even 1594. Yes, today there are fax machines, which are faster than telegraph wires, which are faster than messengers. But the basic economic processes remain the same. . . . What has changed of late is not the economics of the world-system but its politics. (Wallerstein 1995, 24–25)

This brings Wallerstein to his second major disagreement with Tilly. The shrinking of the state pioneered by Thatcher and Reagan was not a reaction to the decreasing effectiveness of state action in the context of proliferating supranational and transnational organizations as Tilly maintains. Rather, it was a reaction "to the *increasing* effectiveness of state-induced redistribution by trying to shrink the state and delegitimize redistribution. . . . It was not that states were wasting money; it was simply that they were spending too much." And they were spending too much because "the combined demands of the Third World (for relatively little per person but for a lot of people) and the Western working class (for relatively few people but for quite a lot per person)" far exceeded what world capitalism could accommodate (Wallerstein 1995, 25–26).

As we shall see in the next section of this paper, Wallerstein's first disagreement with Tilly points to theoretical constructs that PEWS scholarship is most in need of "unthinking," while the second disagreement points to the direction in which CHS scholarship has to do most of the "unthinking." Before we proceed, however, let us notice that these disagreements arise in the context of a basic agreement on the assessment that globalization is not as unprecedented a phenomenon as most observers think and that an understanding of its meaning and prospects requires a temporal horizon that encompasses centuries, rather than decades. In itself, this agreement constitutes important common ground on which the two variants of historical macrosociology can join forces to make sense of today's wave of globalization.

Equally promising is the reversal of roles evinced by the exchange. Tilly, whose historical macrosociology has been squarely based on national states as privileged units of analysis, takes the emerging institutions of world capitalism so seriously as to dismiss the continuing significance of national states as movers and shakers of the contemporary world. Wallerstein, whose historical macrosociology has been just as squarely based on the world capitalist system as the privileged unit of analysis, upholds the continuing significance of national states—to the point of dismissing the novelty of the emerging institutions of world capitalism. We should not make too much of this reversal because Tilly has long been aware of the importance of world capitalism in processes of state formation, and Wallerstein has always attached to national states an importance in the formation and expansion of world capitalism that is even greater than I think they deserve. Granted this, the reversal can still be taken as evidence of a potential breach in the methodological divide that has long kept CHS and PEWS scholarship aloof from one another.

Making Sense of Globalization

In order to make sense of globalization and gain some insight into the possible and likely outcomes of the interrelated processes and events that go under that name, we need to know three things. First, we need to know what is truly new in the present wave of globalization in comparison with earlier waves. Second, we need to know whether genuine novelties, if any, can be inscribed in some evolutionary pattern that we may be able to detect in the sequence of waves of globalization. And finally, we need to know whether and how the novelties that cannot be so inscribed can conceivably lead to a departure from past patterns of recurrence and evolution.

In giving my own tentative answers to these questions, I shall focus on three issues that seem to me to call for some deep unthinking on the part of either or both variants of historical macrosociology. The first two issues correspond to Wallerstein's disagreements with Tilly: first, whether the structural stance of the leading business organizations of world capitalism vis-à-vis the states is the same today as it has been since the sixteenth century; and, second, whether the true novelty of the present wave of globalization is the difficulty that the dominant institutions of world capitalism face in accommodating the combined demands of Third World peoples and the Western working classes. The third issue figures only tangentially in Tilly's "Globalization" article and not at all in Wallerstein's response, but it is probably the most important. This is the issue raised by the seeming relocation of the epicenter of the global economy to East Asia, where it was at the time of the first wave of globalization in Tilly's list.

In order to settle the first issue, PEWS macrosociologists must be prepared to unthink what many of them have come to regard as the quintessence of world-systems theory. This is the idea that, in spite of their extraordinary geographical expansion, the structures of the world capitalist system have remained more or less the same ever since they first came into existence in the "long" sixteenth century. This was a useful working hypothesis in the formative stages of PEWS macrosociology. The more I have worked with it, however, the more I have become convinced that not only does the hypothesis not stand up to historicoempirical scrutiny, but even worse, it prevents us from getting at the heart of the capitalist dynamic, both past and present.

As I have argued and documented elsewhere (Arrighi 1994), we can indeed detect a pattern of recurrence in state-capital relations from the earliest stages of formation of the world capitalist system right up to the present. This pattern consists of recurrent financial expansions in the course of which the leading capitalist organizations of the time tend to shift a growing proportion of their incoming cash flows away from trade and production and reorient their activities toward borrowing, lending, and speculating. In all financial expansions—from Renaissance Florence to the Reagan era—the switch from trade and production to finance was made profitable by an intensification of interstate competition for mobile capital. Except for the scale and scope of the competition and the speed of the technical means deployed in financial deals, the basic political-economic process is in this respect the same in the late twentieth century as it was one, two, four, or even six centuries ago.

Financial expansions, however, are not the expression of an invariant structural relationship between states and capital. On the contrary, they signal the beginning of a fundamental restructuring of that relationship. They are, in Fernand Braudel's (1984, 246) words, a "sign of autumn" of major capitalist developments. They are the "season" when the leading organizing centers of world capitalism reap the fruits of their leadership and, at the same time, begin to be replaced at the commanding heights of world capitalism by a new leadership. Thus, in the Genoese-led financial expansion of the second half of the sixteenth century, city-states like Venice and transnational business diasporas like the Genoese gradually lost their centrality in world-scale processes of capital accumulation. Over time, their place was taken by a proto-nation-state (the United Provinces) and its chartered companies, which lost their own centrality in the course of the Dutch-led financial expansion of the eighteenth century. The new organizing center then became the British nation-state, with its world-encompassing formal empire and informal business networks. But as soon as these governmental and business institutions experienced their own apogee in the British-led financial expansion of the late nineteenth and early twentieth centuries, they too began to be replaced at the commanding heights of world capitalism by the continent-sized United States with its panoply of multinational corporations and far-flung networks of quasi-permanent military bases (Arrighi 1994, 13–16, 74–84, 235–38, 330–31).

In this sequence, the recurrent emergence of new leading complexes of governmental and business agencies that are more powerful, both militarily and financially, than the complexes they replace, is the key aspect of the expansion of world capitalism from its modest beginnings in late medieval Europe to today's all-encompassing global dimensions. The emergence of multinational corporations as key components of the U.S. complex has been part of this pattern. But the issue raised by Tilly is whether, in the course of the present U.S.-led financial expansion, multinational corporations have become a force that undermines, rather than buttresses, state capacity, the capacity of the United States included.

The most appropriate way to settle the issue is to compare today's multinational corporations with their closest analogue in capitalist history, the joint-stock chartered companies of the seventeenth and eighteenth centuries. In this comparison two differences immediately stand out. First, whereas joint-stock chartered companies were half-business, half-governmental organizations that specialized territorially in the monopolization of commercial opportunities in the non-European world on behalf of the governments that had chartered them, multinational corporations are strictly business organizations that specialize functionally across the boundaries of sovereign states. Second, whereas joint-stock chartered companies depended for their very existence on exclusive trading privileges granted by their chartering governments, multinational corporations have established and reproduced themselves primarily on the basis of the competitiveness of their managerial hierarchies.

Taken jointly, these two differences have channeled the development of the two kinds of corporate capitalism along opposite paths, insofar as their respective relations to Western states are concerned. Owing to their territorial specialization and exclusiveness, viable joint-stock chartered companies of all nationalities were always few in numbers (probably no more than a dozen or so at any given time) and all were, and remained, instruments of European states operating in the non-European world at a time when European states were still weak by global standards. Although most of them did not accomplish much, the imperial heritage left behind by the English East India Company, for example, became a decisive factor in the nineteenth-century global expansion of British and Western dominance.

The number of multinational corporations operating under U.S. hegemony, in contrast, has become incomparably greater, owing to their transterritoriality and functional specialization in a greatly expanded world-economy. Moreover, their number has been growing very rapidly in recent years: according to some estimates, from over ten thousand in 1980 to three times as many by the early 1990s (Stopford and Dunning 1983, 3; Ikeda 1996, 48). Originally, this new species of corporate business played a role in the maintenance and expansion of the global power of the United States that was not unlike the role played by chartered companies in the seventeenth and eighteenth centuries in relation to Dutch and British power (Gilpin 1975, 141–42). Soon, however, their proliferation backfired on U.S. power. This happened exactly when the U.S. government most needed its "cut" on the claims that the U.S. multinationals had established on foreign incomes and resources, namely, at the time when the fiscal crisis of the U.S. "warfare-welfare state" became acute under the impact of the Vietnam war and the U.S. civil rights movement. As the crisis deepened, a growing proportion of the overseas cash flows of U.S. corporations, instead of being repatriated, flew to offshore money markets, precipitating the collapse of the U.S.-controlled Bretton Woods system (Arrighi 1994, 300–8).

In short, contrary to Wallerstein, there is plenty of evidence to support Tilly's contention that the ongoing expansion in the number and variety of multinational corporations constitutes a novelty in state-capital relations. Whether or not multinational corporations, like their global predecessors, "need the states" (and in many respects they undoubtedly do), the *unintended* result of their proliferation is a disempowerment of Western states, in sharp contrast with their empowerment before and during the nineteenth-century wave of globalization. Nevertheless, it does not follow that this disempowerment has been the main driving force behind the offensive against workers' rights pioneered by Thatcher and Reagan through a revival of neoutilitarian doctrines of the minimalist state. On the contrary, on this second issue it is Tilly's, rather than Wallerstein's, contention that does not stand up to historicoempirical scrutiny, and it is CHS rather than PEWS macrosociology that has to do most of the unthinking. Three main considerations seem to me to tilt the scales of the evidence against Tilly.

First, the revival of neoutilitarian doctrines cannot be attributed to a novelty of the late twentieth century precisely because it is a *revival*. What is more, it is a revival of doctrines that first became hegemonic within the Western world in the second half of the nineteenth century—at a time, that is, when by Tilly's own account, Western states were experiencing empowerment rather than disempowerment. And finally, a hundred years ago these doctrines neither were, nor were they perceived by workers to be, an attack on their rights and living conditions, as witnessed by the support that the British working class and Labour Party granted to Britain's *unilateral* free trade. Clearly, either the neoliberal creed that was revived in the 1980s means something completely different than what the original creed meant a hundred years ago, or the revival cannot be attributed to historical circumstances (a disempowerment of Western states) that are the opposite of what they were one hundred years ago.

Second, the massive flight of capital to extraterritorial financial markets that in the late 1960s initiated the disintegration of the U.S.-controlled Bretton Woods system occurred in the context of escalating demands for high mass consumption in the First World and for national self-determination and development in the Third World. In leading the flight, multinational corporations were expressing a vote of no confidence in the capacity of the United States and its European allies to prevent these combined demands from seriously undermining the profitability of their global operations. The unintended result of this vote of no confidence was a further weakening of that capacity and a consequent generalized perception that the U.S. world order was in serious crisis. For most of the 1970s, however, the dominant force in the dynamics of crisis remained First and Third World social movements that sought delivery on the promises of the global New Deal that undergirded the U.S. world order (cf. Arrighi 1982; Arrighi, Hopkins, and Wallerstein 1989; Arrighi 1994).

Finally, in spite of its state minimalist rhetoric, the Thatcher-Reagan response to the crisis of the 1970s was not to "shrink the state" in

reaction to "the decreasing effectiveness of state action," as Tilly maintains. Far from shrinking, the U.S. government under Reagan accumu-
lated a larger national debt than at any time during U.S. history, and
it is this debt, more than anything else, that today ties the hands of the
U.S. government both domestically and globally. The main thrust of
the Thatcher-Reagan response was, instead, the use of a bloated state
to deflate the social power of First World workers and Third World
peoples in an attempt to regain the confidence and support of an increasingly transnationalized and volatile capital. The attempt was
largely successful but at the cost of a further disruption of what was
left of the Cold War world order. This disruption included the proliferation of forms of war involving forces other than disciplined national
armies—a proliferation that Tilly correctly identifies among the most
important signs of a general weakening of state capacity (Arrighi 1994,
epilogue; Tilly 1995a, 17–18).

In sum, the offensive against workers' rights that has characterized
the present wave of globalization is rooted in world-historical circumstances that are radically different from those of the nineteenth-century
wave of globalization. Although the presence of a large and growing
number and variety of multinational corporations is one of the circumstances that are different, this is not the difference that has prompted
the offensive. In order to understand the offensive and its prospective consequences, we must focus on the difference in power relations
not between states and capital, but between Western states and non-
Western peoples. We must focus, that is, on the fact that in the
nineteenth-century wave of globalization, the power of Western states
vis-à-vis non-Western peoples was high and still rising, whereas in the
present wave it is lower and declining further.

This is a difference that CHS macrosociology is not well-equipped
to deal with, unless it is prepared to do its own share of unthinking.
For its entire research program has been premised on the assumption
that states—including and especially the European states that have
constituted the program's overwhelming concern—are distinct and
bounded units whose properties are primarily determined by what
goes on inside of them or, at most, by their mutual competition. Useful
as it has been in the identification of common properties and principles
of variation among states across space and time, this assumption has
made CHS macrosociology oblivious to two among the most basic
facts of state formation in the modern era: first, that throughout the
modern era, power relations within and among Western states have
been thoroughly shaped by power relations between Western states

and the non-Western world; and second, that what Western and non-Western states have become is largely the outcome of a process of violent conquest of the world by European states. This is the process that materialized most conspicuously in Tilly's second and third waves of globalization and the reversal of which is responsible for the most important peculiarities of the present wave. How can we make any sense of the nineteenth-century, British-led wave of globalization without focusing on the relationship of Britain to its Indian empire? And conversely, are not many of the problems faced by the United States in the present wave of globalization due to the fact that, unlike Britain in the nineteenth-century wave, it has no Indian empire to cover its balance of payments deficits and to supply the military manpower needed to police the world?

Envoi

Let me conclude by pointing to a final issue that the Tilly-Wallerstein exchange does not raise but which is probably the most critical to understanding the prospective consequences of the present wave of globalization. The issue figures prominently in Andre Gunder Frank's latest book (1998), but it was first raised within PEWS macrosociology by Janet Abu-Lughod's study (1989) of what Tilly singles out as the first wave of globalization in the past millennium. In the concluding pages of her book, Abu-Lughod suggests that the thirteenth-century wave of globalization, loose and tenuous as it was, may be as relevant to an understanding of our future as anything that has happened since (1989, 369–72).

What happened since is that European states gradually conquered the world and turned it into a new, denser, and stronger system centered on Europe itself. Although the center of the expanding system "migrated" from country to country and eventually to North America, "it remained within a common cultural zone that excluded African, Latin American, and Asian powers. And even though the economic and political institutions of the core underwent significant transformations, they remained within a tradition which was culturally Western" (Abu-Lughod 1990, 281). The social sciences have been part of this tradition and became so fixated on "studying the persistence and evolution of *the* 'modern' world-system that we are unprepared to understand what we sense may be its break-up or at least its radical transformation" (Abu-Lughod 1990, 281–82).

The perception that something radical may be happening in this respect is obscured by the fact that "many of the former colonies of Europe in Africa and the Middle East, after gaining their independence in the wake of World War II, have actually been demoted in the world system" (Abu-Lughod 1989, 370). After this was written, the perception was obscured further by the self-proclaimed "triumph of the West" in the Cold War—a claim that forgets that the Soviet Union was no less part of the Western cultural tradition than the United States and that the Cold War was primarily a Western civil war. Nevertheless, as previously noted, the deflation in the power of many non-Western states (and the further centralization of the power resources of the historic West) has been accompanied by an economic empowerment of states far removed from the traditional power centers of the West that has no precedent in the modern era. The empowerment is still surrounded by much uncertainty, as witnessed by the ongoing East Asian financial crisis, but crises of this kind have been typical of all *emerging* centers of world capitalism, including the United States during and after the crash of 1929–31 (Arrighi and Silver et al. 1999).

As Abu-Lughod (1989, 370–71) herself suggests, embryonic as this change still is, it may well be a sign that "the old advantages that underlay the hegemony of the West are dissipating." Although the centralization of means of mass destruction in U.S. hands is unprecedented, the United States has neither the human nor the financial resources needed to translate that centralization into effective global power. And while none of the East Asian states that have grown rich under the carapace of U.S. hegemony can even remotely challenge the U.S. militarily, neither are any of them prepared to "write a blank check," let alone spill blood, to ensure the continuation of U.S. military supremacy.

Instead of witnessing the usual fusion of a higher order of military and financial power that has characterized all past replacements of one leadership by another at the commanding heights of world capitalism, we are witnessing a fission that leaves global military power heavily concentrated in the hands of the declining Western hegemon and concentrates global financial power in East Asian hands (Arrighi, 348–56; Arrighi and Silver et al. 1999, 88–96, 272–89). Under these circumstances, to paraphrase Abu-Lughod (1989, 371), it is indeed hard to imagine that the era of Western hegemony will be superseded by a new form of world conquest. And it does indeed seem more likely "that there will be a return to the relative balance of multiple centers exhibited in the thirteenth-century world system." Such a return would inevitably require "a shift to different rules of the game, or at least an end to the rules Europe introduced in the sixteenth century" (Abu-Lughod 1989, 370–71).

Both variants of historical macrosociology have remarkably little to say on what these rules might look like and on how to monitor the process that may eventually bring them into existence. I suspect that this is because both variants have tried to fit the present rise of East Asia into theoretical constructs that are ill-suited for the purpose. Perhaps the time has come to try the opposite strategy, that is, unthinking these constructs in light of the recentering of the global economy on East Asia.

References

Abu-Lughod, Janet. 1989. *Before European Hegemony: The World System, A.D. 1250–1350.* New York: Oxford University Press.
———. 1990. "Restructuring the Premodern World-System." *Review* 13 (2): 273–86.
Arrighi, Giovanni. 1978. *The Geometry of Imperialism: The Limits of Hobson's Paradigm.* London: Verso.
———. 1982. "A Crisis of Hegemony." In *Dynamics of Global Crisis,* S. Amin, G. Arrighi, A. G. Frank, and I. Wallerstein, 55–108. New York: Monthly Review Press.
———. 1994. *The Long Twentieth Century: Money, Power and the Origins of Our Times.* London: Verso.
Arrighi, Giovanni, Terence Hopkins, and Immanuel Wallerstein. 1989. *Antisystemic Movements.* London: Verso.
Arrighi, Giovanni, and Beverly Silver, et al. 1999. *Chaos and Governance in the Modern World System.* Minneapolis: University of Minnesota Press.
Braudel, Fernand. 1984. *The Perspective of the World.* New York: Harper & Row.
Chase-Dunn, Christopher, and Peter Grimes. 1995. "World-Systems Analysis." *Annual Review of Sociology* 21:387–417.
Cohen, Benjamin. 1996. "Phoenix Risen: The Resurrection of Global Finance." *World Politics* 48:268–96.
Cumings, Bruce. 1997. "Japan and Northeast Asia into the 21st Century." In *Network Power: Japan and Asia,* edited by P. J. Katzenstein and T. Shiraishi, 136–68. Ithaca, N.Y.: Cornell University Press.
Evans, Peter. 1995. *Embedded Autonomy: States and Industrial Transformation.* Princeton, N.J.: Princeton University Press, 1995.
Frank, Andre Gunder. 1998. *ReOrient: Global Economy in the Asian Age.* Berkeley: University of California Press.
Friedmann, Harriet. "Prometheus Rebounds." Review of *The Modern World-System,* vol. 1, by Immanuel Wallerstein. *Contemporary Sociology* 25:319–22.
Gilpin, Robert. 1975. *U.S. Power and the Multinational Corporation.* New York: Basic Books.
Harvey, David. 1995. "Globalization in Question." *Rethinking Marxism* 8 (4): 1–17.
Ikeda, Satoshi. 1996. "World Production." In *The Age of Transition: Trajectory of the World-System, 1945–2025,* T. K. Hopkins and I. Wallerstein et al., 38–86. London: Zed Books.
Kindleberger, Charles. 1969. *American Business Abroad.* New Haven, Conn.: Yale University Press.

Kohli, Atul, et al. "The Role of Theory in Comparative Politics: A Symposium." *World Politics* 48:1–49.

Polanyi, Karl. 1957. *The Great Transformation: The Political and Economic Origins of Our Time* Boston: Beacon Press.

Ruggie, John. 1994. "Third Try at World Order? America and Multilateralism after the Cold War." *Political Science Quarterly* 109 (4): 553–70.

Skocpol, Theda. 1994. *Social Revolutions in the Modern World.* New York: Cambridge University Press.

Stopford, John M., and John H. Dunning. 1983. *Multinationals: Company Performance and Global Trends.* London: Macmillan.

Symposium. 1995. "Scholarly Controversy: Global Flows of Labor and Capital." With contributions from Charles Tilly, Immanuel Wallerstein, Aristide R. Zolberg, E. J. Hobsbawm, and Lourdes Beneria. *International Labor and Working-Class History* 47 (spring): 1–55.

Tilly, Charles. 1995*a.* "Globalization Threatens Labor's Rights." *International Labor and Working-Class History* 47 (spring): 1–55.

———. 1995*b.* "Macrosociology, Past and Future." *Newsletter of the Comparative and Historical Sociology Section of the American Sociological Association* 8:1–4.

Wallerstein, Immanuel. 1995. "Response: Declining States, Declining Rights?" *International Labor and Working-Class History* 47 (spring): 24–27.

———. 1998. "The Rise and Future Demise of World-Systems Analysis." *Review* 21 (1): 103–12.

CHAPTER EIGHT

Cracked Casings:
Notes toward an Analytics for
Studying Transnational Processes

SASKIA SASSEN

Transnational processes such as economic globalization confront the social sciences with a series of theoretical and methodological challenges. In the case of today's global economy, such a challenge comes out of the fact that it simultaneously transcends the exclusive territorial authority of the national state yet is implanted in national territories and institutions. As a result, economic globalization directly engages two marking features of much social science: the explicit or implicit assumption about the national state as the container of social processes, and the implied correspondence of national territory and nationally exclusive territoriality (the institutional encasement of that territory). Both of these assumptions describe conditions that have held for a long time—throughout much of the history of the modern state since World War I and in some cases even earlier. But these conditions are now being partly unbundled.

These assumptions about the national state as container and territoriality as synonymous with territory work well for many of the subjects studied in the social sciences. But they are not helpful in elucidating a growing number of situations when it comes to globalization and to a whole variety of transnational processes now being studied by sociologists and other social scientists. Nor are those assumptions helpful for developing the requisite research techniques.

One of the features of the current phase of globalization is that the fact that a process happens within the territory of a sovereign state does not necessarily mean it is a national process. This localization of the global, or of the nonnational, in national territories undermines many of the methods and conceptual frameworks prevalent in the social sciences. Developing the theoretical and empirical specifications that allow us to accommodate this is a difficult and collective effort. The new literature on transnationalism represents the beginning of one such effort. For instance, anthropologists and sociologists working on immigration have provided us with particularly fruitful studies in this regard, cross-border migration flows being a subject that lends itself to such an approach (see, e.g., Basch, Schiller, and Szanton-Blanc 1995; Mahler 1995; Smith 1995; Grasmuck and Pessar 1991; Bonilla et al. 1998).

The distinction between the global and the local needs to be rethought, as do established notions of membership, or of the necessity of physical proximity in the constitution of the "local." For instance, both the new international professional class and the immigrant workforce operate in contexts which are both local and global; they are members of a cross-border culture that is in many ways "local." The international financial centers of London, New York, Zurich, Amsterdam, and Frankfurt are all part of an international, yet very localized, work subculture. We see here both proximity and deterritorialization. And immigrant communities in these cities also have international linkages with their home countries and local cultures of origin. In a different manner, they nonetheless also have the experience of deterritorialized local cultures, not predicated on proximity.

These are partial accounts of the full experience of these two groups. But the experience of globalization and its impact on localities is partial; it is not an all-encompassing umbrella. It installs itself in very specific structures. And it is this specificity that we need to study, along with the macro processes, and for which we need to develop particular categories of analysis. In the next two sections I try to illustrate this by focusing on two distinct processes: one concerned with the relation between the global economy and the national state, and the second the relation of the global economy and place. This choice of focus is inevitably conditioned by my own past research. Both of these foci contain research sites that call for detailed empirical work, including ethnographic work, and for an understanding of social and cultural dynamics. Herein lies, indeed, one of the important methodological and theoretical implications of such an alternative approach. A study of the global economy is not confined to the macrolevel cross-border processes studied by economists. It also requires macro- and microlevel sociological studies.

My concern here is with understanding how we study specific localities, structures, and formations in a context of globalization and transnationalization. I think we need to develop new categories that do not presuppose the customary dualities global/local or national/global. Further, the sociological study of some familiar subjects—gendered economic organization and dynamics, race relations, cities, labor markets, and the like—needs to incorporate, in addition to the typical variables applied to them, some of the variables coming out of the new theorization and analytics of globalization.

The Unbundling of National Territoriality

Two notions underlie much of the current discussion about globalization. One is the zero-sum game: whatever the global economy gains, the national state loses, and vice versa. The other is that if an event takes place in a national territory it is a national event, whether it is a business transaction or a judiciary decision. These assumptions about zero sums and geography influence experts on the global economy as well as the general public. For experts it has meant that they have typically confined themselves to cross-border processes, notably international trade and investment. The analysis has produced a rather empirically and theoretically thin account that begs more questions than it answers.

An emerging body of scholarship has constructed the spatiality of the global economy along different lines, showing that to a large extent global processes materialize in national territories (e.g., Mittelman 1996; Knox and Taylor 1995; Sassen 1991; Stren 1996; Brenner 1998; Taylor 1995). Many transactions that are a key part of the global economy do not cross borders, or do not do so in the ways that investment and trade do. Even the most digitalized global financial market is grounded in a set of very material resources and spaces largely embedded in national territories.

Further, precisely because, to a considerable extent, global processes materialize within national territories, a large number of national states have had to become deeply involved in the implementation of the global economic system. One of the key features of the role of the state vis-à-vis today's global economy (unlike earlier forms of the world economy) has been to negotiate the intersection of national law and foreign actors—whether firms, markets, or supranational organizations. We generally use the term "deregulation" to describe the outcome of this negotiation. The problem with this term is that it only captures the withdrawal of the state from regulating its economy. It does not register all the ways in which the state participates in setting up the new frameworks through which globalization is furthered, nor does it capture the associated transformations inside the state (see Cox 1987; Panitch 1996; Sassen 1996). A much older doctrine captures certain aspects of this negotiation through the concept of extraterritoriality, but only as it pertains to other governmental actors. Elsewhere I have examined whether the impact of economic globalization on national territoriality can also be subsumed under the doctrine of extraterritoriality; my conclusion is that globalization engages the state in such different ways and represents such different modes of articulation of the foreign actor and national law from those evident in cases of extraterritoriality that is not useful to subsume both under the same concept. I prefer to name this process denationalization (see Sassen 1996, chap. 1).

Multiple negotiations were and are necessary for the implementation of the particular type of global economic system we now live with. These include familiar mechanisms such as lifting interest ceilings and new legislative measures allowing privatization of public-sector firms, the latter a key condition in many countries for the entry of foreign investors. But they also include the formation of new subcultures in international finance and accounting. These are necessary to ensure the cross-border circulation of new financial instruments and new accounting principles, mostly Anglo-American in origin, and this even in traditionally resistant countries such as France or China.

Global cities are one of the major instantiations of some of these processes. They are one form of the embeddedness of global processes in national territories and in national institutional arrangements. Insofar as this embeddedness is mediated through deregulation, we can posit that globalization entails a partial denationalizing of national territoriality. These cities concentrate many of the institutions that are the object of deregulatory measures, notably financial markets and the institutions through which direct foreign investment is handled (see Sassen 1991, pts. 1, 2).

This incipient denationalizing of national territorial authority is one of the distinctive features of this current phase, as compared with the three decades after World War II and generally the period after World War I. It is a process whose presence is signaled, but not fully captured, by a variety of new developments. A "global" transaction (e.g., a deal between a French and an Indonesian firm) can take place inside a third territory (e.g., Manhattan). China's government could launch a hundred-year bond, to be sold mostly in New York, for which it did not have to engage the U.S. government but, rather, J. P. Morgan and Bankers Trust. Further, the privatization of public-sector firms, now largely owned by international investors, is not simply a change in property regime but also a shift of "governance" functions from the public to the (in this case largely foreign) private sector. Other important developments in this direction are the rise of international commercial arbitration as the main mode for settling cross-border business disputes. The main purpose of this type of arbitration is to avoid national courts. Further, credit-rating agencies, which are private firms, fulfill some of the most important governing functions for the global capital market.

All of these developments can be seen as signaling, among other outcomes, this incipient denationalizing of national "territory" through a chipping away at the exclusive territoriality of national states. I want to emphasize again that the impacts of these various developments and the deep meanings of them all vary rather markedly for different types of states.

In brief, what is generally called deregulation actually refers to an extremely complex set of intersections and negotiations that, while they may preserve the integrity of national territory as a geographic condition, do transform *exclusive* territoriality, that is, the national and international frameworks through which national territory has assumed an institutional form. In my examination of various components of deregulation I bring to the fore the distinction between national territory and national territoriality (Sassen 1996). Territory and territoriality have corresponded tightly for much of the recent history of mostly so-called protected economies, especially in most of the highly developed countries. Today, globalization and deregulation may be contributing to an incipient slippage in that correspondence. Much deregulation has had the effect of promoting that slippage and giving it a legitimate form in national legal frameworks.

Many of the negotiations necessary for the implementation of a global economy have to do with the creation of new business cultures and new consumer cultures. And they have to do with distinct ways of representing what is the "economy" and what is "culture." In my reading of the evidence, economic globalization is encased in a broad range of cultural forms, typically not recognized in general commentaries (by the media) or in expert accounts as cultural, but rather seen as belonging to the world of technology and expertise. This deserves study.

For instance, international finance became an immensely creative practice in the 1980s, with many new, often daring instruments invented and the creation of several new markets. For this to succeed required not only "state of the art" technological infrastructure and new types of expertise. It also required a very specific transnational subculture within which these innovations could circulate, be accept-able, and be successful—that is, actually sold. We simply cannot take for granted the vast increase in the orders of magnitude of the financial markets and the variety of mechanisms through which forms of capital hitherto considered fixed, such as real estate, were made liquid and hence could circulate globally. These massive innovations entailed a very significant set of negotiations in view of what had been the domi-nant banking culture. And they entailed a rather dramatic increase in the number of very young and very smart professionals. These profes-sionals command both the mathematics and the computer/software knowledge required, and, at a far younger age than had been the norm in the industry, thus gained significant control over vast amounts of capital. There is a bundle of sociological issues here: insider communi-ties, trust, generational shifts, networks, the social construction of such conditions as expertise and technical outputs. These are part of the explanation beyond narrowly economic and technical factors.

Another important instantiation is the ascendance of a certain type of legal and accounting model, basically Anglo-American in origin, as the "correct" one in global business transactions. This also entails a series of negotiations, some conceptual, some operational: for example, the current practice of locating Anglo-American law and accounting firms in Paris or in Beijing to handle cross-border business into and out of these countries with their very different legal and accounting systems. Again, there is a need here for detailed research on such oper-ations—the need to recover the anthropology and the sociology of these conditions of economic globalization.

In view of these transformations in the territoriality and sovereignty of the national state resulting from economic globalization, we can posit that there may also be an impact on citizenship. The history of the institution shows the importance of the underlying conditions in the shaping of modern citizenship. Insofar as the global economy has created new conditions, we might see another phase in the evolution of the institution of citizenship.[1] Once we accept the cultural and his-torical specificity of concepts of civil society and citizenship in Western social and political theory, we need to reckon, at least theoretically, with the impact of global forces that challenge the authority of the national state. In a world where the sovereignty of the national state and civil solidarity are possibly challenged by globalization, what is the analytic terrain within which we need to examine the question of citizen rights in the social sciences? Do we need to expand this terrain?

Expressed differently, do we need to introduce new elements in the discourse on rights in the social sciences? (See Jacobson 1996; Soysal 1994; Sassen 1996; Ong 1997.)

Places and Cross-Border Networks

One particular line of inquiry that can be derived from the preceding discussion on the distinction between territory and territoriality concerns the question of specific types of territory. Few categories contain as sharp a contrast as the global economy, with its association of macrolevel processes, and place, with its associations of microlevel processes. Yet, as I have tried to show in detail elsewhere (Sassen 1991), place is central to the multiple circuits through which economic globalization is constituted.[2]

I think of the mainstream account of economic globalization as a narrative of eviction. Key concepts in that account—globalization, information economy, and telematics—all suggest that place no longer matters and that the only type of worker that matters is the highly educated professional. It is an account that privileges the capability for global transmission over the material infrastructure that makes such transmission possible; information outputs over the workers producing those outputs, from specialists to secretaries; and the new transnational corporate culture over the multiplicity of work cultures, including immigrant cultures, within which many of the "other" jobs of the global information economy take place. In brief, the dominant narrative concerns itself with the upper circuits of capital and, particularly, with the hypermobility of capital rather than with that which is place bound.

One strategic type of place for these developments, and the one focused on here, is the city. Including cities in the analysis of economic globalization is not without conceptual consequences. Economic globalization has mostly been conceptualized in terms of the duality between national/global, where the latter gains at the expense of the former. And it has largely been conceptualized in terms of the internationalization of capital and then only the upper circuits of capital. Introducing cities into an analysis of economic globalization allows us to reconceptualize processes of economic globalization as concrete economic complexes situated in specific places. A focus on cities decomposes the national state into a variety of subnational components, some profoundly articulated with the global economy and others not. It also signals the declining significance of the national economy as a unitary category in the global economy. And even if, to a large extent, this was a unitary category constructed in political discourse and policy, it has become even less of a fact in the last fifteen years.

Why does it matter to recover place in analyses of the global economy, particularly place as constituted in major cities? Because it allows us to see the multiplicity of economies and work cultures in which the global information economy is embedded (King 1996). It also allows us to recover the concrete, localized processes through which globalization exists and to argue that much of the multiculturalism in large cities is as much a part of globalization as is international finance. Finally, focusing on cities allows us to specify a geography of strategic places at the global scale, places bound to each other by the dynamics of economic globalization.[3]

I refer to this as a new geography of centrality. It is a geography that cuts across the old North-South divide: it includes not only the major centers of economic power in the highly developed countries but also the corporate world of places such as São Paulo and Buenos Aires or Bombay and Bangalore. Alongside this new geography of centrality there is also a new geography of marginality. It also cuts across the North-South divide: it includes the disadvantaged of New York City and Paris as well as those of São Paulo and Bombay. The notion of such geographies engenders research agendas that can focus on questions of power and poverty in ways that combine the specificity of the local with broader, cross-border dynamics (e.g., Ward 1990). And such an agenda allows us to do so without losing some version of a "container," only now a container that is not "the nation" or "the city," but one that encompasses fragments of each in a cross-border space with systemic properties that specify it.

One of the questions raised by such new cross-border geographies of centrality and marginality is whether they are also the space for a new transnational politics. For instance, insofar as an analysis of the global city recovers the broad array of jobs and work cultures that are part of the global economy (although typically not marked as such), it allows one to examine the possibility of a new politics of traditionally disadvantaged actors operating in this new transnational economic geography. This is a politics that arises out of the condition of economic participation in the global economy, albeit as low-wage earners, from factory workers in export processing zones to cleaners on Wall Street. It is a condition shared by workers in many different places around the world—places integrated into the global system. Immigrant workers and women are among the strategic actors in this new transnational geography.

The centrality of place in a context of global processes engenders a transnational economic and political opening for the formation of new claims and hence for the constitution of entitlements, notably rights to place, and, at the limit, in the constitution of notions of membership and "citizenship" (Holston 1996). The city has indeed emerged as a site for new claims: by global capital, which uses the city as an "organizational commodity," but also by disadvantaged sectors of the urban population, frequently as internationalized a presence in large cities as is capital (Abu-Lughod et al. 1994). The denationalizing of urban space and the formation of new claims centered in transnational actors and involving contestation raise the question: Whose city is it?[4]

The space constituted by the worldwide grid of global cities, a space with new economic and political potentialities, is perhaps one of the most strategic spaces for the formation of transnational identities and communities. This is a space that is both place centered, in that it is embedded in particular and strategic sites, and also transterritorial, because it connects sites that are not geographically proximate yet are intensely connected to each other. As I argued earlier, it is not only the transmigration of capital that takes place in this global grid, but also that of people, both rich (i.e., the new transnational professional workforce) and poor (i.e., most migrant workers). And it is a space for the transmigration of cultural forms, for the reterritorialization of "local" subcultures. An important question is whether it is also a space for a new politics, one going beyond the politics of culture and identity, though at least partly likely to be embedded in these.

I see this as a type of political opening that contains unifying capacities across national boundaries and sharpening conflicts within such boundaries. Global capital and the new immigrant workforce are two major instances of transnationalized categories that have unifying properties internally and find themselves in contestation with each other inside global cities. These cities are the sites for the valorization of corporate capital and the devalorization of disadvantaged workers. The leading sectors of corporate capital are now global in their organization and operations. And many of the disadvantaged workers in global cities are women, immigrants, and people of color (signaling a demographic embeddedness in the formation of this disadvantage). Both find in the global city a strategic site for their economic and political operations. Immigration, for instance, is one major process through which a new transnational political economy is being constituted, one which is largely embedded in major cities insofar as most immigrants, whether in the United States, Japan, or Western Europe, are concentrated in major cities. It is, in my reading, one of the constitutive processes of globalization today, even though not recognized or represented as such in mainstream accounts of the global economy.

Typically, the analysis about the globalization of the economy privileges the reconstitution of capital as an internationalized presence; it emphasizes the vanguard character of this reconstitution. At the same time it remains absolutely silent about another crucial element of this transnationalization, one that some, like myself, see as the counterpart of that of capital: this is the transnationalization of labor. Second, that analysis overlooks the transnationalization in the formation of identities and loyalties among various population segments that explicitly reject the imagined community of the nation.[5] With this come new solidarities and notions of membership. Major cities have emerged as a strategic site for both the transnationalization of labor and the formation of transnational identities. In this regard they are a site for new types of political operations.

We see here an interesting correspondence between great concentrations of corporate power and large concentrations of "others." Large cities in the highly developed world are the terrain where a multiplicity of globalization processes assume concrete, localized forms. These localized forms are, in good part, what globalization is about. High on any agenda for sociologists in the next century is not only the differential power engendered by bureaucratic organizations of state and economy (pace Sjoberg, in this volume), but the instantiation of these consequences in the cracked casings of space.

Notes

1. Immigrants and refugees have frequently been invoked lately in efforts to restrict the conditions for citizenship. They have also been the subjects in a majority of human rights decisions in U.S. courts entitling them to various rights associated with citizenship, thereby denationalizing membership. The question of membership can also be extended to firms and economic actors: deregulation and globalization have contributed to a denationalizing of membership in the business community.

2. Massive trends toward the spatial dispersal of economic activities at the metropolitan, national, and global level are indeed all taking place, but they represent only half of what is happening (e.g., *Futur Antérieur* 1995). Alongside the well-documented spatial dispersal of economic activities, new forms of territorial centralization of top-level management and control operations have appeared (Sassen 1991). National and global markets as well as globally integrated operations require central places where the work of

globalization gets done. Further, information industries require a vast physical infrastructure containing strategic nodes with hyperconcentrations of facilities. Finally, even the most advanced information industries have a work process—that is, a complex of workers, machines, and buildings that are more place bound than the imagery of information outputs suggests.

3. One of the central concerns in my work has been to look at cities as production sites for the leading service industries of our time and hence to recover the infrastructure of activities, firms, and jobs that is necessary to run the advanced corporate economy. I want to focus on the *practice* of global control: the work of producing and reproducing the organization and management of a global production system and a global marketplace for finance, both under conditions of economic concentration. This allows me to focus on the infrastructure of jobs involved in this production, including low-wage, unskilled manual jobs typically not thought of as part of advanced globalized sectors (e.g., several chapters, notably Salzinger, in Burawoy [1991]).

4. There are two aspects in this formation of new claims that have implications for the new transnational politics. One is the sharp and perhaps sharpening differences in the representation of these claims by different sectors, notably international business and the vast population of low income "others"—African-Americans, immigrants, women. The second aspect is the increasingly transnational element in both types of claims and claimants. It signals a politics of contestation embedded in specific places but transnational in character.

5. Insofar as sovereignty is being unbundled the state is no longer the exclusive subject for international law. Other actors, from nongovernmental organizations (NGOs) and minority populations to supranational organizations, are increasingly emerging as subjects of international law and actors in international relations. Women and immigrants have emerged as one such subject in forums involving international human rights disputes (Sassen 1999). The growth of instruments and the growth in their use by judges in national courts over the last ten years, the growing influence of the European Court, and the spread of the concept of human rights through the global mass media—all of these have contributed to a normativity that is not centered in the national state, even though it requires national states for its implementation.

References

Abu-Lughod, Janet L., et al. 1994. *From Urban Village to East Village: The Battle for New York's Lower East Side*. Cambridge, Mass.: Blackwell.

Basch, Linda, Nina Glick Schiller, and Christina Szanton-Blanc. 1994. *Nations Unbound: Transnationalized Projects and the Deterritorialized Nation-State*. New York: Gordon & Breach.

Bonilla, Frank, Edwin Melendez, Rebecca Morales, and Maria de los Angeles Torres, eds. 1998. *Borderless Borders: U.S. Latinos, Latin Americans, and the Paradox of Interdependence*. Philadelphia: Temple University Press.

Burawoy, Michael, et al. 1991. *Ethnography Unbound: Power and Resistance in the Modern Metropolis*. Berkeley: University of California Press.

Brenner, Neil. 1998. "Global Cities, Local States: Global City Formation and State Territorial Restructuring in Contemporary Europe." *Review of International Political Economy* 5, 1:1–37.

Cox, Robert. 1987. *Production, Power, and World Order: Social Forces in the Making of History.* New York: Columbia University Press.

Futur Antérieur. 1995. Special issue of *La Ville-Monde Aujourd'hui: Entre Virtualité et Ancrage,* edited by Thierry Pillon and Anne Querrien. Paris: L'Harmattan.

Grasmuck, Sherri, and Patricia Pessar. 1991. *Between Two Islands: Dominican International Migration.* Berkeley: University of California Press.

Holston, James, ed. 1996. "Cities and Citizenship." Special issue, *Public Culture,* vol. 8, no. 2.

Jacobson, David. 1996. *Rights across Borders.* Baltimore: Johns Hopkins University Press.

King, A. D., ed. 1996. *Re-presenting the City: Ethnicity, Capital and Culture in the 21st Century.* London: Macmillan.

Knox, Paul L., and Peter J. Taylor, eds. 1995. *World Cities in a World-System.* Cambridge: Cambridge University Press.

Mahler, Sarah. 1995. *American Dreaming: Immigrant Life on the Margins.* Princeton, N.J.: Princeton University Press.

Mittelman, James, ed. *Globalization: Critical Reflections. International Political Economy Yearbook 9.* Boulder, Colo.: Lynne Rienner Publishers.

Ong, Aihwa. 1996. "Strategic Sisterhood or Sisters in Solidarity? Questions of Communitarianism and Citizenship in Asia." Special issue "Feminism and Globalization," *Indian Journal of Global Legal Studies,* vol. 4, no. 1.

Panitch, Leo. 1996. "Rethinking the Role of the State in an Era of Globalization." In *Globalization: Critical Reflections,* edited by James Mittelman. Boulder, Colo.: Lynne Rienner Publishers.

Salzinger, Leslie. 1991. "A Maid by Any Other Name: The Transformation of 'Dirty Work' by Central American Immigrants." In *Ethnography Unbound,* ed. Burawoy.

Sassen, Saskia. 1991. *The Global City: New York, London, Tokyo.* Princeton, N.J.: Princeton University Press.

———. 1996. *Losing Control? Sovereignty in an Age of Globalization.* The 1995 Columbia University Leonard Hastings Schoff Memorial Lectures. New York: Columbia University Press.

———. 1999. *Guests and Aliens.* New York: New Press.

Smith, Robert. 1995. "Transnational Immigrant Communities." Ph.D. dissertation. Columbia University, Department of Political Science.

Soysal, Yasmin. 1994. *Limits of Citizenship.* Chicago: University of Chicago Press.

Stren, Richard. 1996. "The Studies of Cities: Popular Perceptions, Academic Disciplines, and Emerging Agendas." In *Preparing for the Urban Future: Global Pressures and Local Forces,* edited by M. Cohen et al., 392–420. Washington, D.C.: Woodrow Wilson Center Press.

Taylor, Peter J. "World Cities and Territorial States: The Rise and Fall of Their Mutuality." In *World Cities in a World System,* edited by P. Knox and P. Taylor, 48–62. Cambridge: Cambridge University Press.

Ward, Kathryn B., ed. 1990. *Women Workers and Global Restructuring.* Ithaca, N.Y.: ILR Press.

CHAPTER NINE

The Social Terrain: The History and Future of Sociology's Object

HARRIET FRIEDMANN

Sociology is the child of national capitalism, whose long struggle to reshape relations among persons gained a century-long victory in the second half of the nineteenth century. One parent was the state, which eventually created a contiguous and relatively stable system of rule in the European peninsula of the Eurasian land mass and in the next centuries extended it, via colonization/decolonization, to encompass the globe. The other parent was property of a new kind, which reshaped the relations between humans and land and, with it, the relations among humans and between humans and other species.

In a long process begun in Europe in the nineteenth century and finally realized globally in the twentieth century, more humans came to inhabit cities and towns than farms and villages. Persons were cast asunder from the ties to one another that were rooted in agrarian life and lost their visible connection to the land—especially to the plant and animal species serving the human lives that tended them, to the spaces shared by humans and other species, and to the waters replenishing life. With the separation of urban dwellers from direct contact with the earth, the stage was set for people to have neither any idea about the origins of the species that daily passed through their bodies nor any understanding of the natural basis of social relations.

To a growing degree, persons became tied to one another and to the earth only indirectly by bonds of money (but see Smith, in this volume). This achievement of national capitalism was a radical rupturing of personal bonds between people and of the substantive connections between persons and the earthly supports of the species life of humans: not only the mix of species expelled or managed by humans, but also the water and air whose flows continually renew human bodies. Of course, the rupture is illusory. To live without consciousness of

Thanks to Jane Collins and Philip McMichael for introducing me to the works of Riley and Brun, respectively, and to Janet Abu-Lughod for unflagging encouragement and sensitive editing.

the interconnectedness of our species-being is to be buffeted by the crises that inevitably attend unanticipated interruptions of or damages to the flows.

Sociology emerged from a preoccupation with poverty, which was understood to belong to the reconstructed wage-dependent family. This cast into the shadows the political-economic framework of national sovereignty and the earthly basis of material life. Both came into the foreground as the social unfolded and began to unravel late in the twentieth century. In this chapter, I begin by taking a closer look at the "nation-state-family complex" that lies at the heart of the definition of the "social" as the object of sociology. I then examine the evolution of that historical complex, which opened into two major contradictions: state sovereignty within a global economy and gender equality within a policy framework oriented to the (male) family wage. Finally, I turn briefly to suggest possibilities for a liberatory reformulation of the social, tied to consciousness of gender and of the rest of nature.

Constituting the Social and Sociology

The "social" is an elusive category. Despite its apparent commonsense meaning, the category is historical, and its history is now revealing what was hidden within common sense. We cannot think as we did before, because we cannot take for granted the implicit assumption of social theory: namely, that women and children have only a dependent existence irrelevant to the political theories of citizenship/civil society and the economic theories of markets and accumulation (see Smith, in this volume).

Over the past century, sociology took shape within the evolving institutions of power and contestation accompanying a stabilization of industrial capitalist economies: nation-states that impose and finance secular ideas and symbols to legitimate and manage the urban world of wage-dependent families (increasingly the domain of women), and social movements designed to mitigate their effects on the masses of men, women, and children divorced from agrarian forms of life.

Sociology began with the discovery of the "social." Positivists defined civil society as the spontaneous coordination of specialized labor, open to improvement by a new field of expertise. Late-nineteenth-century states buoyed and reconstructed universities as sources of secular knowledge, including the new discipline of sociology. Social reformers focused on the problems of capitalist society, mainly the suffering and insecurity of working-class families. In contrast to (implicitly male) citizens or workers, the family implied women and children, whose provisioning depended on purchases of necessary commodities. Although reform was bound up with the socialist and woman suffrage movements, its understanding of the social distinguished it from politics, even though the social worked within the politics of a national context.

Early capitalism gave rise to a specific constellation of poverty that, in a money-centered economy, was quite different from earlier pauperism. The new pauperism involved working-class families (with domestic labor now differentiated and subordinated to outside paid labor) and a division of labor along racial or cultural lines (e.g., the Irish willing to accept wages that required living in basements and eating potatoes). The "family wage" was a spontaneous solution of ordinary people in the Victorian era to the combined problems of excessive competition of workers, lower wages of children and women relative to men, and to the utter dissolution of precapitalist households and communities based in agriculture and crafts. It drew upon the bourgeois ideology and practice of its time, making the ideal of the breadwinner-homemaker family seem natural. Its naturalness made poverty implicitly a family issue, and any empirical departure from this ideal became part of the problem of poverty.

The Victorian invention of the (male) wage-dependent family as an ideal achieved an impressive solution to a variety of unprecedented problems. In the name of the family wage, men and women struggled mightily to achieve laws restricting the employment of women and children and limiting the hours of work. Political leaders were thus able to prevent the self-destructive dynamic of competing capitalists. In the competitive labor markets of early capitalism, employers had hired the cheapest workers and worked them the longest hours. This led to appalling conditions of overwork and overcrowding, to the displacement of men by women and, wherever possible, of adults by children. The invention of the working-class family, adapted from the bourgeois family but without servants or luxury, at one stroke reduced labor competition (for males) and created an unpaid domestic support system for male workers as well as provided space, time, and care (by females) for the nurturing of children (May 1985; Humphries 1977; Fox 1993).

A century later, however, the inequalities of labor laws and the stability of marriage cannot be presumed, and the related institutions that sustained the working classes—male-privileged labor unions and female-focused social and family benefits—are under assault. For an entire century the family wage solution to the excessive exploitations of early capitalism hid the gender dimension of the whole structure. The complicity of women in constructing that solution in the mid–nineteenth century, the role of women as both agents and objects of late-nineteenth-century projects to "reform" the victims of poverty, and the connection of the suffrage movement to reform all contributed to a "gender-neutral" understanding of the realm of the social. Yet unlike the explicitly gendered sphere of "private life," whose boundaries were breached by reformers, the social was located in the family, or at least in those families susceptible to the gaze of sociologists and reformers. Bridging the divide between public and private, this concern with the intimate lives of poor families brought wives and mothers into sustained outside gaze. The outside gaze was often female; reform offered a route for some women into public life.

Denise Riley (1988) offers an original, and to my mind convincing, analysis of the invention of the social as an aspect of the history of feminism. It is just as telling in its identification of gender as an aspect of the history of sociology. Riley cites Comte (1907, 1–7),[1] whose understanding of the feminine aspect of the social is less well known than those of John Stuart Mill and Harriet Taylor Mill: "It is from the feminine aspect only that human life, whether individually or collectively considered, can really be comprehended as a whole." This phrase concludes a passage in which Comte contrasts access to temporal power, from which women and the working classes are excluded, with protection within a social realm, in which intellect is subordinated to social feeling. Riley reflects:

> This shining projection of "women" alights on a newly conceived space which is deeply caught up in allied peculiarities. The nineteenth-century "social" is the reiterated sum of progressive philanthropies, theories of class, of poverty, of degeneration; studies of the domestic lives of workers, their housing, hygiene, morality, mortality; of their exploitation, or their need for protection, as this bore on their family lives too. It is a blurred ground between the old public and private, voiced as a field for intervention, love, and reform by socialists, conservatives, radicals, liberals, and feminists in their different and conjoined ways. Like the modern collectivity of "women," it carries an air of natural good sense; yet both in their mutual references can be traced to a complicated post-1790s gestation. (Riley 1988, 49)

She argues convincingly that the constitution of the social removed pressing questions about the capitalist economy and state power from the terrain of politics. Poverty became assigned to the sphere of the social, which was identified with women. As the "private" sphere was broached, the "nonpublic" nature of "women" was carried over to the femininized social. *To assign poverty to the social, therefore, was to remove it from the political.*

As women in feminist, socialist, and reform organizations undertook studies of poverty, their object of research was mainly families. In the understanding of the era, families in turn centered on "working-class women." The latter were observed in relation to budgets, nutrition, cleanliness, child care or neglect, household management and cooking skills, and a variety of anxieties related to Victorian ideals of female purity, including incest (Riley 1988, 50–51). The fact that investigators were often sympathetic to their subjects, defended them against charges of feckless fecundity, and sought to improve their lot concealed the oddity of centering ideas of the social on a new historical individual: the woman responsible for children, yet dependent on money allotted by her wage-earning husband or whatever she could earn in a discriminatory labor market.

The social became political much later, in the sense of extending the contested sphere of rights to excluded persons within the polity and to new areas of "social" rights. After the Second World War, politics centered on the consensus goal, buttressed by the public sector, of full employment. This soon extended to the widening demand to provide social supports and public services to all citizens—a claim pressed sequentially by labor unions, civil rights activists, and feminists. And yet this trend was scarcely universal or irreversible. The distinction between the "social" and areas appropriate to "political" discourse re-emerged in the postsocialist politics of Eastern Europe, in which "democratic" debates excluded child care, reproductive rights, and other "women's" issues on the grounds that they were social, not political.

National Spaces for Parallel Social Spheres

It was in the national spaces defined by the intersection of markets and state rule that the new realm of the social could be constituted (Sassen, in this volume). The *social*, as distinct from the purely *political*, had previously been viewed as complexes of nation-state-family. But as each national society became the object of study and intervention by its own experts, the social and the political were gradually combined: first in university sociology and social reform movements, then in an increasingly interventionist state that guided bureaucratic programming of intervention through social policy.

In the aftermath of the collapse of the Great Depression and then the end of the Second World War, an army of public-sector employees in various Western nation-states was mobilized to "make war on" poverty. As the state took on some responsibilities to organize and provide housing, food, incomes, and services that were formerly the domain of families, it required knowledge to define its projects and it needed workers with training and credentials to carry them out. Sociology benefited particularly from the expansion of university enrollments, which promised upward mobility and careers to many students and a supply of qualified graduates to public and private employers. Employment in sociological practice, education for such employment, and funding for sociological research all reflected the intimate connection between the technical aspiration to manage the realm of the social and the fears that political challenges might emerge from a realm that spontaneously organizes itself for itself. Alvin Gouldner (1970) was one of the first to note this:

> The growth of the Welfare State has meant the emergence of a new power in society with an ever growing number of personnel and an increasing variety of social functions. What has most directly linked this new state apparatus to the sociological establishment and brought sociologists into closer ties with it is its vastly increased level of funding, some significant part of which is available to the social sciences and directly provides new career-supporting resources. . . . The social sciences increasingly become a well-financed technological basis for the Welfare State's effort to solve the problems of its industrial society. (Gouldner 1970, 344–45)

Noting the dramatic rise in government funding in the United States and in European countries in the early 1960s, Gouldner argued that one consequence was a shift away from social theory and toward applied, policy-oriented social science, "both for welfare and for warfare," and, secondarily, for industrial management. As the state entered the realms of life at work, at home, in schools and neighborhoods and cities, it needed expert help in identifying problems and in designing, operating, and evaluating programs and recipients. Public-sector workers, whether qualified in social work or at lower grades, benefited from education in sociology. Sociological research provided the former, and sociological teaching the latter.

Differentiation of the Social: Individual and Social Rights

A new period is upon us. Sociology now has an opportunity to become conscious of its original object, whose secret lay hidden in the feminine basis of the social sphere that was historically constructed around the double problematic of poverty and the family. Secrets become visible when they cease to exist in their old constellations or to serve their old functions. It is fitting that late-twentieth-century feminist ideas and practices should contribute to the collapse of the specific field of the social, as it had been constituted by feminists and other reformers of the late nineteenth century. The reinvention of feckless mothers who can be blamed for their own poverty and the poverty of their children now occurs against a backdrop not of the invention of the social, but of its disintegration. Because stable new ways of organizing material and emotional aspects of daily life have not yet emerged, is it any wonder that students of sociology include more than their share of women who want to understand the contradictory pressures of their own observation and experience?

In the 1970s, the women's movement articulated new claims for full equality. The fight for rights unintentionally brought to a head the contradictory hidden basis of implicitly male rights as workers and economically empowered citizens. Rising divorce rates and increased participation of women in the labor market made explicit and political an old reality: the feminization of poverty. In the United States, this converged with the continuing struggle for racial equality by African Americans. Sociology, which (often in a blaming way) had characterized African American households as "female headed," is now taking up the more complex issues of inequality and identity.

Perhaps paradoxically, both the decline of the breadwinner-homemaker family and the reassertion of familist fundamentalism have contributed to the breakup of the poverty/family constellation that lay at the heart of the nineteenth-century constitution of the social. On one hand, the claims of women and cultural minorities contain a tension between individual rights and the pressing question of who is responsible for children (and more widely, the large and difficult-to-measure sphere of unpaid domestic, community, voluntary, neighborhood, and philanthropic labor).[2] On the other hand, to hold the "family" responsible for poverty, and poor children responsible for the fate of their birth, is to return to the presocial ideology/morality and practices of early capitalism. Fundamentalist politics of the family seek to replace public institutions with state enforcement of male responsibility and female dependency, while the extension of social and economic rights to women and minorities seeks to reorient public institutions to individuals. Both signal a disintegration of the realm that had been constituted as "social" in the nineteenth century.

The dismantling of social programs, although harmful to women and cultural minorities, has not been as effectively challenged as it once might have been, not only because of their alienating and, particularly in the United States, stigmatizing nature, but also because of the shifting identification of poverty as related to individuals rather than families. The feminization of poverty and the identification of child poverty no longer bear the same relation to an unquestioned "family," because power and accumulation have begun to free capital from the constraints of the family wage system, with its supports in trade unions and public sectors.

Massive international migration to Europe and North America from countries of the South has added to the potential power of capital to undercut trade unions—predominantly male and native born—by substituting female and cultural-minority labor in relocated or restructured enterprises (see Waldinger and Perlman, in this volume). The same mobility of capital, combined with backlash against organized women and minorities and workers, has led to tax revolts from below and tax refusals from above. In the 1980s, the assault on the public sector was beginning in earnest, with disintegrative effects on the gender relations that had solidified over a century ago.

Disintegration of the Social: Sovereignty and Economy

As national capitalism is undermined by the very transnational corporations that were once nurtured by national laws, national working classes, and national markets, sociology is losing the orientation to public policy that accompanied its expansion in size and influence (see Sjoberg, in this volume). Enlargement of the money sphere—via specific private corporations and transnational institutions—is also enlarging the space over which problems of capitalism, industry, and industrial agriculture are shaped.

The money sphere is expanding at the expense of state capacity and aspiration to manage its effects on people and the land. National states are losing their capacity not to regulate capital but to manage its consequences: employment and disemployment, wasted resources and pollution of habitats, the varieties of distress experienced by citizens in the wake of mobile capital which faces fewer limits to short-term exploitation. Paradoxically, because citizens are increasingly deprived of or insecure about the welfare promised in the golden age of the 1960s and 1970s, competing national political parties have been narrowing their claims of legitimacy to success in the economic sphere.

Yet money, which is still marked by national currencies, depends on the system of laws and institutions created and guaranteed by states. The hegemony of sequential powers allowed monetary systems to widen—that is, the gold standard under British hegemony and the dollar under the U.S.-guaranteed Bretton Woods system.[3] Between hegemonies—for example, during the period between the two world wars and possibly again in the immediate post-1970 period—the wider system has teetered between unraveling institutions of the former hegemon and the emergent possibilities for future constellations.

A collapse like the Great Depression of the 1930s would now be more disastrous, because of our greater concentration in cities and our far greater dependence on commodities and money. It might be avoided by an unprecedented move to transnational regulation (e.g., by the World Trade Organization and the proposed Multilateral Agreement on Investment) or by a new hegemon, perhaps Japanese or Chinese (Frank 1998). But it is a big gamble.

The twentieth-century expansion of the state system through the decolonization of Asia and Africa and the formation of the socialist states reinforced the role of national states. Soft currencies, overvalued by national states, created protected spaces for the "development project"—an international consensus, shared by national rulers and organized oppositions, about the goal of industrialization and more widely, modernization (McMichael 1996). Contradictions began to arise in the tensions between transnational organizations and national development imperatives, but until the early 1970s the balance remained in favor of national states. All this happened within the context of Cold War blocs. The ultimate collapse of the Soviet bloc, which ended the bloc structure containing postwar capitalism, was a crucial moment in the transnational project to sweep away national powers to regulate capital (Friedmann 1993, 1998). But it is important to recognize the politics behind the apparent deluge of mobile capital. There is nothing "natural" or "inevitable" in what Philip McMichael has called the globalization project.

All inhabitants of the earth are now subjects of a mammoth experiment in corporate self-regulation. Thus far this experiment is marked, first, by irresistible pressure from international agencies, supported by powerful states, to make all currencies convertible; second, by the freeing of banking capital to move national wealth across the globe; and, third and most important, by the legal empowering of new institutions such as the World Trade Organization to take on the powers to define and regulate contracts, currencies, use of knowledge, and movements of commodities. These new institutions are formed by (unequal) national states, which formally cede their powers to appointed multilateral boards, committees, and agencies. These substitutes consequently lack the kind of political relationship to civil society that national states have.[4] Just as it is difficult for employees to challenge a footloose transnational corporation, so it is difficult for citizens of any country to challenge a body created by international treaty. The pressing question for humanity, and therefore for sociology, is whether such regulatory bodies can really provide the stable basis in human relations or in relation to the earth for continued profitability and for political rule, except of the most repressive kind.

As a transnational state (McMichael and Myhre 1991; Cox 1987, 253–65) incipiently emerges, albeit without any guarantee of success, the balance of nation-state capacities shifts away from social activities that draw upon sociological knowledge. The growth areas of national state structures are trade and finance (emphasizing debt obligations rather than public investment) and control structures such as police and prisons. As a generation of economists, engineers, and lawyers trained in the same North American and European institutions gains control over the ruling political parties in many parts of the world, it acts on a shared understanding of what is needed: reducing state protection for national or regional sectors and reducing state supports to relieve poverty or provide services not reliably provided by family, church, voluntary organizations, or neighbors in market economies and urban settings. Rising crime rates, public health problems, homelessness, pauperism, and other resurgent problems of early capitalism are calling forth similar repressive solutions: more prisons and police, even orphanages. The demand for sociologists specializing in criminology, demography, and public health will likely remain stable. Other parts of the discipline are likely to suffer.

For the main part of sociology, which in the late nineteenth century found an intellectual domain bordering economics and political science,[5] the old realm of the social may shrink with the capacity or will of states to remedy the human problems of capitalist economies. The dominant movement is for states to reduce their own capacities to intervene in the old realm of the social: housing, urban infrastructure, income support, education, and health. The rise of economics to the "master science" displaces sociologists and psychologists as experts in political management. On one hand, to the extent that problems are defined as intractable to public intervention, the policy relevance of sociology declines to the state, still the main source of funding. On the other hand, students see less payoff in sociology-related careers, except in criminology and in polling and marketing, which have become less distinct from one another. As universities experience their own fiscal problems, pressures increase on academics to find external sources of research funds and to rationalize and combine funded research with graduate training and research assistance.

In this context, the pressure is great to scour the environment for projects that can convince potential funders of their practical utility. It seems unlikely, however, that participation by sociology in the rococo elaboration of consultancies for public, private, and nongovernmental organizations of all kinds will contribute to a deep understanding of the possible unfolding of relationships into emerging futures. In this situation, the reconstitution of the realm of the social is likely to occur apart from the self-perpetuating scramble of sociology to fund itself. Its sources are to be found in the embodied practices and relations of humans living in specific places under specific ruling relations (Smith, in this volume).

Possibilities for Reconstituting the Social: Gender and Money

Once the object of sociology becomes visible and disintegrates, how can we understand the relations among persons? As George Herbert Mead long ago noted (1934, esp. 229), we individuals cannot be understood as contained within our skins. Immanuel Wallerstein has taken the concept of interconnectedness to the globe and, by extension, we could take it to the cosmos. Yet Wallerstein, like the rest of us, is stuck with false commonsense distinctions between the social on the one hand and the political and economic on the other. The demise of the manifestly historical distinction between anthropology (exotic) and sociology (famili[ar]) should alert us to the historicity of the demarcation of the social from other categories.

This is an opportunity to open our minds and senses to new ways of observing and new ways of organizing our observations. We can try to open to the emotionally challenging appreciation that our observations of the would-be global economy and transnational state are experimental, as we struggle with and against the conceptual limits of the nineteenth-century definitions of the social, political, and economic. When we work with analysts, such as my favorite, Karl Polanyi (1957), we must remind ourselves of their historical contexts. To Polanyi's understanding of utopian projects to commodify land, labor, and money, we may add a perception of the social that is sensitive to its hidden, gendered past.

As at its founding, renewal of sociology (or whatever succeeds it) can choose to engage with spontaneous reconstitutions of the social at this time and in observable localities. Not surprisingly, as the social departs from the concepts locked into formal sociology a century ago, much new thought is taking place outside the academy. At the heart of some of this nonacademic literature is, in addition to gender, a concern with human relations to nature, including technology and specific places, and with coordination of the specialized work of individuals, including money and time. These return us to classic questions of nineteenth-century theory, as raised, for example, by Marx and Adam Smith.

The spontaneous responses to the disintegration of the nation-state-family "social" are being met by both repressive and experimental movements. Only massive force could try to return women (and men) to Victorian gender roles. Other institutions can only be saved or replaced by relocating them in a new configuration of gender/age/residence/work/conviviality relations among persons. The choice between emergent possibilities that are liberating or repressive depends on awareness.

Although they now take place globally rather than locally, the old problems of destructive levels of competition are returning to labor markets, including displacement of men by women and of adults by children. Numerous self-protective responses, to use Polanyi's phrase, are evident. Rallying national states to resist global capital may still be possible, but resistance seems frighteningly stronger on the extreme right, which can draw on resentment and old forms of gender and race privilege and can invoke tradition or fundamentalist religion to counter barren consumerist culture. Rallying the old—and some new—progressive forces, French Socialists, British Labour, and German Greens perhaps have another opportunity to negotiate a balance between European monetary union and protection of remaining social supports. The dangers of financial speculation—and of ecological destruction—may render present impossibilities very much possible. In the long run, though, the dissolution of the nation-state-family constellation implies that new forms of the social must emerge.

What are the spontaneous new forms of the social emerging from the confrontation of daily life with the exigencies of mobile capital and shrinking public supports? And how can political support be mobilized for them? Just as the family-wage ideal was expressed as a demand for labor market regulation by the state and thus depended directly and indirectly on state controls, so reconstitutions of the social will have to be institutionalized to acquire depth and stability. Movements are arising for shorter hours of work, shared work, and other ways to resist the growing tendencies to overwork some and marginalize others. These promise not only to reconstitute daily life but also to reverse the commodification of everything, which poisons the lifesystems of the planet and loots its biological and mineral heritage. These depend, however, on changes in taxation, benefits, union practices, and much more.

Another promising idea, probably unrealistic in the present ideological climate, is the "citizen's wage," which has historically taken a variety of names, such as "basic income grant," "guaranteed annual income" and the "negative income tax" (Block 1990, 204–8). As Brun (1997) argues, the material insecurity of dependence on jobs locks individuals into present arrangements even when they do not work. The alternative is to construct a "necessity sector" in which each person would be guaranteed a minimal material base in money and kind. This would increase the creative life of individuals and collectivities. Some political power must keep it separate from the "affluence sector," which would be allowed to operate freely but without economic compulsion.

Embodying Theory: Social Life in Earthly Cycles

There is reason to believe that the crisis of the social is larger than the nation-state-family complex and the ways that persons can live in markets. Questions about human relations to nature, including land and other species managed by human beings, are part of the classic tradition of social theory. But these particulars were smothered in the embrace of industry as progress and by the flight, sometimes forced and sometimes spontaneous, of village dwellers from the bonds of traditional oppressions and toil.

The whole edifice of industrial society, formerly socialist no less than apparently triumphant capitalist, is built on massive ignorance or denial of the human relationship with the flows of water and air on the planet, with other species, with the geological and biotic aspects of the places we inhabit. Industrial production and present forms of consumption replace cyclical processes with linear systems of inputs and outputs. The markets for inputs and outputs have reached out to encompass the globe. As a result, over the past century especially, we have begun to experience real limits on mining mineral and organic substances that we have not returned to the earth in usable form. We have also begun to experience the limits to the capacity of the earth to absorb the wastes of both our producing and consuming practices. The penetration of mass consumer goods and media carrying their promotion into populous areas such as India and China threaten to bring these limits to a climax sooner than visions of "postindustrial possibilities" based on services and microelectronics might suggest (Block 1990).

This is common knowledge, even though it has not yet been integrated into our common sense or our understanding of the social. Reconstituted relations among persons entail reconfiguring human relations with the earth. Helpful theory must depart from what Colin Duncan (1996, 123) calls "the outstanding feature of industrial thinking: its urge arbitrarily to simplify so that only a few variables need to be considered and then manipulated."

To really accept new knowledge requires a change in subjectivity (Griffin 1996, 154). For instance, we have yet to overcome the split we live between the knowledge of the universe gained in this century and the common sense formed in the eons preceding it. As cosmologist Brian Swimme points out, we still experience the sun rising rather than the great ball of the earth rotating us, pressed to our little spots on its surface, toward that massive ball of fire. Though fundamental, to reconsider matter and energy is far outside the realm of social theory and methods. We have reached a point that requires new ways of knowing—not a rejection of science, but an integration into wisdom, a transformation of our anachronistic subjectivities. Few of us are aware of the startling fact that Einstein experienced his moment of insight into the expansion of the universe, with all it implied about the time, space, and meaning, as "muscular" (Swimme 1996, 105–7).

Compared to the shifts in subjectivity demanded by physics, it is somewhat less daunting to consider the possibility of achieving experiential awareness of the insights of ecological science. These require reorientation not only in *what* we think but, more profoundly, in *how* we think. It is not consistent with sustaining the split between mind and body that underlay the last phase of science, the one which now shifts the balance between constructing new forms and destroying habitats. That split has become as natural to our way of experiencing the world as the false but compelling sense that the sun rises.

Let us begin with what we "know" but have not integrated into our common sense—the gap that new theoretical understanding of the "social" is challenged to fill. Humanity is one in a web of species inhabiting a planet with definite flows of air and water. The earth supports life via intricate cycles of air and water, which originated in the formation of the planet and the evolution of life forms. Movement through those life forms, via photosynthesis and respiration, keeps the cycles moving in ways that support the growth and decline of various species. All this happens in specific ecosystems that are bounded by earth formations and bodies of water, the latter moving more quickly than the former. Ecosystems evolve through the reciprocal effects of specific species on each other and on water and soil. The formation of an ecosystem involves the growth and decline of species in a process called succession. The process eventually reaches a provisional climax, which is stable. Each of the flows and cycles of microorganisms, plants, animals, minerals, water, and atmospheric gases passes through the mutually determining cycles of the others. The climax ecosystem is the most complex.

Colin Duncan (1996) has written a book that offers a way to locate the human species in the earth. It is a distinguishing feature of humans to intervene consciously and systematically in the evolution of ecosystems. Ten thousand years ago humans began the process of simplifying ecosystems through agriculture and herding. Humans chose plants and animals to cultivate and rear and made them dependent upon human labor in order to multiply. The other species striving to compete with our chosen species came to be defined as "pests," as did the species competing with us to eat our chosen species first. (Other species, such as those eating insect pests, became helpers.) To compound the difficulties created by humanity for itself, the most promising plants to cultivate were seedbearing annual grasses—grains—which prevail in immature stages of ecosystems. Humans planted the seeds, weeded out other plants, and fought off competing birds, insects, and land animals also hungry for human-chosen plants. All engaged in constant war against natural succession to climax ecosystems.

There were preindustrial ecological catastrophes, such as the making of the ancient Mediterranean into a desert through deforestation and overgrazing. Yet it was not until the twentieth century that humanity passed its second threshold, when the majority of the species became city dwellers. That made possible a break in the experience of the species at just the interface with the "rest of nature." For the first time, not with the industrial revolution but with the subordination of agriculture to industry, humans ceased to accept the fact that "agriculture necessarily rides on living ecological cycles" (Duncan 1996, 116).

Industrial farmers, whose knowledge and practices came increasingly to be created and dispensed by industrially focused science, began to replace management of natural cycles of species, water, soil, and air, with linear processes modeled on the transformations of inert substances in industry. Industry supplied the machines that replaced work animals and some human labor, the animal feed that replaced pastures and rotational feed crops, and the chemicals that replaced the manure and other organic materials formerly employed to renew fertility. Industry also received the plant and animal products from farms and livestock operations to process into complex or distantly transported edible commodities. As agriculture became ever more simplified into monoculture, industry provided more chemicals to kill the ever-expanding number of pests that sought to complexify the ecosystems of fields and barns.

Several consequences can be seen. The first was an illusion that agriculture was increasingly "productive," as minuscule numbers of people remained in charge of the increasing mass (but decreasing genetic variety; see Wilkes 1988) of plants and animals available to be eaten. It was an illusion, because all those people working in input, processing, and transportation industries must be understood as part of the organized intervention into the rest of nature. This illusion led to the marginality in thought and conscious practice of agriculture. Yet human interventions into the cycles of life and the cycles of air and water sustaining all life continued and deepened the simplification and attendant problems of soil and water degradation and of pests. This also led to an addictive process of searching for ever-new industrial interventions to solve multiplying problems, a process familiar, for instance, with antibiotic resistance in human medicine (which owes something to the use of antibiotics in animals reared for human food).

Second, the replacement of cycles by linear practices, distanced as external "inputs" and "outputs," created an unprecedented problem of waste. Industry created new substances that could not reenter the cycles from which their component parts had been taken. Old substances, such as organic wastes of animals and humans, ceased to renew the managed ecosystems of fields and began to pollute aquatic ecosystems essential to human life.

Two approaches have been offered to resolve the present state of affairs, each of them requiring further industrial/technical interventions. The first approach, which has thus far dominated the debate, is to move more completely to so-called "precision farming" (i.e., satellite monitoring of microregions of fields with computer-directed dispensing of determined mixtures of chemicals in order to apply more precise quantities of pesticides and fertilizers). In this approach, *standard* science seeks to make each place on the globe as *standard* as possible, so that it can receive *standard* industrial techniques and substances. Yet Duncan's analysis suggests the likelihood of deepening ecological and social crises, which are terrifying to anticipate.

Such crises, however, may encourage us to adopt the second approach, namely, to reorient completely the linear trend of organizing life in industries and cities through a renewed human appreciation of the "centrality" of the direct relationship between humans and the rest of nature: agriculture (Duncan 1996). The refocusing of human attention to our species-being opens possibilities for renewing culture, knowledge/science, and substantive relations among persons. The key is diversity—renewing daily life and settlements in keeping with the opportunities and limits of the ecosystem. This does not imply a return to old days of tradition and toil, but rather the cultivation of a new and so far not profitable science to select and experiment with site-specific and bioregion-specific cycles of species, water, and air to create food, fiber, and shelter in sustainable ways. It means requalifying labor, reintegrating science with practical experiments, and reenlivening and dispersing modern culture across the terrain less and less accurately referred to as "rural."

The solution, then, is to recover the 10,000-year-old awareness of the unity of species and the flows of water and air on the earth. Today we cannot find this awareness spontaneously, for most of us have no direct experience with natural cycles, only with the problems caused by their disruption. Even those at the border between humanity and the rest of nature practice interventions into the lives of other species, mainly in laboratories, airplanes, and offices distant from the fields where sunlight, air, water, and organisms of all kinds meet. We have to recover our awareness through science, which observes minutely but may reason as widely as we choose. To make the wide choice depends on our cultivation of the perception of unity, moving beyond the delusion that we are separate from nature, that we are not ourselves organisms whose cycles intersect with others as part of a planet spinning through an expanding universe.

This perception of unity, in turn, is made possible by the rethinking of gender, race, culture, and nation, a rethinking that is presently underway both inside sociology and outside (e.g., Griffin 1996). As we come to recognize the historically bound (and increasingly unreliable) nature of our commonsense categories, we can open to possibilities for an adequate reconstitution of the social. As we come to grips with new sciences that explain the material aspects of human life, we can find ways to rethink and to remake relations among our species and to the earth.

Notes

1. Riley points out that Comte was first translated into English by the feminist Harriet Martineau.

2. Generational cleavages (seniors against schoolchildren), class cleavages (private fees for health and education replacing progressive taxation), and gender conflicts over responsibility for children, mimic at the individual level the (probably illusionary) attempt of transnational corporations to make it on their own by capturing ruling institutions and responding repressively to discontent.

3. In 1944, the Allied governments agreed at Bretton Woods, New Hampshire, to create the International Monetary Fund (to finance short-term balance-of-payments shortfalls) and the World Bank (to finance investments in less developed countries). The agreement also pegged international currency exchange rates to the U.S. dollar, an arrangement that remained in force until the early 1970s.

4. The ultimate effects of this shift of authority from national elected assemblies to international appointed boards has the effect, it should be pointed out, of disempowering citizens. Of course, as Arrighi argues in this volume, this also has the effect of enhancing the strategic power of *key* states at the expense of other states in the state system.

5. It must be granted that these borders were under continuous contestation (Block 1990, 33–42).

References

Block, Fred. 1990. *Postindustrial Possibilities: A Critique of Economic Discourse.* Berkeley: University of California Press.

Brun, Ellen. 1997. "Sustainability from Below: Challenge to Globalization." Paper prepared for the International Workshop on Globalization and Social Change, Research Center on Development and International Relations, Aalborg, Denmark, 15–16 May.

Comte, Auguste. 1907. *A General View of Positivism.* London: Routledge & Kegan Paul.

Cox, Robert W. 1987. *Production, Power and World Order.* New York: Columbia University Press.

Duncan, Colin. 1996. *The Centrality of Agriculture: Between Humankind and the Rest of Nature.* Montreal and Kingston: McGill-Queens University Press.

Fox, Bonnie J. 1993. "The Rise and Fall of the Breadwinner-Homemaker Family." In *Family Patterns, Gender Relations,* edited by Bonnie Fox, 147–57. Toronto: Oxford University Press.

Frank, Andre Gunder. 1998. *ReOrient: Global Economy in the Asian Age.* Berkeley: University of California Press.

Friedmann, Harriet. 1993. "New Wine, New Bottles: Regulation of Capitalism on a World Scale." In *Production, Space, Identity,* edited by Jane Jenson, Rianne Mahon and Manfred Bienefield. Toronto: Canadian Scholars Press.

———. 1998. "Warsaw Pact Socialism: Detente and the Disintegration of the Soviet Bloc." In *Rethinking the Cold War,* edited by Allen Hunter. Philadelphia: Temple University Press.

Gouldner, Alvin. 1970. *The Coming Crisis of Western Sociology.* New York: Basic Books.

Griffin, Susan. 1996. *The Eros of Everyday Life: Essays on Ecology, Gender and Society.* New York: Doubleday.

Humphries, Jane. 1977. "The Working-Class Family, Women's Liberation and Class Struggle: The Case of Nineteenth-Century British History." *Review of Radical Political Economics* 9 (fall): 25–42.

Hyde, Lewis. 1983. *The Gift: Imagination and the Erotic Life of Property.* New York: Vintage.

McMichael, Philip. 1996. *Development and Social Change: A Global Analysis.* Thousand Oaks, Calif.: Pine Forge Press.

McMichael, Philip, and David Myhre. 1991. "Global Regulation vs. the Nation-State." *Capital and Class* 50.

May, Martha. 1985. "Bread before Roses: American Workingmen, Labor Unions and the Family Wage." In *Women, Work, and Protest,* edited by Ruth Milkman. Boston: Routledge & Kegan Paul.

Mead, George Herbert. 1934. *Mind, Self and Society.* Chicago: University of Chicago Press.

Polanyi, Karl. 1957. *The Great Transformation.* Boston: Beacon Press.

Riley, Denise. 1988. *Am I that Name? Feminism and the Category of "Women" in History.* Minneapolis: University of Minnesota Press.

Swimme, Brian. 1996. *The Hidden Heart of the Cosmos: Humanity and the New Story.* Maryknoll, N.Y.: Orbis Books.

Wilkes, H. Garrison. 1988. "Plant Genetic Resources over Ten Thousand Years: From a Handful of Seed to the Crop-Specific Mega-Gene Banks." In *Seeds and Sovereignty,* edited by Jack R. Kloppenburg, Jr. Durham, N.C.: Duke University Press.

CHAPTER TEN

Is There a Role for Social Movements?

Pierre Hamel, Henri Lustiger-Thaler,
and Louis Maheu

In this period of late modernity, characterized by a profound redefinition of the nation-state, an increasing fragmentation of social interests, and the rise of multiculturalism, the role of social movements is once again in flux and controversial. Keeping in mind the varieties of sociopolitical meanings and material expressions that manifest themselves in diverse forms of collective action, we want to emphasize that social movements continue to serve oppositional and positive functions in the restructuring of local and global civil societies. Despite their identity-led fragilities, their political ambivalences, and their cultural diversity, social movements still have a central role to play in the redefinition of contemporary social action. In response to the instrumentality of market relations, social movements are more and more revisiting sites that resemble "old social problems," such as unemployment and poverty. But rather than a singular "return of the social," such movements are now coping with the institutional entrenchment of binding relations, around exclusionary practices, which are having powerful effects on how modern actors experience their world.

This brings us to reconsider the abstract unity of purpose that analysts had previously attributed to "new social movements" as defenders of postmaterialist values. As Randall Collins observes (in this volume), in the 1960s and 1970s students of social movements tended to exaggerate their unity and their subversive efficacy, in part because they accepted uncritically the points of view of their activist participants. To better understand the roles played by the more heterogeneous movements of today, one can no longer take their meanings for granted or consider them in isolation from other structurational features of civil society. How they meet and connect around issues of democratization, social justice, or social integration should be of prime concern to sociologists of social movements. In this respect, diversified and fragmented forms of collective action—from environmental or urban issues to welfare, race, and ethnic conflicts—no longer coalesce around long-term ideological convictions.

Despite this shift (perhaps comparable to the "cracked casings" noted by Sassen, in this volume), social movements of all sorts continue to contribute to the building of sociopolitical public spaces within civil society. A social movement's capacity, therefore, to become a mirror of, or to experiment with, new modes of social regulation based on communication and solidarity is in line with its core capacity for being involved in the reconstruction of individual and collective identities (Dubet and Martuccelli 1998).

Contemporary social movements enable actors to find ways out of the impasses of late modern societies. In the face of institutionally embedded social inequalities and exclusionary practices, various social movements attempt to construct collective interpretations of complex modern situations in an increasingly globalized world—situations that confront actors with harsh economic realities, discretionary political decisions, and shifting or ambiguous meanings. This is most evident if we look at the ambivalent experiential relationships that movements seem to develop very quickly, both within institutions and through the institutionalization process (Lustiger-Thaler, Maheu, and Hamel 1998). So we can say that, in the context of late modernity, contemporary forms of collective action are continually shaped by compromises and rebalancing acts, taking advantage of the availability of resources and opportunity structures that are more or less favorable to movement actors. These in turn are shaped by social projects elaborated by the actors themselves and by their abilities to take advantage of such contexts. However, how well they cope with institutions and institutionalization processes depends on their determination and their priorities.

This chapter addresses several issues. First, we briefly characterize late modernity (or late modern institutions) and consider how these conditions are redefining social movements. We then explore how globalization is affecting the nation-state and social movements, examining this issue within the framework of what Ulrich Beck ([1985] 1992) has called the "new political culture." Further, we pay close attention to the diversification of social movements and to the resistances they bring to processes of bureaucratization and other modes of domination within civil society. Finally, we define three sociopolitical rubrics for modern citizenship, all social movement practices, the negation of which underlies the extant basis for forms of institutionally sanctioned social exclusion. We understand these conditions to be captured in the actor's capacity for choosing, belonging and being recognized as a player on the social landscape.

Collective Action in the Context of Late Modernity

Over the past decade or so, the manner in which social scientists re-present collective action and social movements has changed a great deal. No longer do theorists contrast "new" with "old" social move-ments—in particular, with labor mobilizations in industrial society where a strong integration of social, political, and ideological dimen-sions of collective action presumably prevailed. During the 1960s and the 1970s, researchers often used this distinction, explicitly or implic-itly, when they sought to evaluate the impact of movements on public policies. However, the totalistic ambitions of the old social movements have long been abandoned. Today, theorists place greater emphasis on the fragmentation of social movements, on their local character, and on their limited capacity to counteract dominant economic, political, and mass cultural forces. Within the current situation of postindustrial societies, the presence and influence of social movements cannot be judged only in terms of their immediate political impacts.

Social movements have certainly not disappeared; rather, one can assert with some measure of conviction that grassroots citizen actions are everywhere (Fisher and Kling 1993). One has only to look at the dense networks of local organizations in any metropolitan center or study sustained protests or "street" politics to gage the high levels of concerted and strategic collective action. The multiplicity and diversity of citizen mobilization emerging from movements that have direct lines to local, state, and federal bureaucracies, or lack such lines (e.g., the sociocultural politics of the recent Million Youth March in Harlem) are associated with a relatively new context of collective action: un-derscoring who is included and who resides on its strategized and am-bivalent margins. In this miniaturized yet global context, where the struggle for urban "street space" is politicized, the nation-state is no longer viewed automatically as the main enemy of movements.

This does not mean that movements no longer interact with the state or contest its policies. In the United States and Canada we find numer-ous examples of minorities and working-class communities that con-tinue to challenge the state, for example, when fighting against environ-mental hazards (Mayer 1999). Nevertheless, in most instances the state remains only one actor among many, and its importance varies, de-pending on the specificity of local/global conjunctures and the choice of social issues.

The New Political Culture

Recent forms of collective action, particularly on the "who is on the inside," can be explained by the emergence of a new political culture that arises out of a process of political modernization that, over the last few decades, has been occurring in Western democracies. As defined by Ulrich Beck (1992, 194), this new political culture involves a process of "structural democratization," whereby "heterogeneous centers of subpolitics" become the loci for exchanges and cooperation among social and political agents in their decision making. This is the result of administrative changes that have accompanied a profound transformation of the political scene characterized by pragmatic governance.

In this new situation, administrative rationality is affected by reflexive modernization. Political solutions no longer come from above but must be negotiated with social agents through diverse modes of interaction: public consultations, public-private partnerships (including the community sector), decentralization, and a renewal of citizens' involvement and participation in the management of programs or the orientation of policies. As Beck argues, "While the traditional understanding of politics proceeded with a certain naiveté from the assumption that the goals set can be reached by politics, provided the proper means are taken, politics in newer approaches is now viewed as the collaboration of different agents even contrary to formal hierarchies and across fixed responsibilities" (1992, 199).

These changes have been described and analyzed at length by researchers in various fields. Recent studies of urban governance, for example, now focus on the necessity to develop social coordination between agents, as they face uncertainty and complexity through state restructuring (Le Galès and Thatcher 1995; Lauria 1996). Within planning theory, new attention is being paid to communicative approaches, defined in terms of interaction and practical rationality, in contrast to the older rational and comprehensive paradigm of collective action (Innes 1995; Healey 1996).

The sociology of social movements has been at the forefront in recognizing these transformations. While some studies have paid more attention to individuation processes (e.g., Melucci 1996a, 1996b), others have insisted on the intense learning dimensions of collective action (Eyerman and Jamison 1991). The heterogeneous orientations taken by movements in response to new social tendencies, especially the polarizations created by urban growth in the 1990s, continue to hold many researchers' attention and social imagination.

The Effects of Globalization

These transformations that the recent sociological and urban literature refers to are real everyday components of the empirical reality of contemporary collective action. What is significant for social movements in the context of the "new political culture" is perhaps best highlighted in the increasing level of adjustments that individual and collective actors make to a globalizing world. In this regard, social movements must decide whether to resist, locally or globally, the forces shaping the new world order (Sklair 1995) or learn how to take advantage of the new opportunities that informationalization processes and globalization make available, so as to improve collective capacities for social creativity (Castells 1997).[1]

Globalization is certainly not an entirely new phenomenon. However, compared to preceding historical epochs, current globalization processes involve an unprecedented expansion of world capitalism coupled with a redefinition of the role of the state and a revision of Western hegemony on the world stage (Arrighi, in this volume). Saskia Sassen (in this volume) has called our attention to the relationship between the global and the local. A diversified "cross-border culture" remains linked to the specificity of places, and even global cities are "embedded in particular and strategic sites." However, the consequences, in terms of work and life conditions, are not the same for different categories of people: poor and low-paid (mostly immigrant) workers versus the transnational, professional workforce. As Zygmunt Bauman (1998) has put it, the affluent are increasingly internationally mobile, while the poor are chained to "place." Here, the image of the dual city resurfaces in the literature but this time as a global phenomenon. Thus, we are confronted with new claims, a redefinition of "citizenship" and, above all, the possibility of creating "a space for new politics, one going beyond the politics of culture and identity, though at least partly likely to be embedded in these" (Sassen, in this volume).

These remarks invite us to consider the possibility of elaborating what has been called a "cosmopolitan model of democracy," that is to say, a culture and a system of democracy built upon agencies and organizations that "often cut across the territorial boundaries of nation-states" (Held 1995, 267), transforming political institutions and civic culture according to the prerequisites of transnational processes and, in addition, responding to the requirements of democratic rules.

However, from the perspective of social movements, to what extent is transnationalization really the issue? Criticizing bureaucratic forms of management and domination or taking positions against social inequalities are not sufficient to create the political support to achieve universalistic aims or to generate a process of effective political action in the "struggle for power" (Boggs 1994). True, there are limitations to many struggles in post-Fordist settings, and it is extremely difficult to build coalitions among movements and movement sectors in order to combat the destructive side of the new global order. Given these problems, what social and cultural contributions can social movements make as social relations are globalized? It is essential to consider social movements at this level if we want to understand their specific contributions and capacity to challenge the shortcomings of a globalized, late modern order. However, these kind of inquiries must necessarily begin with an understanding of the role that social movements play in more localized civil society.

Social Movements and Local Civil Society

The role of social movements in strengthening civil society has been recognized for many years. Some researchers have argued that social movements on the terrain of civil society are largely associated with intermediary associations producing forms of social recognition and solidarity that the state or the market cannot achieve. Thus, Offe (1985, 826) credits social movements with their ability to explore and define a space of "noninstitutional politics." Similarly, Cohen and Arato (1992, 562) value the dynamic character of social movements "not in terms of the achievement of certain substantive goals but rather in terms of the democratization of values, norms, and institutions that are rooted ultimately in a political culture."

This perspective directs our attention to specific dimensions that nourish the diversified social conduct of contemporary movements. We agree with this interpretation but want to stress further that struggles against the patterns of domination experienced in everyday life are rooted above all in the terrain of civil society (Maheu 1995a). However, the way collective actors challenge institutions from within civil society remains problematic in its juxtaposition of the social and political components of collective action. It is therefore important to pay more attention to the different types and new arenas of conflict experienced by movements in relation to institutions.

Social movements are involved in multiple social struggles that are shaped both from the "outside" (particularly by the new relationships between the local and the global) and from the "inside" (their modes of organization, their values, and the links they create with their communities of choice). Even if we accept, following Barry Wellman (in this volume), that "communities have moved out of neighborhoods," creating dispersed networks and relying on distant personal support, localities nevertheless continue to be extremely important in providing resources to movement actors and organizations that have localized constituencies or goals that are "place specific." This has been observed in a plethora of different types of movements. One only has to think of the struggle of gays and lesbians, or ethnic- and minority-based coalitions, around the cultural framing of specific urban spaces.

In the particular case of the gay and lesbian movements, the expression of social conflict has operated on a number of different levels. In Canada, for example, these movements struggled against legal discrimination, appealing to the Canadian Charter of Civil Rights to enforce their claims on the national level.[2] At the same time, however, they have also fought for social recognition of their identity and difference. For the latter, rights recognized at the legal level were insufficient at the local level. Their demands dealt above all with issues of authenticity and the furtherance of their "life politics" (Maheu 1995b). Movement actors have tended to refer first to their own communities, relying especially on personal ties and networks, as they interact with institutions to encode and politicize their claims.

The women's movements have, to a certain extent, followed a similar path. They developed social networks and social solidarity by organizing activities exclusively for women. At the same time, they brought in public concerns for the political recognition of women's rights, either in instrumental, legal, or cultural terms. The emphasis on identity or difference certainly varied among the main strands of the movement; nevertheless, the majority of these streams used institutional as well as extrainstitutional means of action. By entering an open-ended field of politics, the women's movement experienced in many ways the ambivalence of collective action that characterizes its specificity in the context of late modern societies. These movements are experientially related, on the one hand, to the social dimension of creating a collective actor, while on the other hand, to procuring the political global and local places for its enactment.

This phenomenon is also very evident in less epic identities rooted in broad coalitions of community actors, such as those initiated by the Industrial Areas Foundation, which are emerging across urban America. The latter strategize with reference to extremely localized and particularized neighborhood issues—as miniaturized in their scope as the particular condition of a subway entrance, local drug dealing problems, and so on, as well as purposefully building a sense of ethical commonality by funneling the core of their mobilization efforts through local churches, mosques, and synagogues. Urban actors are learning experientially how to exercise the power of place and collectivity as they traverse the institutions of civil society. By drawing on the complexity and ambivalence of their experiential institutionalization, new forms of action and bases for citizenship claims are emerging.

The Institutional Expansion and Contraction of Civil Society

The self-institutionalization or experiential institutionalization of social movements within civil society is now uppermost in the minds of collective action theorists. Social movements both create and open up networks within civil society by intervening in potential political spaces that precede the construction of institutions and their apparatuses of social control. The civil rights movements was an apt example of this complex process, whereby the compelling issue of human rights entered the discourse of political institutions in as powerful a manner as had ever been experienced in U.S. history, while at the same time creating yet new institutional impasses in struggles against racial inequality.

The impact of social movements is therefore hardly negligible from either side of the dialectical coin. Results have been manifested in a variety of ways, ranging from changes in social policy, shifts in public opinion (as is the hallmark of environmental movements), or in the return of uncredentialed actors, such as dissident students and members of racial minorities who suffer the violence of the state or of right-wing movements that utilize violence as an entry point for being recognized by the state.

The globally networked and culturally configured roles that social movements have in a society remain their continuing effects on the configuration of power. Yet these effects should not be accorded an overbearing purchase in relation to the ways in which movements structure a range of possibilities outside the sphere of institutional politics. This is particularly the case when thinking of new ways of coding and representing social interests that, by and large, remain unmediated and raw to the social touch. The importance of what anthropologist James Scott (1985) referred to as the "weapons of the weak" should not be underestimated in social movement analyses. These practices do not necessarily materialize in changes of public policy, nor do they result in formal political decisions. But, like a socially constructed undercurrent, they have a more fluid presence, focused upon ways in which to build collective representations as self-structured phenomenon and based on the subject's sense of reflexivity and relationship to everyday life. This presumes a wide and unfixed horizon for action that interpellates institutions and everyday life—the foundation of local civil societies. This capacity for action is situated within and maintained through dialectical tensions that traverse institutional and extra-institutional moments in the life of a collectivity or social movement. This is the particular specificity as well as promise of social movements: their contraction and expansion of the social possibilities of everyday life practices, within localized civil societies, through the late modern elasticity of institutions.

As already mentioned, social movements emerge within informal spaces (e.g., area block associations or local churches) that are often of a highly decentralized and miniature nature and placed purposefully beyond the reach and regulation of local governments or global sovereign power. Their strategic location, or sense of network creativity, is their ability to engender, while at the same moment be absent from, any direct intervention into political processes. Social movements are the sometimes loud, other times silent, architects of civil society in as much as civil society is increasingly a fibrous web defined by the institutional framing of social experiences.

The following questions become important if we are to follow this line of thought about movements and their actors. First, how are the capacities for collective action by social movements inscribed in the aforementioned dialectical logic of civil society? In other words, what is the relationship between the social experience of collectivities in globalized places and in localized institutions? One must be able to illustrate how this capacity for action expands the process of political representation in civil society while developing specific political interests. In brief, we should be able to establish how conflicts, which are situated outside formal institutional spheres, are representative of social struggles that bring meaning to collectivities in the process of institutionalizing themselves or expressing alternatively the institutionalization they have already experienced as part of their collective self-definition. Second, how is it that social movements are subject to forms of closure of a political system, even while this same political opportunity structure enables certain concerted forms of collective action to transpire and to have a critical effect on how movements relate to their own changing internal agenda? And finally, how is it that social movements are inscribed in civil society at the same time that they are actually constructing it through the substance of their internal debates and conflicts? How can we decenter our thinking about institutions and view their construction from a social movement perspective?

Some of the debates in the new institutionalism literature might prove helpful here, especially if stripped of their curious resemblance to the old functionalism. At any rate, these questions display the type of analytical interpretations necessary for thinking through the effects of extrainstitutional politics upon its counterparts within institutions. These capacities for action are part of what we refer to as the expansion and contraction of civil society. There is expansion in the sense that the issues and stakes that traverse a system of action have an effect on its frontiers that are constantly being recomposed. There is contraction in the sense that whatever social and political regulation does occur seeks to limit the purchase of movements to the strategic needs of charted civic spaces. Yet expansion and contraction are instances of the same wellspring, given that both are reminders of the need to secure legitimacy within the political community of debates, conflicts, and confrontations that animate and structure public life. Both are also reminders of the reproduction capacities of social movements on a wide range of structurational levels.

In terms of the role of social movements in the reproduction of civil society, this can be seen as both the medium and outcome of this type of critical momentum. The struggles of social movements contain the broadest possible framework for balancing society-centered and state-centered analyses. Yet to explain how social movements actually traverse civil society forces us to push this analysis further. Two possible avenues present themselves. We can articulate social movements to the contraction and expansion of civil society by underlining that there are pertinent effects emanating from these movements, which by necessity acquire diverse forms. And yet, given the unpredictable and arbitrary nature of collective action, the products of these dialectical exchanges are far from clear. Given the contradictions inherent in these types of articulations, the very least that can be said is that the role of social movements in this area is their contribution to the stabilization and destabilization of a political system of action at its most critical and definitive moments.

On the one hand, social movements engage in a process of social regulation as well as direct their energies to intermediary and local institutions that may be peripheral to a specific system of action. This in itself opens up the boundaries of the localized political components of civil society. There is a critical purchase here in terms of social regulation as well as the construction of collective will within communities. The articulation of social movements to political life can also acquire a different form. Less the carrier of a dialectical tension between the institutional and the extra institutional, social movements can also gain degrees of influence within a modified and destabilized political structure. These types of processes within movements represent a transition point for civil society as well as for movements themselves in terms of being integrated within a particular sphere of action and reason through attaining an interest-group status.

Social movements in this regard contribute to fixing, in time and space, the most contemporary forms of legitimate state power through the institutionalization not of protest, but of the capacity to address the state within its own field of action. A contemporary definition of social citizenship must be understood, therefore, as the residue of the push and pull of actors in the institutions of civil society. Indeed, if we see social movements as sited on the edge of or within institutionalization processes, we would have to conclude that they are the most contemporary manifestation of what social citizenship might be: in a city, a state, or the nation-state.

However, in a globalizing world, what are the constraints on these horizons? What, aside from the now-obvious nature of the globalized economy, gives us a better understanding of these citizenship claims other than the localization of their practices? What of globalization in the everyday struggles for community and miniaturized commonalties? Globalization, as a process, is intrinsically interrelated with localization, its opposite, as a transformative component of late modernity.

Exclusion and the Miniaturization of Civil Society

The concept of globalization is emerging as a powerful replacement for the centrality that was once accorded to the idea of modernization. Roland Robertson has argued, in a particularly strong version of this, that localities are now only an aspect of globalization (1992). We want to reinterpret Robertson's view in the following manner by alleging that cultural and economic *globalization processes can only be understood through localities.* True, it is possible, if we look at nongovernment organizations (NGOs) for example, to develop a theory of global social movements and the transnational state. But local phenomena demand a different epistemology if we are to avoid making only the most banal statements about the globalization of action. True, exclusion is an *aspect* of globalization; however, the stakes for combating it are layered in systemic complexity.

We want to insist, however, that "locality" inscribes meaning in and of itself; it contains exclusionary and inclusionary regulatory processes that are both coupled and uncoupled from global shifts in the meaning actors ascribe to their experiences of the world. The miniaturization of social relations—the counterpart of globalization—assures inconsistencies and social ambivalences. Social movements, in this regard, miniaturize social conflicts as much as they globalize their effects. And nowadays, movements are often poised at this late modern juncture. The nature of social exclusion is a case in point.

Choosing, Belonging, and Being Recognized

Social exclusion in a late modern institutional sense becomes not so much a "return of the social," in terms of older social problems, but of global/local ambivalences in the structuration of action, in the contraction and expansion of civil society. Social movements, whether they are imbricated in institutions or poised outside their increasingly mobile borders, have a contemporary role to play in terms of enabling action, thus structuring conflicts and arguments within civil society around issues of social exclusion. The excluded, from our perspective, have only a modest influence on the practices of choosing, belonging, and recognition as social movement goals. These find expression in terms of local inclusions versus global exclusions and, vice versa, around issues of structural ambivalence. The case of local economic development corporations, based in very situated communities, illustrates the "self-limiting" politics of actors through local development and their abject marginal status in terms of the logic of global capital flows. These are the substantive terrains of struggles and ambivalences around social citizenship that movements defend and represent as a matter of course.

The problem of choosing is central to the transformed status of civil society and its institutional arrangements. Actors choose in relation to networks of proximity and distance. These sites are institutionally embedded in the miniaturization of social relations in civil society. To choose is to exercise degrees of freedom and diverse forms of moral attachments that people have in regard to their collectively defined roles and again, most important, a distance from any particular role. Increased attention to the social limits of growth—environmental devastation, for example—has further pushed the moral envelope within which we choose and the attendant institutional structures in which they function. The problem of choice has placed the individual in a framework of multiple deliberations that are personal and experiential, as well as collective. Choice is constructed in the first instance, that is, as an entry point about the experience of being able to choose. The ability to choose places the actor in a very different relationship to the violence of the state. Institutions are largely about the structuring of a social territory for making choices. These social sites are also strategically refused. Recent "police riots" and tense race relations in New York City that focused on the right to march and where to march are played out on the strategic field of social exclusion as a collective practice around black youths: their aspirations, frustrations, cultural politics, and sense of self as larger than their miniaturization in local civil society.

The experience of being able to choose in one locality, buttressed by a global, postcolonial sense of choosing one's identity in *any* locality, is further confounded by the problem of belonging. Traditionally, belonging has referred to an embodied subjectivity through meaning making, community, and one's place in the associative society. Civil society, in its eighteenth- and nineteenth-century root definition, largely captures this sense. Belonging is, however, very problematic when cultural boundedness on the local and global levels is itself strained. Social movements that mediate the distance and proximity between institutional practices while rescripting the experience and discourse of home or belonging complicate the successes or failures of collective action. Hence, the very principle of belonging, in its constitutional/institutional and unfixed postcolonial modes, is a challenge for social movements as cognitive agents involved in meaning making.

Belonging, in a late modern context of changing concepts of place and identity, also risks the possibility of spaces construed for those who do not belong, from the most obvious example of the modern social panopticon, penitentiaries, to the most brutal category of institutionalized exclusion best captured by the double entendre of "homeless movements." This exclusionary category is increasingly embedded in language itself, as homeless people appear more and more distant from a traditional understanding of the class structure.

Recognition underlines that subjectivity, the possibility of being seen as an actor, is only possible through the principle of reciprocity. This means that institutionalization, embedded in local civil societies as well as global networks, seeks out "the recognized" as a matter of course. A politics of recognition, as Charles Taylor has argued (1989), underscores the diversity of claims that emerge for a visible presence— in the polity, on the urban landscape, or at the nation-state level. Yet the dialectic of recognition is also about invisibility, and the strategic use of exclusion is practiced by social movements as a way of remaining "apart." Youth movements often nurture this exclusionary element as cultural capital. The question, from the perspective of the social movement analyst, is how visible are claims for belonging, imposed exclusion, or strategic exclusion in the expansion and contraction of civil society? How visible/invisible are actors in the construction of a social conflict? Again the homeless subject comes to mind as the most stark example of the visibility of the invisible. This leads us some way from a traditional ontology of conflictual social relations to one of institutionally based exclusion that relationally incorporates, constructs, and reconceptualizes an actor's presence in a civil society of shifting locales and mobile attachments to place.

Conclusion

In these circumstances of complex relations between local places and global flows, the very least we can say is that the role of social movements has not diminished. If anything, the sociology of social movements has had its own version of contraction and expansion as a field of disciplinary knowledge. Emerging from a parochial interest in collective behavior and riots to theories of collective action about an actor's sense of self has forced the study of social movements to consider new avenues of reflection and empirical study; indeed it has prompted new historical subjects. The role of institutions in local/ global civil societies and the stakes that actors have within these processes are fundamental to a late modern framing of exclusion and inclusion as sociopolitical phenomena. Has globalism helped, confused, or hindered social movements in defining their localized claims? The most informed answer to this question must be that it depends. The jury is still out, as analysts and movement actors assess the impact of globalization and its interface with human practices as a form of collective action. What is not moot, however, is the continuing and important role of social movements as the first and last defenders of civil participation as a bulwark against exclusion. To imagine a civil society without the prerequisite social imaginary that movements bring to its very construction is unfathomable.

Notes

1. Think of recent examples of international solidarity networks, such as the post–Tiananmen Square Chinese student organization, that have made successful use of the new information technologies. The two possible strategies, however, are not mutually exclusive; they often work in tandem in contemporary collective action.

2. For more details on this charter, see Bourque and Duchastel (in this volume).

References

Bauman, Zygmunt. 1998. "On Glocalization: Or Globalization for Some, Localization for Others." *Thesis Eleven*, no. 54, 37–49.

Beck, Ulrich. (1985) 1992. *The Risk Society: Towards a New Modernity.* London: Sage Publications.

Boggs, Carl. 1994. "The New World Order and Social Movements." *Society and Nature: International Journal of Political Ecology* 2 (2): 91–129.

Castells, Manuel. 1997. *The Information Age, Economy, Society and Culture.* Vol. 2, *The Power of Identity.* Oxford: Blackwell.

Cohen, Jean L., and Andrew Arato. 1992. *Civil Society and Political Theory.* Cambridge, Mass.: MIT Press.

Dubet, François, and Danilo Martuccelli. 1998. *Dans quelle société vivons-nous?* Paris: Seuil.

Eyerman, Ron, and Andrew Jamison. 1991. *Social Movements: A Cognitive Approach.* Cambridge: Polity Press.

Fisher, Robert, and Joseph Kling, eds. 1993. *Mobilizing the Community: Local Politics in the Era of the Global City.* London: Sage Publications.

Healey, Patsy. 1996. "Planning Through Debate: The Communicative Turn in Planning Theory." In *Readings in Planning Theory,* edited by Scott Campbell and Susan Fainstein, 234–57. Cambridge, Mass.: Blackwell.

Held, David. 1995. *Democracy and the Global Order.* Cambridge: Polity Press.

Innes, Judith. 1995. "Planning Theory's Emerging Paradigm: Communicative Action and Interactive Practice." *Journal of Planning Education and Research* 14 (spring): 183–90.

Lauria, Mickey, ed. 1996. *Reconstructing Urban Regime Theory.* London: Sage Publications.

Le Galès, Patrick, and Mark Thatcher. 1995. *Les réseaux de politique publique (Débat autour des policy networks).* Paris: L'Harmattan.

Lustiger-Thaler, Henri, Louis Maheu, and Pierre Hamel. 1998. "Institutions and Collective Action," *Sociologie et Société* 30 (fall): 173–87.

Maheu, Louis. 1995a. Introduction to *Social Movements and Social Classes: The Future of Collective Action,* edited by Louis Maheu. London: Sage Publications.

———. 1995b. (With Henri Lustiger-Thaler.) "Les mouvements sociaux: Plaidoyer pour une sociologie de l'ambivalence." In *Penser le sujet: Autour d'Alain Touraine*, edited by François Dubet and Michel Wieviorka, 313–34. Paris: Fayard.

Mayer, Margit. 1993. "The Career of Urban Social Movements in West Germany." In *Mobilizing the Community: Local Politics in the Era of the Global City*, edited by Robert Fisher and Joseph Kling, 149–70. London: Sage Publications.

———. 1999. "Urban Social Movements in a Era of Globalization." In *Urban Fields/Global Spaces: The Phenomena of Urban Movements in a Global Environment*, edited by Pierre Hamel, Henri Lustiger-Thaler, and Margit Mayer. Forthcoming.

Melucci, Alberto. 1996a. *Challenging Codes: Collective Action in the Information Age*. Cambridge: Cambridge University Press.

———. 1996b. *The Playing Self: Person and Meaning in the Planetary Society*. Cambridge: Cambridge University Press.

Offe, Claus. 1985. "New Social Movements: Challenging the Boundaries of Institutional Politics." *Social Research* 52 (winter): 817–68.

Robertson, Roland. 1992. *Globalization: Social Theory and Global Culture*. London: Sage.

Scott, James. 1985. *Weapons of the Weak: Everyday Forms of Peasant Resistance*. New Haven, Conn.: Yale University Press.

Sklair, Leslic. 1995. "Social Movements and Global Capitalism." *Sociology* 29 (August): 495–512.

Taylor, Charles. 1989. *Sources of the Self: The Making of the Modern Identity*. Cambridge, Mass.: Harvard University Press.

PART THREE

The New Realities of Race/Ethnicity

Erosion of the Nation-State and the Transformation of National Identities in Canada

GILLES BOURQUE AND JULES DUCHASTEL

The rise of multiculturalism and an increase in the variety of claims for equity on the basis of "categorical identities" are among the most salient phenomena in the recent evolution of Western democracies (Taylor 1992; Kymlicka 1995; Pal 1993). While such challenges to undifferentiated citizenship are to be found in many countries, in Canada they have taken on their own character because of the particular institutionalized structure of the state, which evolved historically in ways quite different from the United States and Western Europe.

Underlying cross-national variation, however, is a common and profound crisis in the process of political institutionalization that is perhaps inherent in modernity. This crisis occurs along three dimensions: a crisis in the public sphere where discussions over power and the resolution of conflicts take place; a crisis in the capacity of democratic institutions to achieve necessary compromises among competing claims; and a crisis in the political community itself, both as "a source of mutual recognition and trust" (Kymlicka 1995, 105) and as a common moral horizon (Taylor 1991).

These obstacles to the process of political institutionalization are closely related to the erosion of the nation-state, which is now challenged in its capacity to remain the major context for the reproduction of social relations. Externally, globalization and the world market have clearly been tending to reduce the capacity of the state to regulate economic processes, as the chapters by Saskia Sassen, Giovanni Arrighi, and Harriet Friedmann in this volume have already emphasized. Internally, the fragmentation of the political community along ethnic/racial/gender lines is challenging the state's ability to insure political regulation.[1]

Two questions arise from this situation. First, one must ask: Is the erosion of the nation-state and the fragmentation of identities an inevitable and irreversible process? And second, up to what point are these processes problematic? In the case of the nation-state, is it not possible that the weakening of political institutions can be compensated for by

consolidation under the "rule of law"? And might not the multiplication of communities and categorical groups actually represent progress in enlarging the domain of rights, rather than merely indicate the
fragmentation of society?

Looking at the Canadian example, we propose a partial answer to
these questions. The authors of this chapter have investigated the formation and evolution of political identities in Canada by carefully analyzing the speeches given by successive prime ministers of Canada
between 1941 and 1992 at Federal-Provincial Constitutional Conferences (Bourque and Duchastel 1996a). These speeches reveal how a
preoccupation with the fragmentation of identity has become increasingly central in Canada's constitutional debate. We argue in the first
section of this chapter that the transformations taking place in Canada,
in both their economic and political forms, may mirror those occurring
in other modern societies. In the second section we raise the question
of whether a political legitimacy crisis has arisen in Canada because
of a narrowing of the public sphere and a weakening of the political
community. The chapter concludes with some more general propositions about the reinvention of political community and citizenship as
these emerge from our analysis of the Canadian case.

The Fragmentation of Identity in Canada

In Canada, both the constitutional question and the formation of a
national identity have long been problematic. It must be noted that
Canada achieved her full independence only gradually—first gaining
sovereignty over its international relations in 1931 (Status of Westmin-
ster), then attaining the right to independent Canadian citizenship by
1946, finally dropping all references to the British Private Council by
1949, and culminating in 1982 with the right to repatriate its Constitution.[2] This slow evolution explains why the constitutional question has
been an unending one; in this context, Canadian identity as such, and
its relation to other competing identities, thus developed along a very
complex process.

We argue that the identity-formation process is closely linked not
only to the evolutionary character of the political regime but also to
the federated form of the state (Bourque and Duchastel 1996a). The
initial choice of a federal regime, rather than a legislative union, was
imposed by the existence of "the people of Lower Canada [present-
day Quebec] . . . with a different language, nationality and religion
from the majority" and by the "disinclination on the part of the various

Maritime Provinces to lose their individuality, as separate political organisations" (MacDonald 1865). Thus, the Quebec and regional questions were already present at the outset of the Confederation.

The Constitution of 1867 was a conservative compromise between competing elites of the British colonies. While the compromise led to the adoption of federalism, this solution was unable to eradicate conflicts, either those between the two "founding peoples" (francophone and anglophone) or those between different provinces. On the contrary, nationalisms and regionalisms have merely exacerbated over the years, while tensions between the government and indigenous (aboriginal) peoples, who were originally excluded entirely from the constitutional arrangement, have continued to grow.

A second major factor relating to the formation of identity has been the transformation of the role and form of the state. We believe that the historical passage from classic liberalism to the welfare state has had a significant effect on how Canadian identity has been represented. Throughout the period up to the Second World War, the state had a liberal form, and Canadian identity was more or less bifurcated along "simple" ethnic lines: Anglo-Saxon/Protestant extraction and French Canadian/Catholic extraction.

A proper Canadian identity began to emerge only during the 1940s with the rise of the welfare state. The introduction of social policies that transformed state interventions in Canada contributed to the formation of a broader *national* Canadian identity based upon common membership and social citizenship. This new civic nationality was linked to a universalistic system of redistribution via the social security system adopted after the Second World War. However, this purely Canadian identity made very poor use of the concept of nation; rather, it focused on the idea of a *community of citizens*, with each citizen entitled to the same services through shared national institutions.

Despite this change, the government of the Province of Quebec remained largely preoccupied with ethnicity, continuing to define French Canadians by their shared language and religion. It resisted incorporation in three ways. First, Maurice Duplessis, prime minister of Quebec in 1936–39 and again in 1944–60, refused to relinquish certain powers to the central government. The Quebec prime minister rejected the new definition of Canadian citizenship, and, most of all, he objected to transforming the role of the state. Duplessis defended a liberal form of the state, favoring a strict interpretation of the British North American Act of 1867 and arguing that the federal government was permanently bound by the original pact between the two founding nations of Canada. In the 1960s, having completed the welfare conversion of its provincial apparatus, Quebec moved from demanding a national ethnic representation within Canada to establishing its own competing political national representation.

We believe that the 1960s constituted a turning point in the process of redefining Canadian identity, a process that eventually led to the political deadlock of the 1980s and 1990s. Many factors contributed to the transformation of Canadian identity during the 1960s, of which the rise of Quebec's nationalism constituted perhaps the main impetus. The federal government's answer to Quebec's demands for recognition was the Official Language Act of 1970. This law, passed by the Canadian Parliament, can be considered the first step toward the particularization of identity in Canada. Rather than recognizing Quebec's specific political rights as a national minority as detailed in the Constitution, the federal government chose to confer language rights on citizens all across Canada, based on their common membership in a variety of cultural communities. Language rights were given to individuals insofar as they could claim that they belonged to specific communities. Although at the time the law was passed, the federal government formally specified only two particular beneficiary groups (those who spoke English and those who spoke French), later, similar claims would be advanced by additional language groups.

Other factors also contributed to the transformation of Canadian identity. The recognition of beneficiary groups on such particularistic bases severely undermined the universalistic perspective on which Canadian civic nationalism rested. A number of these particularist claims emerged at the turn of the 1960s and the 1970s. For example, the Indian Bill of 1969 (Weaver 1981), which sought to integrate aboriginal peoples by abolishing their special privileges or rights in exchange for full citizenship, was defeated, which led to the resurgence of their counternationalism. Another example at the end of the 1960s was a rejection of the policy of biculturalism, which had been suggested by one of the presidents of the Laurendeau-Dunton Royal Commission on Bilingualism and Biculturalism. Instead, the adoption of a multicultural policy at the beginning of the 1970s led to increased demands from many other cultural communities. At the same moment, categorical claims were favored by the official policies of the secretary of state of Canada (Pal 1993), facilitating the organization of a multiplicity of beneficiary groups, including feminist organizations.

Since the early 1980s under a neoliberal regime, this transformation of Canadian identity from universal citizenship to particularistic identities has grown even stronger. Many factors, including the adoption in 1982 of the Charter of Rights and Freedoms,[3] contributed to this shift. First, the inherent incapacity throughout Canadian history to reach a consensus about national identity continued to generate contradictory ways of representing political identity. Second, the increased complexity of social relations associated with the development of the welfare state contributed by multiplying the number of groups claiming special rights. Third, the transformation of the state toward neoliberalism favored the dissolution of traditional collective solidarities, including those based on class.

During the constitutional debates that preceded the repatriation of the Constitution in 1982, cultural communities and social movements were not only formulating demands but asking that their demands be written into the Constitution itself. Although we do not accuse Trudeau's government and the Canadian secretary of state of manipulating these movements, the fact remains that the federal government benefited from the support of these claims-making groups. This strengthened Trudeau's hand vis à vis some opposing provincial counterparts in the discussions prior to the repatriation of the Constitution. In the context of the welfare state, the denial of national minorities' claims and the particularistic answers given to linguistic, cultural, and social minorities' pressures contributed to the constitutionalization of a particularistic citizenship resting on the Charter of Rights and Freedoms.[4]

The Constitutional Law of 1982 offered a mixture of potentially contradictory rights. In addition to the classic universalistic rights (e.g., individual freedoms and political and judicial rights, as specified in Articles 2–14) and such universalistic social rights as equal opportunity (as mentioned in Article 36), we find an array of many more or less particularistic rights, such as the right of linguistic and cultural groups to their own official languages and a general recognition of multiculturalism (see Articles 16–22, 27). Furthermore, there are the categorical rights accorded to special beneficiary groups of citizens, for example, nondiscrimination and equality of designated groups such as women and the disabled (see, e.g., Article 15, which forbids discrimination based on disability, race, sexual orientation, etc., and Article 28, which calls for equality between men and women). In addition, Article 35 of the Charter recognizes some rights for the aboriginal peoples that are situated somewhere between cultural and national rights. Significantly, such recognition was not granted to Quebec.

We must insist that the recognition of these rights cannot be attributed exclusively to Canadian-specific conditions. In the tradition of T. H. Marshall (1977), it is possible to define "modernity" as the progressive enlargement of human rights—from civil and political rights, to social rights, and, progressively, to ethnic and categorical rights (Birnbaum 1996; Parsons 1969; Young 1990). Stated this way, it seems that the expansion in the definition of human rights is a consequence of some general movement of progress, although regrettably the transformation does not necessarily move in a consistent direction.

What distinguishes Canada is not so much the recognition of these new rights but their explicit incorporation into the constitutional document itself, which, as we shall see, represents a fundamental departure from practices in other countries. The Charter introduced many contradictions between different kinds of rights without specifying their relative precedence. It thus left to the courts the responsibility for deciding their application and interpretation, which is what we mean by *judicialization*.[5]

It is important to bear in mind that the extension of different rights must be examined in conjunction with the evolution of larger social phenomena. The introduction of the Charter of Rights and Freedoms coincided with many other trends, such as the globalization of the economy, the emergence of a neoliberal form of the state, the exhaustion of salary-based work relations, and the judicialization of social relations at every level of society. It could be said that the proliferation of rights was one of the ultimate effects of the bureaucratization of the welfare state whose tendency had been to specify more and more beneficiary groups, rather than to extend a more comprehensive citizenship to all persons.

Is There a Crisis of Political Legitimacy in Canada?

The crisis of political legitimacy in Canada can best be illustrated by the successive failures of the political process in the constitutional domain since 1982: (1) the failure of the constitutional conferences on the aboriginal question (1983–87); (2) the failure of the Meech Lake Accord (1987–90);[6] (3) the failure of the Charlottetown agreement (1992);[7] (4) the absence of any credible compromise following the very close margin by which the referendum on sovereignty in Quebec was defeated in 1995; and (5) the silence that greeted the recommendations of the Dussault-Erasmus report on aboriginal peoples in 1996.[8] Both the stringent rules for amending the 1982 Constitution and the increasing complexity of Canadian society have made it difficult if not impossible to resolve these questions, both politically and socially (Bourque and Duchastel 1996*b*).

If at the practical level of constitutional debates there is general acknowledgment of a legitimacy crisis, there is no theoretical unanimity about how this crisis should be interpreted. Beyond dispute is the presence of deep transformations in Canadian economic, social, and political structures. The debate starts with the interpretation of these transformations and the challenge they pose for institutions. In the following section we examine two central questions related to the existence of a legitimacy crisis (or a crisis of legitimation, to use the term of Habermas [1975]): the narrowing of the public sphere and the weakening of the political community.

The Narrowing of the Public Sphere

The importance and the centrality of Parliament, as a democratic institution where power discussions and conflict resolutions take place in modern societies, are currently being challenged. The shift from legislative institutions to judicial ones and the move from universalistic to particularistic conceptions of citizenship are signs of this challenge. It is, however, possible to reach very different evaluations of these trends that establish various "entitled groups" and that give them specialized rights to enforce their entitlements in courts of law.

As noted earlier, according to the view of T. H. Marshall, the history of modern society can be interpreted as the broadening of rights in three successive phases. First, political and judicial citizenship is extended through universal suffrage and the rule of law. Second, social citizenship emerges with social security programs and is consolidated in a universalistic perspective within the welfare state. Finally, the development of a particularistic citizenship recognizes members of certain previously marginalized social and cultural categories. From a postmodern perspective, the extension of such particularistic rights to an increasing number of social categories represents the progressive affirmation of a "real" citizenship for the dominated and the excluded.

This postmodern interpretation, which cannot be entirely dismissed, ignores the threat to universal citizenship and the potential dangers that can arise from the enlarged role of judiciary that is associated with an increased specificity of particularism. The liberal state, which prevailed between 1840 and 1930 (Burdeau 1987; Rosanvallon 1984), had been characterized by proclaiming formal and universal citizenship. This definition continued to prevail through its transformation into the welfare state between 1930 and 1980 (Ewald 1986), even though such civil, political, and judicial rights ignored existing inequalities due to class, gender, generation, or culture (Kymlicka 1995).

By directly addressing questions of inequality, the welfare state did enlarge the scope of universalism. In the European and Canadian welfare states, for example, the approach remained universalistic, even where social policies were aimed at specific segments of the population. Social problems and social risks were usually approached within a universalistic perspective. With the emergence of the Canadian neoliberal state in the 1980s, however, we see a transformation of this universalistic orientation into a particularistic approach. In the domain of social security, universalistic measures are being replaced by particularistic policies targeting specific social categories (Boismenu and Jenson 1996). In the field of rights recognition, categorical and cultural rights are being granted to many newly entitled groups on a more or less biological, behavioral, or ethnocultural basis, thus negating a fundamental postulate of universalism.

The rise of particularism has also been accompanied by a shift in the balance of power between politics and the courts. In Canada, this movement is the result of both the growing importance of judicial review (Reed and Howe 1991) in the context of both the bureaucratization of the welfare state and the incorporation of the Charter of Rights and Freedoms into the body of the Constitution. The increasing subordination of parliaments to courts and to technocratic apparatuses leads to enforcement through legal processes, whether administrative or constitutional in nature, to the detriment of the legislative process.

An important question arises from this new dynamic. While there are certainly positive aspects in proclaiming these new rights and in insuring their judicial protection, it must also be recognized that the courts, as some evidence shows, have often taken a conservative position, not necessarily deciding in favor of the weak (Mandel 1994). Is there any substantive basis, then, for expecting that the courts will defend citizen rights better than the political system?

We wish to stress the fact that both the weakening of modern universalism and the judicialization of social relations are realities that must be dealt with. While it is true that democracy is challenged by the multiplication of entitled groups appealing for redress in the courts, it is also true that it is impossible to reverse historical trends by returning to the previous classical or social universalistic models. The pressing political task is to imagine forms of universalism that can cope with the increasing complexity of present societies.

In the same manner, even if the tendency to incorporate particularistic rights in the Constitution and to adjudicate them in the courts may have a deleterious effect on the political capacity of society to rule itself, it is not possible to ignore the central importance of different sets of rights. Democracy may need to be reinvented to take into account the increased complexity of different regimes of inequalities. In that sense, citizenship must be questioned intrinsically in its relation with political institutions. Should citizenship rest on the relations between individuals or groups and the courts, or rather, should it rely on the larger political community in the public sphere? This question is of great importance in the Canadian situation, where the combined effects of the constitutionalization of rights and the fragmentation of identities have jeopardized any significant political compromise.

A Weakening of the Political Community

From the start, political modernity established a close link between citizenship and popular national sovereignty (Gellner 1989; Schnapper 1994). The twin processes of individualization and nationalization have characterized the formation of the modern state. The principle of citizenship implies that all citizens form a political community, and this commonality confers legitimacy on the political system and thus insures social cohesion. In Western democracies different articulations of these two principles can be observed. The liberal tradition insists on individual freedom and the need for citizens to be protected from the state. The republican perspective stresses the necessary link between the nation and the citizen, giving birth to more centralized national systems. In between, as is the case in Canada, social citizenship and pragmatic regroupings on a territorial, societal, or governmental basis are favored. But in every case, some solution was adopted to address the tension between the individualization process and the necessary construction of political communities.

The weakening of the political community can indeed be considered as the second manifestation of the political legitimacy crisis. Both the judicialization of social relations and the erosion of the nation-state seem to precipitate the dissolution of social links inside the national space. On the one hand, the community of citizens is more or less deprived of its political capacity for democratic action. On the other hand, the capacity of nation-states to intervene in their own economic and social spheres is greatly diminished by globalization. The economy is no longer controlled autonomously within national borders, because it is now under the supervision of technocratic supranational institutions, such as the Organization for Economic Cooperation and Development (OECD), the World Trade Organization (WTO), the World Bank, and the International Monetary Fund (IMF). National economic policies must adapt to more general trends induced by free trade agreements (Deblock and Brunelle 1993; Boismenu 1995). Thus, social legislation is being regressively adjusted to this general context under the pressure of the fiscal crisis of the state. Moreover, the political community tends to implode under pressures coming from the growing assertion of regionalism, localism, and neocorporatism. Such phenomena can be interpreted as being new ways through which the political sphere is activated. They can also be viewed as jeopardizing the global solidarity that should characterize the political community.

Political Crisis in Canada

We have to take into account both the generalized influence of these factors and the specificity of Canada's constitutional history in order to understand its present situation. At a general level, Canada and Quebec are confronted by the same problems concerning the effects of globalization and the increasing internal complexity in their own societies. At a more specific level, however, the country and the province have strongly differing views of the present situation and how to deal with it. Thus far, neither position has prevailed.

As we have seen, Canada developed over time an institutionalized conception of the political community, and its political discourse made very poor use of the concept of nation; rather, the discourse referred primarily to the notion of citizenship. Since the end of World War II, the Canadian political community has not been conceived as a totality but as the actual gathering of citizens in national institutions. Even after this representation evolved from a universalistic conception to a more particularistic one, its central notion remained the citizen.

This transformation in the concept of citizenship was later marked by a shift from welfare policies to the Charter of Rights and Freedoms as the central symbol of national identity. Most Canadians, with the exception of residents of Quebec, consider the whole process of the 1982 repatriation of the Constitution and the incorporation of the Charter into the Constitution perfectly legitimate. Many subgroups of Canadians feel that the Charter contributes to the recognition of their rights, even though there is little concern about the recognition of national groups like Quebecers or aboriginal people.

The Charter's conception is that Canada has become a mosaic of different entitled groups, and these should not be discriminated against in any way. Any principle of precedence between different types of subgroups is regarded as unacceptable. Nevertheless, we must remember that both national questions remain to be answered and both will continue to challenge the stability of Canadian political institutions.

As we all know, Quebec is no more homogeneous than the rest of Canada. First, important minority groups represent around 20 percent of the population. If it became independent, Quebec's government would face the same problems that Canada's central government faces today. Second, Quebecers of French origin continue to be ambivalent about their identity. But, on the whole, it is possible to say that Quebec's successive governments have had a completely distinct representation of national identity. Since the 1960s, Quebec's prime ministers have insisted on the existence of a nation or of "a people" of Quebec, thus adopting the republican model by asserting that citizenship cannot be isolated from the existence of the nation. This explains why Canada and Quebec are putting forward different integration models to newcomers. Canada insists on multiculturalism and the Charter of Rights, while Quebec proposes an integration into a common French political culture that takes into account the plurality of cultures (Labelle, Rocher, and Rocher 1995).

The repatriation of the Constitution in 1982 completely changed the perception of the constitutional stakes in both Canada and Quebec. If, in the Canadian view, Quebec has become one actor among many others, Quebec's representation remains profoundly nationalistic. Most of the francophone Quebecers resent their exclusion from the constitutional process in 1982. The constitutionalization of the Charter is still dismissed as a political ploy to undermine Quebec's language legislation. The shift in the balance of power between the parliaments and the courts is also viewed as diminishing the legislative capacity of Quebec. Finally, the rules for amending the Constitution, which were also adopted without Quebec's consent, are seen as rendering any political recognition of Quebec's specificity impossible, as was illustrated by the failures of the Meech Accord and the Charlottetown Agreement.

If we add to the Quebec problem other potential conflicts that can emerge from the unsolved aboriginal question (i.e., the translation of their proclaimed rights into real institutions) and from the regional tensions, we must conclude that the political crisis in Canada is likely to become very severe.[9]

Reinventing Political Community and Citizenship

There is no simple solution to the challenges faced by Western societies. On one hand, the restoration of the classical democratic model centered on One Nation, which has prevailed until recent years, is unable to prevent the erosion of the nation-state. On the other hand, both the classical and the social conceptions of universalism are incapable of coping with the fragmentation of identities. We are faced with the necessity of reinventing the political community in the direction of supranational political entities and citizenship within a pluralistic perspective (Ferry 1991; Kymlicka 1995).

The resolution of this problem will take on as many different forms as there are different historical situations. Political institutions and conceptions vary considerably from one country to the other. First, the degree to which national institutions are centralized will affect possible future solutions. Second, the ways that the articulation between universalism and particularism are thought of will also affect the possible outcome of these transformations. For example, the capacity to integrate social differences seems to be greater, at least at the ideological level, in the Anglo-Saxon world than in some centralized European countries like France. In France, one must be very prudent when considering how to deal with the growing complexity of social relations, even more so when the question of defining specific rights is raised. By contrast, in the United States and in Canada the question of pluralism and multiculturalism seems to be better understood, but remains the object of many debates (Taylor 1992; Kymlicka 1995).

First, we will examine the problem of reinventing new political institutions that can respond to the present challenges of globalization; second, we will propose an alternate way of thinking about the fragmentation process. In our discussion we will keep in mind possible solutions for the resolution of the Canadian crisis.

This first question concerns the reconstruction of politically significant institutions. Both the primacy of the market and the growing importance of bureaucratic institutions aimed at its regulation are challenging the traditional role of the nation-state. The weakening of the political process should be remedied by the construction of supranational political institutions. The only existing example is the European community, which is still in the process of developing its own political institutions. The core idea is that these institutions ought to be more than a technocratic apparatus and must refer to a community of citizens. The formation of a supranational political community should be considered as an occasion to restore the democratic process at the level of global decision making. This new political community would super-impose itself, without erasing national entities, in certain domains that can no longer be dealt with at the national level.

The concept of supranationality could be applied to the Canadian situation characterized by recurrent national conflicts over the recognition of inner-dominated nations; this is also the case of Spain and the United Kingdom. As we have already seen, there has been a fragmentation process of identities in Canada during the last thirty years, adding to the problem of national claims many other demands from cultural or categorical groups. This increasing heterogeneity of social identities has led to an increase of actual as well as potential conflicts. We believe that the creation of a supranational political entity would contribute to the resolution of these conflicts. In such a case, the Canadian state would first have to recognize that Canada is a multinational state (Kymlicka 1995) as well as a multicultural society.

One solution might be the transformation of the Canadian Federation into a confederal union whose constituents would be Quebec, the aboriginal peoples (Dussault-Erasmus 1996), and the rest of Canada. A commonly elected parliament, having full powers over its jurisdictions, would constitute the central institution of this union. The constitution of the union would be based on the recognition of universal rights (political, judicial, economic, and social) by the central government and all other governments of the union. Cultural and categorical rights could also be asserted in a charter, without necessarily having the same precedence as universal rights.

We think that these rights would then no longer come into conflict with national rights, those being recognized in the political institutions of the union. Such a political regime would simultaneously recognize the plurality of national political cultures and the formation of a common citizenship within the supranational political community. Being at the same time a Quebecer and a Canadian, or a Native and a Canadian, would no longer be experienced as a contradiction, but as the recognition of the inevitable complexity of identities.

Even if this approach could potentially solve the national and cultural conflicts by favoring the expression of multiple allegiances, it does not specify the nature of the new citizenship that would result. In other words, must the particularistic citizenship that has imposed itself in Canada (partly as the result of a political strategy to deny any special recognition of a national status for Quebecers and the native peoples) remain the model of a future union? We think that this kind of citizenship based on the fragmentation of identities and the judicialization of social relations also needs to be re-examined.

The fragmentation process should not be encouraged by the ongoing judicialization of conflict resolution, but rather be translated into pluralistic policies. A pluralistic citizenship should impose itself over the present form. Political legitimacy should regain its primacy over judicial proceduralism. In our view, problems such as pay equity between genders, access to jobs in the public sector for cultural communities, or the rights of linguistic minorities to have their own schools are better served through the political process than through the courts. That is, the recognition of the pluralistic dimensions of society should be part of the ongoing political debate, rather than left to judges' decisions. Furthermore, the promotion of a pluralistic citizenship could favor the reinvention of new forms of universalism, instead of the particularization of social policies in the neoliberal context. For example, the introduction of a universal allocation could be preferred to the targeting of excluded groups of citizens. This new citizenship is possible so long as a community of interest and solidarity exists. We think that the creation of a supranational political community should be a primary condition for the emergence of this pluralistic citizenship.

These ideas are preliminary answers to the problems raised by the erosion of the nation-state and the fragmentation of identities. Beyond the existence of profound transformations in the regulation of present societies, and more specifically in the Canadian situation, we want to underline the complexity of possible interpretations and expected outcomes. We have proposed more or less utopian answers for the future, hoping that modernity will be able to transform itself into what Giddens (1990) has called high modernity, as a compromise between modernity and postmodernity.

Notes

1. By political regulation we refer to the *rules* defined in the Constitution, as well as to the institutions of the political regime which preside over democratic discussions of power, the organization of social relations in the economic and social domains, and the specific articulations between the public and private spheres.

2. Even though Canada did gain its international sovereignty as early as 1931, the Private Council continued to arbitrate constitutional controversies until 1949, and the Constitution itself, that is, the British North American Act (BNAA), remained in London until 1982.

3. When the Canadian Constitution was repatriated from Great Britain, the federal government chose to incorporate in the Constitution itself a new portion of the text

entitled the "Charter of Rights and Freedoms." This decision, as we shall later see, contributed decisively to affirming the particularistic (or multicultural) conception of citizenship.

4. Because the Charter of Rights and Freedom has been incorporated into the first thirty-four articles of the Constitution itself means that the charter has become the fundamental reference for the legal system. Courts are expected to interpret democratic institutions in light of this text.

5. The term "judicialization of social relations" refers to the increasing role of procedural and judicial resolution of conflicts.

6. The prime ministers of Canada and its constituent provinces agreed in the 1987 Meech Lake Accord to recognize Quebec as a distinct society, but this agreement was aborted when it was not ratified by all provinces within the required three-year period. Ironically and perhaps of symbolic significance, it was the vote of an aboriginal representative in the parliament of Manitoba that finally caused the accord to fail.

7. The Charlottetown Agreement, intended to confer some autonomy on Quebec, was submitted to a general referendum, but it was rejected by a majority of voters not only in Canada as a whole but also in Quebec province. Quebec voters felt that the agreement had not gone far enough in recognizing a special status for their province, whereas other Canadians rejected the agreement because they felt it had gone too far.

8. The recommendations of the Dussault-Erasmus report went very far in the direction of establishing self-government for aboriginal peoples. Up to the present writing the federal government has given no serious response to these recommendations.

9. *Editor's note:* On August 4, 1998, Canada's federal government signed a treaty with a group of indigenous peoples in British Columbia, not only ceding control over land but conferring on them the legal right to run their own "nation." Whether this treaty will be ratified is another matter. See Anthony DePalma, "Canada Pact Gives a Tribe Self-Rule for the First Time" (*New York Times,* August 5, 1998, 1).

References

Birnbaum, P. 1996. "Sur la citoyenneté." *L'Année Sociologique* 46 (1): 57–85.

Boismenu, G. 1995. "L'enjeu de la protection sociale dans le cadre de d'ALENA." In *Textes du colloque international: Intégration continentale, recomposition territoriale et protection sociale.* Montréal, Paris: Grétsé, IRIS-TS.

Boismenu, G., and Jenson, J. 1996. "La réforme de la sécurité du revenu pour les sans-emploi et la dislocation du régime de citoyenneté canadien." *Politique et Société* 30: 29–52.

Bourque, G., and Duchastel, J. 1996a. (With V. Armony.) *L'Identité fragmentée: Nation et citoyenneté dans les débats constitutionnels canadiens, 1941–1992.* Montréal: Fides.

———. 1996b. "Les identités, la fragmentation de la société canadienne et la constitutionalisation des enjeux politiques." *International Journal of Canadian Studies* 14:77–94.

Burdeau, G. 1987. *Traité de science politique: L'État libéral et la démocratie gouvernée.* Paris: Librairie Générale de Droit et de Jurisprudence.

Deblock, C. and Brunelle, D. 1993. "Une intégration régionale stratégique: Les cas nord-américain." *Études internationales* 24 (3): 595–629.

Dussault, R., and Erasmus, G. 1996. *Report of the Royal Commission on Aboriginal Peoples.* Ottawa: Royal Commission on Aboriginal Peoples.

Ewald, J. 1986. *L'état providence*. Paris: Grasset.

Ferry, J.-M. 1991. *Les puissance de l'expérience. Essai sur l'identité contemporaine*. Paris: Éditions du Cerf.

Gellner, E. 1983. *Nations and Nationalism*. Oxford: Blackwell.

Giddens, A. 1990. *The Consequences of Modernity*. Cambridge: Polity Press.

Habermas, J. 1975. *Legitimation Crisis*. Boston: Beacon Press.

Kymlicka, W. 1995. *Multicultural Citizenship*. New York: Oxford University Press.

Labelle, M., F. Rocher, and G. Rocher. 1995. "Pluriethnicité, citoyenneté et intégration: De la souveraineté pour lever les obstacles et les ambiguïtés." *Cahiers de Recherche Sociologique* 25:213–45.

MacDonald, John A. 1865. Canada, Legislature. *Parliamentary Debates on the Subject of the Confederation of the British North American Provinces*. Québec: Hunter, Rose & Lemieux.

Mandel, M. 1994. *The Charter of Rights and the Legalization of Politics in Canada*. Toronto: Thompson Educational Publishers.

Marshall, T. H. 1977. *Class, Citizenship and Social Development*. Chicago: University of Chicago Press.

Pal, L. A. 1993. *Interests of State: The Politics of Language, Multiculturalism, and Feminism in Canada*. Montreal and Kingston: McGill-Queen's University Press.

Parsons, T. 1969. *Politics and Social Structure*. New York: Free Press.

Reed, P., and Howe, V. 1991. "The Urge to Order: A Study of the Growth of Law in Canada." Paper presented at the International Conference on Law and Society, Amsterdam.

Rosanvallon, P. 1984. *La crise de l'état providence*. Paris: Seuil.

Ryerson, S. B. 1972. *Le capitalisme et la confédération: Aux sources du conflit Canada-Québec (1760–1873)* Montréal: Parti pris.

Schnapper, D. 1994. *La communauté des citoyens: Sur l'idée moderne de nation*. Paris: Gallimard.

Taylor, C. 1991. *The Malaise of Modernity*. Concord, Ont.: House of Anansi Press.

———. 1992. *Multiculturalism and the Politics of Recognition*. Princeton, N.J.: Princeton University Press.

Weaver, S. M. 1981. *Making Canadian Indian Policy: The Hidden Agenda, 1968–70*. Toronto: University of Toronto Press.

Young, M. 1990. *Justice and the Politics of Difference*. Princeton, N.J.: Princeton University Press.

CHAPTER TWELVE

The Future of U.S. Society in an Era of Racism, Group Segregation, and Demographic Revolution

JOE R. FEAGIN

In *The World and Africa*, W. E. B. DuBois argued that the extreme degradation in European colonies overseas was "a main cause of wealth and luxury in Europe. The results of this poverty were disease, ignorance, and crime. Yet these had to be represented as natural characteristics of backward peoples" ([1946] 1965, 37). Part of the first multinational and global capitalist operation, the brutal exploitation of African labor and land has long been left out of most European and American accounts of Western industrial development and affluence. By bringing the history of Africa to the center, DuBois showed African colonization to be central to serious accounts of European development.

Similarly, the first step in developing a full understanding of racial oppression as it has developed in North America is to put the four-centuries-long white domination of peoples of color at the center of the analysis (on global conflict along the color line, see Arrighi, in this volume). White racism in North America, as elsewhere, begins with the brutal encounter of indigenous peoples and the people of Africa with European and Euro-American colonialism and imperialism.

Yet the whites who have placed imperialism on the backs of most of the world's peoples have often held the reins of their domination with anxiety and fearfulness. In F. Scott Fitzgerald's celebrated "era" novel, *The Great Gatsby* ([1925] 1983, 19), several whites converse about a new book by a racist analyst. One male character concludes that "the white race will be ... utterly submerged. It's all scientific stuff; it's been proved. ... It is up to us, who are the dominant race, to watch out or these other races will have control of things." A female character adds, "We've got to beat them down."

Today this concern with maintaining white Eurocentric hegemony over "other races," over the cultural others, remains strong in the United States. It is found not only in far-right white supremacist groups but also among mainstream political leaders and rank-and-file workers. Republican presidential candidate Patrick Buchanan made this statement to the 1992 Republican convention: "And as those boys [the National Guard during the 1992 riot] took back the streets of Los Angeles, block by block, my friends, we must take back our cities, and take back our culture, and take back our country" (as quoted in Zukin [1995, 47]). Buchanan is referring to the growth of the non-European population. *Forbes* editor Peter Brimelow has argued that the United States is facing huge immigration waves that are reducing the white core. He asserts that the United States "has always had a specific ethnic core. And that core has been white." A few years back, some 90 percent of Americans "looked like me. That is, they were of European stock. And in those days, they had another name for this thing dismissed so contemptuously as 'the racial hegemony of white Americans.' They called it 'America'" (Brimelow 1995, 10, 59).

Many white analysts fear processes and actions that may make the United States a multiracial, multicultural democracy. Buchanan has further argued that "our Judeo-Christian values are going to be preserved and our Western heritage is going to be handed down to future generations and not dumped on some landfill called multiculturalism" (as quoted in Page 1991, A27). Some may say that Buchanan represents only the extreme of the political spectrum. Yet his view is held, with some variation, by numerous white moderates and liberals. For example, liberal journalist Richard Bernstein has argued in exaggerated terms that aggressive training in multiculturalism is dominant and tyrannical on college campuses. He compares campus multiculturalism to the "terror" after the French Revolution in its allegedly "narrow orthodoxy" and its "occasional outright atrocity" (Bernstein 1994, 3–4). Prominent liberal social scientist Arthur Schlesinger, Jr., views multiculturalism as dominating all levels of education and as making "an astonishing repudiation" of the idea of "a unifying American identity." He fears the great "assault on the Western tradition" by multiculturalism, which he also terms "tribalism" (Schlesinger 1991, 13, 124–25). For white liberals and conservatives, strong multiracial democratic efforts are seen as challenging white interests and cultural norms. Many seem to fear the coming challenges to white nationalism and domination.

These views have a deep history among U.S. intellectuals, including social scientists. In the late nineteenth and early twentieth centuries many white social scientists, including leading sociologists such as Edward A. Ross and leading psychologists such as Carl Brigham and other public intellectuals, articulated views similar to these. One of the influential intellectuals during the first three decades of the twentieth century was Madison Grant, a lawyer and zoologist who developed his racist ideas in the then widely read book, *The Passing of the Great Race* (1916). He feared newer immigrant groups from Southern and Eastern Europe, asserting that interbreeding between European "races" would destroy the superior "Nordic race." Pseudoscientific racism of this type fueled support for passage of the openly racist 1924 immigration law, which excluded most immigrants other than Northern Europeans. The sadness recently expressed by white intellectuals and analysts over the loss of what they prize as "Western civilization" echoes the fears and ideas of earlier apologists for white (Northern European) domination.

Today, much evidence indicates that the majority of white leaders (including many contemporary social scientists whose complicity is obtained through action or default) and ordinary whites desire to maintain and reinforce the white hegemony they regard as central to the structure and culture of the United States. From the first years of the fifteenth-century conquest to the present day, racial oppression has been a central organizing feature of North American society. And that oppression has been well rationalized by leading intellectuals of every era. Of course, a white Eurocentric perspective is not unique to the United States; versions of it can be seen from England to Italy, and from France to Russia (see Feagin and Batur-Vanderlippe 1996). Still, for over four centuries the North American intellectual elite seems to have devoted more time and effort (in hundreds of books and uncounted articles) in defending and rationalizing the system of white racism than have its counterparts in European nations. Significantly, moreover, few social scientists have thoroughly researched and critically theorized this white domination in its past, present, and likely future incarnations. Today we need much more research probing and examining the patterns and realities of this racial domination, particularly in relation to the demographic changes that now challenge it.

The Ongoing Demographic Revolution

Major challenges to white domination are arising from large-scale population changes now well underway. Whites of European descent are a modest and decreasing fifth of the world's population, and they constitute a decreasing proportion of the U.S. population. Whites are now a statistical minority of the population in four of the five largest U.S. cities—New York, Los Angeles, Chicago and Houston—and in larger geographical areas such as New Mexico, Hawaii, and the southern parts of Florida, Texas, and California. If current migration and birth rates continue, by about the year 2002 whites will be a minority of California's population; by about 2010, a minority of Texas's population; between 2015 and 2040, a minority of the population in Arizona, New York, Nevada, Florida, New Jersey, Maryland, and some other states; and by about 2055, a minority of the U.S. population (Maharidge 1996). By about 2035 a majority of youths under the age 19 will be persons of color (Feagin, Vera, and Zsembik 1995). According to recent Census Bureau middle-scenario projections (assuming a rate of growth no less than that experienced in the 1980s), in the year 2050 the U.S. population will be about 383 million with just under half—about 181 million—being Americans of color (Murdock 1995, 33–47). At that point, there will be more Americans of color than there are whites today. By the mid-2050s, if the rate of growth does not decrease, Americans of European descent will be the statistical minority. Not since the 1700s have whites been a minority of the North American population.

These predicted demographic changes will likely have significant social, economic, and political implications, most of which have not yet been probed systematically by critical social scientists. Let me mention just a few. It seems likely that no later than 2040 the U.S. educational system will be predominantly composed of students of color; this has major implications for the staffing, structure, and curriculum of school systems now substantially under white control. If the association between being a family of color and having a lower than average income does not change (often the result of overt or indirect economic discrimination), the proportion of poor families will increase, as will economic and related inequalities across the color line. By the late 2050s or so it is also likely that a majority of the U.S. labor force will no longer be white, and the population and labor force will be older (see Murdock 1995, 193–97). The older retired population will thus have a majority of whites, while the younger working population will have a majority of workers of color. How will the latter feel about supporting elderly whites (e.g., paying into Social Security) who have created and maintained a white racist society? If current trends continue, most service workers caring for aged whites in institutions will be low-paid workers of color. Will cross-racial conflicts arise where the aged are under conditions of great dependency? There may also be a greater racial polarization in regard to politicized issues such as bilingual education programs and English as the official U.S. language. White politicians who oppose legal immigration, affirmative action, and bilingual programs will likely not be elected when the majority of their constituencies, in large states throughout the nation, is composed of citizens of color. As voting constituencies change, it is likely that juries and justice systems, educational systems, and many government agencies will also change.

The reader should note that I am not arguing for a one-scenario demographic inevitability. There are numerous factors that shape whether these demographic changes proceed as many demographers predict—and shape how population changes will play out. Nonetheless, some variation on these demographic changes seems probable at this point in time, and few social scientists are currently researching or assessing the likely future scenarios of racial-ethnic change and conflict in the United States.

What Is White Racial Domination?

White racial domination (white racism) encompasses the white attitudes, emotions, images, ideologies, practices, and institutions integral to the long-term domination of people of color. At the heart of this domination are socially organized practices of whites that deny people of color the dignity, opportunities, spaces, positions, and privileges available to whites (Feagin and Vera 1995, 7–8). These white practices, which are racist in their typical use of the identifying markers of physical characteristics or biological ancestry, are an everyday matter and routinely "activate underlying power relations" (Essed 1991, 50). Undergirding the practices are strong ideological rationalizations. This white domination stems historically from the expansion of European capitalism and colonialism, which dominated non-European peoples (e.g., by means of weaponry and death-dealing epidemics) in order to secure raw materials, cheap labor, and access to new markets. When dominated peoples come to be seen in racialized terms by capitalist colonizers, capitalism, colonialism, and racism merge and reinforce each other. As Pierre Van den Berghe has noted, "Far and away the most widespread, enduring, and virulent form of racism and the costliest in terms of human suffering has been that which developed in western Europe and its colonial extensions in Africa, Asia, Australia, and the Western hemisphere" (Van den Berghe 1981, 362).

White Domination in Everyday Practice

Today as in the past, this white domination encompasses the exploitation and sociospatial segregation of people of color, as well as the reinforcing phenomena of coercion, violence, and cultural dominance. There is a structure of racial separation and segregation maintained in an ongoing process of everyday discrimination and its rationalization. Indeed, one of the most striking features of U.S. society today is its extreme residential and social segregation along racial lines.

In the U.S. economy there is a dual labor market structure within which many workers of color are forced into lower-paying jobs by means of direct and indirect (e.g., by means of de facto segregated education) discrimination. This can be seen both across and within the blue-collar, white-collar, and elite occupational categories of the U.S. economy. At the top of the economic pyramid, white men hold virtually all powerful positions in large corporations and other major organizations. A 1980s analysis of top positions in major economic, political, and educational organizations found only 20 African Americans and 318 nonblack women among 7,314 powerful positions (Dye 1986, 190–205). More recent studies suggest the pattern persists. In the mid-1990s about 95 percent of the corporate positions at the level of vice president or higher were held by white men (Glass Ceiling Commission 1995, 12, 60–61). Nearly thirty years of affirmative action have had little impact on the powerful elites that control U.S. society.

At virtually all occupational levels, the dual labor market structure is maintained by widespread discrimination against workers of color. One study of hiring discrimination in Washington, D.C., and Chicago used black and white testers applying for entry-level jobs; about 20 percent of the black testers faced discriminatory treatment (Turner, Fix, and Struyk 1991). A 1994 survey of more than a thousand African American employees in Los Angeles found six in ten reporting employment discrimination in the past year: the greater their education, the greater the likelihood they faced job discrimination (Bobo and Suh 1995). A majority of highly educated Asian and Latino American workers also reported job discrimination. This pervasive system of workplace discrimination overtly or covertly reserves many job opportunities and privileges for whites. The system also transfers the "results of the labor of one social group to benefit another" (Young 1990, 49). Historically, much of the value of the labor of workers of color (what might be called racial surplus value) has been transferred to white employers by means of slavery or low wages to a degree that exceeds that for white workers. One additional dual reality facing the disproportionately working-class workers of color is a very high level of unemployment, which for African Americans has long been at least double that for white workers. As Willhelm (1970) has long argued, increasingly African American workers are no longer needed in many areas of the U.S. economy.

From the beginning, residential segregation has been a central underpinning of white domination. Massey and Denton examined black-white segregation in thirty major metropolitan areas and found little change in the high levels of residential segregation between 1980 and 1990. For African Americans residential segregation from whites was high at all income levels and occurred in both cities and suburbs (Massey and Denton, 1993, 221–23). Widespread real estate and rental discrimination lies behind this racial geography. One 1989 research study using 3,800 test audits in twenty-five cities estimated that black renters encountered discrimination about half the time, while black home seekers faced discrimination 59 percent of the time. Latino American testers faced similar levels of discrimination (Turner, Struyk, and Yinger 1991). Recent housing audits in Fresno, San Antonio, New Orleans, and Montgomery sent testers into traditionally white rental areas and found very high rates (60–80 percent) of antiblack (and in Fresno and San Antonio, anti-Latino) discrimination by white landlords (see Fair Housing Council of Fresno County 1995).

One possible white response to demographic change is to flee areas where the number of residents of color is growing; that is, they increase the degree of territorial separation and segregation. Frey (1997) has argued that population data show the United States is balkanizing, in part because of renewed "white flight." For example, as California has seen large-scale immigration from Asia and Latin America, many whites have left the state. During the first half of the 1990s most U.S. counties with substantial population gains from *internal* migration saw little percentage growth in the immigrant population; these areas are becoming whiter and older. In contrast, most of the seventy counties with significant growth in number of immigrants had low (net) numbers of domestic migrants (Frey 1997, 22). Most of the large West Coast, Gulf Coast, and East Coast cities are becoming more diverse in racial-ethnic terms, and whites are now, or soon will be, a minority of their populations. Yet, in other areas of the United States, particularly the Midwest and the Mountain West, diversity is not increasing, and in some cases these areas are actually becoming whiter (Frey and Tilove 1995, 44). Frey has underscored the spatial segregation here: "Early in the 20th century, the distance between immigrant communities and native-born communities could be measured in mere yards by city neighborhood boundaries. Later on, it widened to miles as a stark contrast between city and suburb became apparent. Current patterns suggest that the distance between these two kinds of communities is widening even further" (Frey 1997, 22).

Some time ago Gunnar Myrdal ([1944] 1964, 618) noted that residential segregation means that whites and blacks do not interact "in the many activities founded on common neighborhood. Residential segregation also often becomes reflected in uniracial schools, hospitals and other institutions." The experiential reality of enforced separation in space is at the heart of white domination, and it has serious consequences. In the early 1990s journalist Isabel Wilkerson's field report of two adjacent suburbs of Chicago, one white and one black, found that many whites "live out entire lives without ever getting to know a black person." Each racial group feared the other, but black Chicagoans were "fearful because much of their contact with white people was negative," while "whites were fearful because they had little or no contact" (Wilkerson 1992, 18). Today, as in the past, most white Americans live in an isolated spatial "bubble" separated for the most part from the worlds of African Americans and other Americans of color.

Today, segregation in education often stems from residential segregation, and both help maintain the dual labor market. A recent Harvard research project reported that, as U.S. courts in the 1980s and 1990s allowed school systems to discontinue desegregation programs, segregation of white children increased significantly—in both city and suburban school systems (Applebome 1997, A10).

Challenges for Research and Theory

Recall that DuBois argued that the rape and exploitation of Africa had been left out of most European accounts of Western development and affluence. African colonization was central to European and American development. Today, the economic development and wealth of industrialized nations are still linked substantially to the past and continuing exploitation of resources and labor of people of color within African nations and in many other countries across the globe.

If we are to understand the past, present, and likely future of the United States and other Western societies, we must place "race," or more accurately white racial domination, at the center of sociological analysis. Today, little social science research and theory—outside the somewhat marginalized research areas called "racial relations" or "minorities"—now does this. Indeed, most societal analysis ignores "race" or treats it as one variable among many and not as a central reality. Like Marx's placing of class exploitation at the center of analysis of Western societies, we must place racial exploitation, oppression, and segregation at the center of serious analyses of Western societies. At their cores they *are* about racial oppression and domination. (I am not calling here for a monothematic perspective; class and gender domination also need to be placed at the center of any thorough analysis of Western societies such as the United States.)

It has been said that a major task for residents of the former Communist states of Eastern Europe is to forget the falsified past and to learn the real past, in which old heroes become villains and old villains become heroes. One major insight for sociological analysis of U.S. racial matters is that the old, frequently white-washed, racial history of the United States—still featured in most textbooks today—must be replaced with one that places the collective memory of the oppressed at its center. The collective memory of oppressed people of color is not necessarily always accurate, but it is doubtless often more accurate than the collective memory of the white oppressor on matters of racial domination, whether that collective memory is recorded by social scientists or not (Coser 1992, 21–22). Racial domination includes the construction of a view of past history and of current reality, a dominant ideology, that legitimates racial domination. The struggle for sociological wisdom on racial matters will begin by bringing the collective memory of the oppressed from the margin to the center of research and analysis.

Let me illustrate the neglect of racial domination in one major theoretical tradition. Modern sociology in the United States is sometimes said to have originated in the research of the famous Chicago school, which centered much of its attention on the social geography of cities. Drawing heavily on the analogy of plant communities, leading Chicago sociologists conceptualized urban development and differentiation in terms of an impersonal competition of human groups. Groups such as whites and blacks located in "natural city areas" whose composition changed over time in processes such as group invasion and succession (Park, Burgess, and McKenzie 1925; see also Schwendinger and Schwendinger 1974, 476–86). In the Chicago school's ethnographic studies the lives of those in poor areas were frequently portrayed in terms of a subculture of poverty. However, these researchers largely ignored the interventionist role of business and political elites in shaping cities like Chicago. Their theories and generalizations not only ignored white racial domination but sometimes even reflected racist notions of superior and inferior racial groups common in this period (see, e.g., Park 1918; see also the critique of the Chicago school in Abu-Lughod 1991 and in this volume.) Much subsequent sociological analysis of cities has moved beyond this perspective to give some attention to the role of racial discrimination in urban patterns (e.g., Gist and Fava 1974; Abu-Lughod 1991), yet neither racial domination nor racial segregation is a *central* concern in most urban research or in general sociology textbooks in the United States (e.g., Logan and Molotch 1987).

Making arguments about the poor that are similar in a number of ways to the old Chicago school, William Julius Wilson, perhaps the most politically influential sociologist in the United States, has recently published a third major book on the urban poor. Drawing on research studies of poor black Chicagoans, Wilson (1996) interprets their severe economic problems mainly in terms of broad trends such as the globalization of jobs and argues that social problems of the black poor come from job troubles and from concentration in neighborhoods without middle-class residents or strong institutions. However, Wilson downplays the role of past and present racial and class domination in creating serious problems for African Americans in Chicago. For example, there is no discussion of the major role that powerful white real estate actors have long played in the city's high level of residential segregation nor of white-elite-controlled urban renewal programs that destroyed black neighborhoods and concentrated those displaced into adjacent poverty areas with decreasing employment opportunities (see Fitch 1996, 3). Working in a long tradition of sociologists since the Chicago school, Wilson accents the point that problems of the poor stem substantially from a subculture with inappropriate values.

In much social science research on societal problems there is a strong tendency to develop interpretations that do not deal centrally with racism or class exploitation and thus that are less likely to alienate elite interests that use and fund much social science research. Wallerstein has suggested that there are only two possible languages for explaining inequality within a capitalist system—the view that some are born of nobler birth, which does not work well in modern states with legal equality as official doctrine, and the view that all have equal opportunity but some do not use their inherent abilities. A culturally oriented interpretation of inequality "provides the only acceptable legitimation of the reality of large-scale collective inequalities within the ideological constraints of the capitalist world-economy" (Wallerstein 1991, 87). Those with low social status are there because of their cultural heritage. "They come from a group that is somehow less oriented to rational thinking, less disciplined in its work ethic, less desirous of educational and/or earned achievement" (Wallerstein 1991, 88). Much of the research of the Chicago school and of its descendants in modern sociology uses sophisticated versions of this hoary rationalization of social inequality that Wallerstein clearly rejects.

I do not have the space to deal in depth with recentering sociological theory in regard to white domination, but let me suggest a few possibilities in regard to racial oppression and U.S. cities. DuBois offers some insights in this regard. His work on Africa and African Americans shows the impact and importance of bringing formerly marginalized issues to the center of research analysis. In my view an adequate sociological theory of urban development in the United States must bring white domination to the center of this inquiry. Racial segregation is not an impersonal phenomenon naturally arising in cities but is shaped directly by white agents working diligently to create this pattern. Racial segregation is the foundation feature of U.S. urban settlements. From the beginning, whites, particularly the powerful elites, intentionally constructed racial segregation, exploitation, and discrimination inside and outside cities in order to serve significant white interests.

In the African American case specific agents took action to create the hegemonic system: white slaveholders, shippers, and overseers in the slavery period and white business elites, politicians, and workers since the end of slavery. Exploitation and segregation are still central to this racist system. Over nearly four hundred years African Americans—first as slaves, and since then as segregated and underpaid workers—have contributed at least a trillion dollars in uncompensated labor to build up U.S. cities and U.S. society into a condition of great wealth and prominence (see Feagin, forthcoming). In addition to this uncompensated labor, African Americans (and other people of color) have had to contend with the many other harsh realities of racial degradation. Today, racial domination still serves the interests of most white Americans, and a major theoretical reconceptualization of its role at the center of the United States and other Western societies is necessary if sociology is to be relevant to the twenty-first century.

Conclusion

The ongoing demographic trend toward a new majority of Americans of color in many cities and states—and perhaps ultimately in the nation as a whole—presents a challenge to white domination in the United States. Dramatic changes appear to be coming at a time of persisting racial oppression and inequality, as well as persisting class oppression and inequality. Not only is the racial cleavage in the U.S. large and growing in several areas, but the income share of the bottom one-fifth of the population has decreased from one-sixth of that of the top fifth in the late 1960s to about one-tenth of the top fifth today. Moreover, current "high" levels of employment obscure lower wages and incomes and higher unemployment for many U.S. workers, particularly Latino and African-American workers. As the United States becomes ever more automated, some analysts see the capitalist elite more or less abandoning less skilled workers, which means many workers of color will fall victim to permanent unemployment and a "new feudalism" (Willhelm 1983).

Metaphorically, one might think of the racial-ethnic population and related social changes as a railroad train headed down a track at a fast pace. Ahead on that same track is another train labeled "white racial domination" heading in the oncoming direction. A major train wreck appears to be imminent.

In the near future there will likely be major social and political changes in the United States. How fast these changes will come is hard to predict, yet as I have suggested certain transformations seem likely. Over the next few decades demographic changes could end white numerical dominance of numerous political, juridical, and educational systems in many cities and several states (e.g., California, Texas, Florida, New York). Democratic institutions, such as universal suffrage and the peer jury system, can no longer be relied upon by whites to maintain social and political control. The new majority of Americans of color will be less likely to acquiesce in continuing white discrimination and oppression. In many areas of the United States we are likely to see some social upheaval, including an array of protests, demonstrations, and uprisings. Because of the demographic changes, whites are under ever-increasing pressure to desegregate institutions, redistribute resources, and pay reparations for past oppression.

However, today most white leaders and other whites are not inclined to desegregate institutions or redistribute resources. It is possible that threatened whites will react to the demographic changes in increasingly repressive ways. Whites may devise new types of political exclusion, such as new literacy tests or poll taxes, or they may seek to exclude non-European immigrants as was the case before the 1960s (see Feagin 1998). Today many whites are moving into security controlled communities and suburban enclaves with private schools, and many are moving out of cities and states with high concentrations of immigrants. One possible scenario for the U.S. future may be racial-ethnic partitions like those in the former Yugoslavia. Or perhaps some whites will try to create a system like the apartheid of South Africa with its highly repressive, but ultimately unstable, white minority rule.

Large-scale balkanization poses serious long-term problems not only for Americans of color but also for white Americans. Balkanization creates its own conflicts and instabilities. Moreover, living in all-white enclaves will not prepare whites for a world composed mostly of people of color. During the twenty-first century it seems quite possible that nations like Japan, China, and India will become much more powerful economically and politically on the world scene. Most whites' lack of interest in learning about, or confronting, the realities of racial oppression today and their resistance to creating truly multiracial democracies here or elsewhere puts them into an increasingly untenable global position in the political long run.

References

Applebome, P. 1997. "Schools See Re-emergence of 'Separate but Equal.'" *New York Times*, April 8, A10.

Abu-Lughod, J. L. 1991. *Changing Cities*. New York: Harper/Collins.

Bernstein, R. 1994. *Dictatorship of Virtue: Multiculturalism and the Battle for America's Future*. New York: Alfred A. Knopf.

Bobo, L., and S. A. Suh. 1995. "Surveying Racial Discrimination: Analyses from a Multiethnic Labor Market." Unpublished research report. University of California, Los Angeles, Department of Sociology.

Brimelow, P. 1995. *Alien Nation: Common Sense about America's Immigration Disaster*. New York: Random House.

Coser, L. 1992. Introduction to *On Collective Memory* by Maurice Halbwachs. Chicago: University of Chicago Press.

Essed, P. 1991. *Understanding Everyday Racism*. Newbury Park, Calif.: Sage.

DuBois, W. E. B. (1946) 1965. *The World and Africa*. New York: International Publishers.

Dye, T. 1986. *Who's Running America?* 4th ed. Englewood Cliffs, N.J.: Prentice Hall.

Fair Housing Council of Fresno County. 1995. "Audit Uncovers Blatant Discrimination against Hispanics, African Americans and Families with Children in Fresno County." Press release, October 6.

Feagin, J. R. 1998. *The New Urban Paradigm*. Lanham, Md.: Rowman & Littlefield.

———. Forthcoming. *Systemic Racism*. New York: Routledge.

Feagin, J. R., and P. Batur-Vanderlippe. 1996. "The Globalization of Racism and Antiracism: France, South Africa and the United States." Unpublished research paper. University of Florida, Department of Sociology.

Feagin, J. R., and H. Vera. 1995. *White Racism: The Basics*. New York: Routledge.

Feagin, J. R., H. Vera, and B. Zsembik. 1995. "Multiculturalism: A Democratic Basis for American Society." In *Primis*, edited by G. Ritzer. New York: McGraw-Hill.

Fitch, B. 1996. "The Case of the Disappearing Work." *In These Times*, December 9, 22–32.

Fitzgerald, F. Scott. (1925) 1983. *The Great Gatsby*. New York: Penguin Books.

Frey, W. H. 1997. "Domestic and Immigrant Migrants: Where Do They Go?" *Current*, January 22.

Frey, W. H., and J. Tilove. 1995. "Immigrants In, Native Whites Out." *New York Times,* August 20, sec. 6, 44.

Gist, N. P., and S. F. Fava. 1974. *Urban Society,* 6th ed. New York: Crowell.

Glass Ceiling Commission. 1995. *Good for Business: Making Full Use of the Nation's Human Capital.* Washington, D.C.: Government Printing Office.

Grant, Madison. 1916. *The Passing of the Great Race.* New York: Charles Scribner's Sons.

Logan, J. R., and H. L. Molotch. 1987. *Urban Fortunes: The Political Economy of Place.* Berkeley: University of California Press.

Maharidge, D. 1996. *The Coming White Minority: California's Eruptions and the Nation's Future.* New York: Time Books.

Massey, D. S., and N. A. Denton. 1993. *American Apartheid: Segregation and the Making of the Underclass.* Cambridge, Mass.: Harvard University Press.

Murdock, S. H. 1995. *An America Challenged: Population Change and the Future of the United States.* Boulder, Colo.: Westview.

Myrdal, G. (1944) 1964. *An American Dilemma,* vol. 2. New York: McGraw-Hill.

Page, C. 1991. "U.S. Media Should Stop Abetting Intolerance." *Toronto Star,* December 27, A27.

Park, R. E. 1918. "Education in Its Relation to the Conflict and Fusion of Cultures: With Special Reference to the Problems of the Immigrant, the Negro, and Missions." *Publications of the American Sociological Society* 13.

Park, R. E., E. W. Burgess, and R. D. McKenzie. 1925. *The City.* Chicago: University of Chicago.

Schlesinger, A. 1991. *The Disuniting of America: Reflections on a Multicultural Society.* New York: W. W. Norton.

Schwendinger, H., and J. Schwendinger. 1974. *The Sociologists of the Chair: A Radical Analysis of the Formative Years of North American Sociology (1883–1922).* New York: Basic Books.

Turner, M. A., M. Fix, and R. J. Struyk. 1991. *Opportunities Denied: Discrimination in Hiring.* Urban Institute Report 91-9. Washington, D.C., August.

Turner, M. A., R. J. Struyk, and J. Yinger. 1991. *Housing Discrimination Study: Synthesis.* Washington, D.C.: Government Printing Office.

Van den Berghe, P. L. 1981. *Encyclopaedia Britannica,* 15th ed., s.v. "racism."

Wallerstein, I. 1991. *Unthinking Social Science: The Limits of Nineteenth-Century Paradigms.* Cambridge: Polity Press.

Wilkerson, I. 1992. "The Tallest Fence: Feelings on Race in a White Neighborhood." *New York Times,* June 21, sec. 1, 18.

Willhelm, S. M. 1970. *Who Needs the Negro?* Cambridge, Mass.: Schenkman.

———. 1983. *Black in a White America.* Cambridge, Mass.: Schenkman.

Wilson, W. J. 1996. *When Work Disappears: The World of the New Urban Poor.* New York: Alfred A. Knopf.

Young, I. 1990. *Justice and the Politics of Difference.* Princeton, N.J.: Princeton University Press.

Zukin, S. 1995. *The Cultures of Cities.* London: Blackwell.

CHAPTER THIRTEEN

The Enduring Ambiguities of Race in the United States

TOMÁS ALMAGUER AND MOON-KIE JUNG

In 1903, W. E. B. DuBois prophetically proclaimed that the "color line" would be the principal social divide in the United States during the twentieth century. As we approach the century's end, DuBois's unsettling prediction appears to have unabated saliency. Although we agree with Feagin's and others' assessment that race has been and will continue to be a central organizing principle of U.S. society, in this chapter we shift the focus from the powerful *effects of* the color line to the color line *itself.*

Although the vast majority of social scientists no longer view race in biologistic terms—that is, as biologically real and transhistorically constant—this consensus has not had a uniformly sweeping impact on how they carry out their research, much of which still employs racial categories *as if* they were biologically given and fixed. The straightforward way in which normal social science continues unreflexively to study race obscures the continual ambiguities and contestations over how racial lines have been drawn historically and are being redrawn today.

One does not have to embrace wholeheartedly recent postmodern approaches to race (e.g., Omi and Winant 1994; Stoler 1995; Takagi 1993) or critical race theory (e.g., Delgado 1995; Haney López 1996) to recognize that the concept of race is fundamentally a sociohistorical construct, the categorical boundaries and meanings of which vary widely across space and time. Because race is a socially conferred status whose biological underpinnings are dubious at best, how and where racial lines are drawn are open to question, and the possibility for contestation always exists. The outcomes of these struggles to define various peoples in racial terms are largely contingent on the relative powers of the groups involved. Lacking any clear "objective" criteria, conflicts over the racial designations of groups are often resolved in favor of the groups that have the power to enact their interests (Almaguer 1994).

A few sociologists have long appreciated this underlying societal context of competition for scarce resources and rewards, in and through which racial matters are contested and negotiated. Writing in 1958, when mainstream sociology still equated racism with race prejudice, which was, in turn, conceptualized as an irrational manifestation of individual pathology, Herbert Blumer (in his classic article, "Race Prejudice as a Sense of Group Position" [1958, 4]) perspicaciously focused on the struggle for "group position," arguing that "the sense of proprietary claim" of the dominant racial group rested primarily on either exclusive or prior rights in many important areas of life. These might include property rights over choice lands and sites; access to certain jobs, occupations, or professions; claims to dominate certain industries or lines of business; and control over decision making in government and law. Most recently, Eduardo Bonilla-Silva (1997) has similarly called for and outlined a structural theory of racism.

However, we must avoid reducing race to a utilitarian logic. Race is "not a matter of bread alone"; it is also inextricably about how people "come to look at the world," themselves, and others (Roediger 1991, 10). While scarce resources may inevitably invite competition, the fact that the competition often takes place on the basis of race—rather than on the basis of class, skill, or other identities—should not be assumed as a given but questioned and explained. "This gives the question of culture and ideology, and the scenarios of representation—subjectivity, identity, politics—a formative, not merely an expressive, place in the constitution of social and political life" (Hall 1992, 253–54).

Given its well-documented centrality in U.S. history, *how* has race, a biological fiction, become so ingrained in the constitution of social, political, and economic life? A large component of the answer lies with the state, in large part through which seemingly arbitrary classifications like race come to be accepted as "real," as a naturalized part of social reality: As Bourdieu has argued,

> The state makes a decisive contribution to the production and reproduction of the instruments of social reality. . . . It imposes and inculcates all the fundamental principles of classification. . . . Through the framing it imposes upon practices, the state establishes and inculcates common forms and categories of perception and appreciation, social frameworks of perceptions, of understanding or of memory, in short *state forms of classification*. It thereby creates the conditions for a kind of immediate orchestration of habituses which is itself the foundation of a consensus over this set of shared evidences constitutive of (national) common sense. (Bourdieu 1994, 13)

The power of the state to legitimate racial categories and frame them as the national common sense is empirically borne out, for example, by the history of access to citizenship rights. Barrett and Roediger (1997, 187) remind us that the "sustained pattern" of conferring or denying citizenship based on race (i.e., the state's decisions concerning "whiteness" and hence "racial fitness" for citizenship) "provides the best guide to who would be racialized in an ongoing way in the twentieth-century U.S." Even a cursory examination of U.S. history reveals that these state decisions have had tremendous material consequences, determining who could become a naturalized citizen, run for public office, legally vote, testify in courts of law, own homestead land, sit on juries, attend certain public schools, join labor unions, marry, and so forth. The state "translates ideas about race into the material societal conditions that confirm and entrench those ideas" (Haney López 1996, 14).

Because it plays such a central role in instituting race "both in things and in minds"—both in "social structures" and in "mental structures" (Bourdieu 1994, 2)—the state has been a major site for racial struggle. Especially during the past four decades, the civil rights movement, recognizing that the state "had historically maintained and organized racial practices," made the state its chief target (Omi and Winant 1994, 105). However, long before the civil rights movement pried open the state to minority claims, the state's racial classification schemes were questioned and contested, provoked by ambiguities in society: both the "little society" of contemporaneous biological and social sciences and the "'big society' of our nation-state" (Wacquant 1997, 222). Through the enactment of its classification schemes, the state equilibrated these societal ambiguities and established them, however temporarily and contingently, as the national common sense (Omi and Winant 1994, 84).[1]

This chapter examines some of the historical and contemporary ambiguities and rigidities in the U.S. state's necessarily elusive attempts to ensnare race in an ever more refined, "correct" classification scheme. It focuses on African Americans and Asian Pacific Americans (two of the groups the U.S. state officially recognizes as "nonwhite") and on Latinos (a group the state defines as a multiracial "Hispanic" ethnic group).[2] In this one chapter, we cannot chart comprehensively the always arbitrary, at times rigid, and intermittently shifting racial boundaries around and within these three categories. Instead, we seek to provoke the reader to question the past and future stability of the racial lines that social scientists as well as the lay public often take for granted.[3]

We organize our account around three major themes, one for each group, but as will become apparent, there are overlaps since the issues raised are not necessarily confined to particular groups. The first section deals with African Americans and the rule of hypodescent. The second concerns the interethnic stability of the panethnic racial category, Asian Pacific American. The third section examines Latinos in terms of the clash between differing cultures of race.

The "One-Drop Rule" and African Americans

More than any other racial group, including whites, the racial line drawn around African Americans has been the most rigidly enforced in the United States. From the mid–nineteenth century to the present day, blacks have been subject to what Marvin Harris has termed the "hypodescent rule" or, more informally, the "one-drop rule" (Harris 1964; Davis 1991): that is, a person with *any* African ancestry is considered to be black. This U.S. "color line" is unique. No other racial group in the United States is defined in such rigid terms, nor does any other nation define "black" in this way. Nevertheless, because the one-drop rule has been accepted and applied so widely in the United States, it has led many to assume that this rigid color line around blacks has been and will always be in existence. But it is important to note that in the past the one-drop rule was not universally applied, and we suggest that since the civil rights movement, its persistence is less assured. Ultimately, however, this category is likely to continue as the most stable of all.

That the one-drop rule was not always ubiquitously applied is illustrated by how persons of mixed "white" and "African" ancestry were treated in parts of the South during the colonial and antebellum periods.[4] Although the legal status of the first Africans may have been as indentured servants, not unlike that of many Europeans, they were soon singled out for chattel slavery (Williams 1944; Jordan 1968), after which the racial boundary between whites and blacks became increasingly rigid. However, because "miscegenation occurred in early colonial experience wherever there were slaves and free blacks," the racial status of persons of "mixed" parentage remained somewhat ambiguous, especially in the upper South (Davis 1991, 33). For example, in 1662 the colony of Virginia passed a law designed to discourage miscegenation by penalizing interracial fornication more harshly than fornication between two whites. But contrary to the rigidity of the hypodescent rule, although mulattos born to slave mothers were automatically considered slaves, those born to white mothers were free for a period of time. It was not until 1681 that, in Virginia, the white "mother had to pay a fine of five years of servitude" and the mulatto "child was sold as an indentured servant until the age of thirty" (Davis 1991, 33).[5]

A rise in the number of manumissions during the period of the American Revolution, "enlarging and darkening the free mulatto population," led whites of the upper South to draw firmer racial distinctions. Still, the legal fate of those with mixed ancestry remained uncertain. A decade after the Declaration of Independence, the Virginia legislature, like the governing bodies of most other upper southern states, defined as "Negro" anyone with a black parent or grandparent. Thus, persons of less than one-quarter black ancestry could claim to be white and were entitled to legal protections not afforded their "Negro" counterparts, although their social acceptance by unmixed whites was problematic (Davis 1991, 34).

As late as 1850, even in parts of the Deep South, people of mixed African and white ancestry were not automatically classified as black. In South Carolina, where by 1708 people of African descent outnumbered whites, free mulattos were considered a third, separate racial category. Davis (1991, 35) points out that South Carolina's early white settlers and early slaves had come chiefly from Barbados, where a three-tiered racial order had prevailed. The courts of South Carolina recognized this distinction between mulattos and blacks but did not fully resolve the ambiguities of the mulattos' racial status. For example, in 1835 a judge ruled that the free mulatto in question, who was not only of "known" black ancestry but also had "some visible Negroid traits," was indeed white. He argued that although a slave mulatto could not be white, a free mulatto could be, if she or he was socially accepted by the white community (Davis 1991, 35–36). This ruling demonstrates that South Carolina's government had not yet adopted the one-drop rule; apparently, neither the white nor the black categories had to be strictly "unmixed" at this point. But perhaps adumbrating the eventual adoption of the hypodescent rule, the ruling also shows that the state was attempting to fit mulattos into a legally dichotomous scheme of white and black, even though socially they might be considered a third racial group. Similarly, the one-drop rule did not apply in southern Louisiana, where free mulattos comprised a third racial category. But unlike South Carolina, Louisiana recognized legally their "in-between" status. For example, the Louisiana Civil Code of 1808 not only prohibited free mulattos from marrying whites; it also forbade them from marrying blacks (Davis 1991, 36).

As seen above, the institutionalization of slavery did not necessarily or immediately lead to a uniform acceptance of the hypodescent rule by society at large or by the various colonial and later state governments. Rather, the South's *defense of slavery*, especially in the period just before the Civil War, forged the wider acceptance of the rule. By the 1850s, the South was drawing a sharper line between whites and blacks, increasingly arguing that "Negroes" were "naturally" meant to be slaves. And in the process of drawing this clearer line between unmixed whites and blacks, the mixing of the two drew a more consistent and persistent reproof, even though explicit arguments were avoided to claim that mulattos, like blacks, were "naturally" slaves. Hence, the whites' uneven acceptance of mulattos in some parts of the South changed to "guarded reject[ion]" (Davis 1991, 42).

This shift also had the effect of altering the mulattos' increasing sense of identifying with blacks rather than with whites. Following the Civil War, the alliance between mulattos and blacks grew deeper, as "mulatto elite leaders began to speak for Negroes as a whole and to lead the development of new American black institutions and a black culture" (Davis 1991, 43; see also Genovese 1976, 430). And as competition between whites and blacks for jobs, land, and political power intensified during Reconstruction, whites' racism against blacks drew fewer distinctions between blacks and mulattos. In the ensuing Jim Crow era of legal segregation, the one-drop rule quickly found social and legal acceptance. Especially concerned that miscegenation would lead to a blurring of the color line, various southern states explicitly adopted antimiscegenation laws that defined "Negro" to mean a person with "any Negro blood at all" (Davis 1991, 55).

Although the postbellum South established the most rigid racial divisions through literally hundreds of segregation laws, institutionalization of the one-drop rule via the powers of the state was not confined to the South. For example, the racial categories used by the federal decennial census lent credence to the increased application of the hypodescent rule throughout the United States. The census of 1830, using a nationally uniform printed schedule for the first time, distinguished "free white persons from free colored persons" (Espiritu 1992, 112–13). The censuses of 1850 and 1860 distinguished free persons as being either white, black, or mulatto, and slaves as either black or mulatto, but did not define the term *mulatto* (Davis 1991, 11–12; Espiritu 1992, 112–13). In the 1870 and 1880 censuses, mulatto was defined to include "quadroons, octoroons, and all persons having any perceptible trace of African blood." By 1920 the census had dropped the mulatto category altogether and defined blacks as persons with *any* black ancestry (Davis 1991, 12).

Similarly, in the landmark Supreme Court decision, *Plessy v. Ferguson*, which constitutionally sanctioned Jim Crow segregation of public accommodations, the Court ruled against plaintiff Plessy's contestation of an 1890 Louisiana law "providing for separate railway carriages for the white and colored races." Plessy contended that he "was seven-eighths Caucasian and one-eighth African blood" and "the mixture of colored blood was not discernible in him" (163 U.S. 537 [1896]). Although not directly defining the black racial category, the court "took . . . 'judicial notice' of what it assumed to be common knowledge: that a Negro or black is any person with any black ancestry" (Davis 1991, 8).

Since World War II, much has changed in the relations between whites and blacks. The U.S. Supreme Court's decision in *Brown v. Board of Education* and other cases, and the civil rights movement of which they were a part, successfully dismantled Jim Crow segregation during the 1950s and the 1960s. In 1967, the Supreme Court also ruled that state laws prohibiting interracial marriages were unconstitutional, thereby reversing its position vis-à-vis the principle of hypodescent. Also, beginning in 1960, the federal census became self-enumerated. Heads of households chose the racial categories of the household members, whereas in the past, census enumerators had classified people racially by observation. At the same time, racial categories and problems of undercounting associated with them became points of heated contention, as "Congress, federal court judges, and public officials turned to census statistics to administer civil rights laws," including the detection of patterns of discrimination and the execution of affirmative action programs (Espiritu 1992, 114–15).

Perhaps because blacks accepted the one-drop rule themselves as it became "naturalized" through custom and law, and because the community thus created provided a basis for political as well as cultural solidarity, the self-enumeration on the census has so far not "introduce[d] any noticeable fluctuation in the number of blacks" (Davis 1991, 12). But the de facto maintenance of the hypodescent rule is certainly not entirely, or even predominantly, due to its acceptance by blacks. There is little indication that whites' perception of the racial line between themselves and blacks has shifted significantly. For example, although de jure segregation of the Jim Crow era has been broken, de facto segregation persists.

Massey and Denton (1987, 823) found "remarkably . . . little evidence of a significant process of spatial integration among blacks in large metropolitan areas" in the 1970s, even though the same study reported much higher rates of integration for Latinos and Asian Americans; significantly, the major exception was black Latinos, whose experiences more closely resembled those of African Americans. Similarly, the rate of black-white intermarriage has lagged far behind those of either Latino-white or Asian-white intermarriage; in 1980 intermarriage between blacks and whites accounted for only about 2 percent of all marriages that involved at least one black partner (Sanjek 1994, 113–14).

A fascinating illustration of the persistence of the one-drop rule is the recent golf sensation Tiger Woods, whose ancestry is one-quarter Chinese, one-quarter Thai, one-quarter white, one-eighth Native American, and one-eighth African American. Although Woods's ancestry is fully half Asian, neither the white nor the black public seriously considers him as the first great "Asian American" golfer in the United States. Similarly, despite the fact that Woods's ancestry is as much Native American as African American, he is also not defined as the first great "Native American" golfer. He remains, in the media and in the popular imagination of white and black Americans, as another in the long line of great African American sports figures, albeit in a still predominantly white sport. Fuzzy Zoeller, a fellow professional golfer, provided the most vivid example of the persistence of the hypodescent rule. When Tiger Woods won the 1997 Masters Championship (held annually at a previously segregated country club in Augusta, Georgia), Zoeller derisively referred to Woods as "that little boy" and remarked to reporters that he hoped Woods would not choose fried chicken, collard greens, or "whatever the hell they serve" for the Champions' Dinner.[6]

Although the reactions to Tiger Woods may seem to be a clear affirmation of the one-drop rule, he also challenges that rule. He has proclaimed himself a "Cablinasian" (the nominal contraction of Caucasian, Black, American Indian, and Asian), a choice of racial identity that has not drawn vehemently negative reactions from either whites or blacks; in fact, it has only increased his popularity, as Asian Americans (as well as Asians in Asia) embraced him as one of their own. Sensing this shift in public attitudes, Woods's primary corporate sponsor, Nike, cleverly markets him to appeal to all minorities who have previously been marginalized or outright excluded from the white world of golf.

In line with such developments there is now a substantial grassroots movement to gain societal and governmental acceptance of multiracial identities. As of 1993, "more than forty grass-roots organizations in the forefront of change on this issue ... [have] come into existence over the last twenty years since the dismantling of Jim Crow segregation, and particularly the removal of the last antimiscegenation laws in June 1967" (Daniel 1993, 179). Cognizant of the state's formative rather than merely reflective role in the construction of racial categories, these groups have targeted the Bureau of the Census and other governmental agencies to allow those who identify themselves as multiracial to do so on official forms. Thus far, the Census Bureau has resisted making "'multiracial' an official self-identification,"[7] but at least one state government and a few municipal governments have changed their classification schemes to accommodate multiracial identities (Daniel 1993, 179). Furthermore, as we show below, Latinos of mixed ancestry simply tend to reject the one-drop rule. Understanding the U.S. racial classification scheme partially through the racial classification scheme employed in the Spanish-speaking Caribbean, many Latinos of African ancestry in the United States do not choose to identify themselves unambiguously as black.

Taken to their logical extremes, these two trends foreshadow the eventual blurring of the racial line between white and black. However, given the deep entrenchment of the hypodescent rule in the constitution of social, political, and economic life in the United States, any shifting or blurring of the "color line" vis-à-vis blacks is likely to be a long, contentious process.

Interethnic Stability and Asian Pacific Americans

In this section we turn to the panethnic category "Asian Pacific American" ("Asian or Pacific Islander," or API), and consider the future stability of this broad category, which includes some fifty different national-origin groups with distinctive languages, cultures, religions, and, in some cases, long histories of hostile contact with one another.[8] Although the category "Hispanic" also subsumes different ethnic and nationality groups within a common designation, those defined as Hispanic can usually be presumed to share the Spanish language and colonial legacy. There is no such unifying principle for the category Asian Pacific American.

Portending the experiences of the Chinese and successive Asian groups in the United States for a hundred years afterward, the official legal status of early Chinese immigrants in California was adjudicated in 1854 by the California Supreme Court. In *People v. Hall*, the court "reasoned" that American Indians had originally migrated from Asia and were thereby "Asiatics." Hence, like American Indians, Chinese were ruled to not have the right to testify in courts of law (Chan 1991,

48; Almaguer 1994, 162–63). This decision in *People v. Hall* was just the first of many laws and court decisions, mostly in western states, through which Asian groups were segregated and discriminated against on a racial basis. Among the discriminatory laws were those enacting public school segregation and prohibiting land purchases and miscegenation.

The national state was similar in its treatment of groups from Asia. If the "power of the national state gave new [European] immigrants both their firmest claims to whiteness and their strongest leverage for enforcing those claims" (Barrett and Roediger 1997, 186), the inverse was the case for Asians in the United States prior to the 1950s. In 1790 the U.S. Congress, "in its first words on the subject of citizenship," restricted naturalization to "free white persons," a rule that remained in force until 1952. Between 1878 and 1952, this racial prerequisite to naturalized citizenship was challenged in fifty-two court cases, constituting one means by which the state demarcated its official racial lines (Haney López 1996, 1, 4). Affirmatively responding to racist white working-class movements, the national state also enacted various anti-Asian immigration laws. In 1882, Congress passed the Chinese Exclusion Act, which was renewed decennially thereafter. Restrictions on Japanese immigration followed in 1907.[9]

In adjudicating where the racial lines should be drawn, especially between whites and nonwhites, the courts were forced to justify their decisions. To do so, they drew on the necessarily ambiguous evidence from society—in the forms of "scientific evidence" (the "supposedly objective, technical, and specialized knowledge" of experts) and "common knowledge" definitions of race, as these were being formulated and contested outside the state (Haney López 1996, 5–9). In every racial prerequisite case involving Chinese, Japanese, Koreans, or Filipinos, "scientific" and "lay" definitions were judged to be in agreement. Without exception, the courts ruled that members of these groups were nonwhite and hence ineligible for naturalization. Furthermore, in all cases involving a multiracial person with ancestry in any of the aforementioned groups, the courts ruled without exception that the person was not white, echoing the hypodescent rule applied to African Americans (Haney López 1996, 203–8).

Asian Indians were the only group now part of the API category about whom the courts equivocated. In 1910, 1913, 1919, and 1920, the courts judged Asian Indians to be "white persons," but in 1909, 1917, and again in 1923, the courts decided that they were really "not white" (Haney López 1996, 67). The definitive word on the matter prior to

World War II was handed down in 1923 by the Supreme Court in *United States v. Bhagat Singh Thind*. Thind's position rested on current scientific evidence classifying Asian Indians as "Caucasian." Since the Supreme Court had earlier equated "white" with "Caucasian," Thind claimed that he was white and therefore entitled to naturalization. Faced with conflicting evidence, the Supreme Court decided against scientific evidence and "adopted the 'understanding of the common man' as the exclusive interpretive principle for creating legal taxonomies of race" (Haney López 1996, 90). Determining that Asian Indians were treated as "nonwhite" by the society, the Supreme Court ruled them ineligible for naturalization.[10]

The courts' halting resolution of Asian Indians' racial fitness for citizenship had a counterpart in anti-immigration measures enacted against them; after a period of halting administrative measures to minimize Asian Indian immigration, Congress finally passed the Immigration Act of 1917, which forbade entry of persons from the "barred zone." This zone included all territories lying east of an imaginary racial and geographical line drawn "from the Red to the Mediterranean, Aegean, and Black seas, through the Caucasus Mountains and the Caspian Sea, along the Ural River, and then through the Ural Mountains" (Chan 1991, 55). All preceding anti-immigration measures were then superseded by the Immigration Act of 1924, which barred the entry of all "aliens ineligible to citizenship."[11] The status of only one Asian group remained ambiguous: the Filipinos. Because the Philippines had become a colony of the United States in 1898, its residents were considered "nationals" rather than "aliens." However, because they were deemed not white, they were ineligible for citizenship. As nationals, they were permitted entry until 1934, when the Tydings-McDuffie Act limited Filipino immigration to fifty persons per year.

Despite similar experiences as aliens (or nationals) ineligible for citizenship, it was really not until the 1960s that Asian Americans began to forge a pan-Asian identity. Before then, various Asian groups had tended to mute their identities and disassociate themselves from one another. They lived in segregated communities, apart not only from the larger white society but from each other, which limited interactions among the groups (Espiritu 1992, 20–24). Furthermore, homeland political animosities, especially between the Japanese and those whom they had colonized, further divided the groups.

Espiritu (1992) suggests that the Asian American panethnicity that began to take shape in the decades following World War II was facilitated by three factors. First, by then the immigrant generation was

outnumbered by native-born members of the second and third generations, for whom past conflicts rooted in homeland politics had receded
in importance. Second, residential segregation of various Asian ethnic
groups declined in the postwar years, increasing their interactions not
only with whites but with other Asians. Third, more Asian students
were attending colleges, again increasing social contact among the various Asian ethnic groups. These changes led to closer relations among
the Asian ethnic groups and to a growing recognition of commonalties
in their past and current experiences in the United States. Furthermore,
inspired by the civil rights movement, the Black Power movement, and
the anticolonial struggles in Asia, "Asian American activists built pan-
Asian solidarity by pointing out their common fate in American society" (Lowe 1991; Espiritu 1992, 30–31).

On the construction of an Asian Pacific American panethnicity, Espiritu (1992, 162) convincingly concludes that "although the pan-Asian
concept may have originated in the minds of non-Asians, it is today
more than a reflection of this misperception. Asian Americans did not
just adopt the concept but also transformed it to conform to their ideological and political needs." By "misperception" she means the tendency of non–Asian Americans to "lump all Asian Americans together
and treat them as if they were the same."

To Espiritu's conclusion we would add more emphasis to the state's
formative role in having shaped the categorical boundary of "Asian or
Pacific Islander." Undoubtedly, the white public's tendency to lump
together the different Asian American groups contributed to the development of a panethnic identity, as Asian American scholars such as
Chan (1991) and Takaki (1989) have documented. But the public did
not necessarily include all the subgroups in its collapse of categories.
For example, Asian Indians would not be confused with Japanese. Furthermore, most of the groups within the current Asian Pacific American category had little presence in the United States prior to the 1960s.

Above all, the "Asian or Pacific Islander" category was initially a
state invention that paralleled, but was not necessarily the same as, the
American public's racial lumping of Asian Americans. The beginning
of the categorical boundary took shape with the Immigration Act of
1917, which, as we have seen, drew an imaginary line around "Asia"
in an attempt to exclude Asian Indians from "whiteness." Although
the vast territory dividing Asia from the rest of the world did not yet
signify *one* race, the state marked this vast area as "not white." The
Thind decision in 1923 solidified this line. The Immigration Act of 1924
that denied entry to "aliens ineligible to citizenship" implicitly con-

firmed the barred zone delimited in the 1917 law. The McCarran-Walter Act of 1952 likewise referred to an "Asian-Pacific Triangle" that included countries from India to Japan and all Pacific islands north of Australia and New Zealand (Hing 1993, 38). Finally, in the 1970s, the state collapsed into a single racial category all Asian groups that had previously been marked by these arbitrary geographic boundaries and by the term "aliens ineligible to citizenship." In 1977, the Office of Management and Budget's Directive no. 15, which standardized racial categories for the census and which is still in effect, explicitly defined "Asian or Pacific Islander" as a "person having origins in any of the original peoples of the Far East, Southeast Asia, the Indian subcontinent, or the Pacific Islands." Further cementing this new definition, the state increased its attention to social welfare and affirmative action policies at this time and increasingly directed resources to Asian Pacific Americans using this umbrella racial category.

Three decades into the construction of an "Asian Pacific America," both by the state and by Asian Pacific Americans themselves, who transformed the category into a social and political identity, its survival in some form seems assured for the foreseeable future. However, whether the current racial line around Asian Pacific Americans will include the same ethnic groups in the future is not as assured. First, the Pacific Islander portion of the Asian Pacific American category has always been and continues to be ambiguous. For example, in the 1990s some Hawaiians are pressuring for reclassification as "American Indian" (see Hodgkinson 1995, 174; Goldberg 1997, 47). Second, the massive Asian immigration that followed the passage of the Hart-Celler Act increased the number of Asian Americans from 1 million in 1965 to 5 million in 1985; in the process, the ethnic composition of the Asian population shifted dramatically:

> In 1960, 52 percent were Japanese, 27 percent Chinese, 20 percent Filipino, 1 percent Korean, and 1 percent Asian Indian. Twenty-five years later, 21 percent of Asian Americans were Chinese, 21 percent Filipino, 15 percent Japanese, 12 percent Vietnamese, 11 percent Korean, 10 percent Asian Indian, 4 percent Laotian, 3 percent Cambodian, and 3 percent "other." (Takaki 1989, 420)

So just as second- and third-generation Japanese Americans, Chinese Americans, and Filipino Americans were forging a panethnic identity, they were confronted with a large new wave of Asian immigrants. In contrast to the Asian Americans of the 1960s, the new immigrants and their children do not share a long history in the United States and are drawn from ethnic origins different from the pre-1965 Asian Americans, which renders the future of pan-Asian ethnicity uncertain.

A third source of instability within the Asian Pacific American category is a long-standing split between Filipino Americans and other Asian Americans. A large segment of the pre-1965 Asian American population and now the largest group of post-1965 Asian immigrants, Filipinos have generally resisted incorporation into the "pan-Asian framework" (Espiritu 1992, 104). In the late-1960s, when Asian American activists were mobilizing around "Yellow Power," Filipino American activists declared themselves to be brown, not yellow. Since then, they have objected to the dominance of Chinese and Japanese Americans in Asian American studies, social service funding and organizations, and affirmative action programs and have intermittently called for removing Filipino Americans from the Asian Pacific American rubric (Espiritu 1992).[12] Nevertheless, Espiritu is probably correct in predicting that, at least in the short term, Filipino Americans will remain within the Asian Pacific American category. First, even though Filipinos are the second largest component of the Asian American category, they are still too few by themselves to constitute an effective political force. Second, even though they share the history and culture of Spanish colonialism, there are many obstacles to joining the Latino coalition. The biggest obstacle may be the state itself which "continue[s] to treat Filipino Americans as Asian Americans." And third, only a minority of Filipino Americans now support a withdrawal from the Asian Pacific American framework (Espiritu 1992, 108, 172). But if the numbers of Filipinos keeps increasing at a rapid pace and if they continue to feel marginalized within the "Asian Pacific American" racial category, their reclassification may become more viable.

Latinos and the Clashing Cultures of Race

In their influential book, *Racial Formation in the United States*, Omi and Winant (1986, 64) define racialization as "the extension of racial meaning to a previously racially unclassified relationship or group." Reviewing U.S. history through this conceptual lens, one can chart the continually unfolding process of racialization, as American Indians, Africans, and later the Mexicans, the Chinese, the Japanese, and so on, have successively come into prolonged contact with whites and consequently been racially classified and subjugated by them.[13]

In this section we would like to modify this conceptualization, insofar as "the extension of racial meaning" is meant as a unilateral imposition of racial categories and meanings onto "preracial" peoples. With the exceptions of the earliest encounters between Europeans and American Indians and between Europeans and Africans, few encounters between the dominant "white" group and "others" in the United States fit this characterization. Mexicans, Chinese, Japanese, Koreans, Asian Indians, Filipinos, and others of the nineteenth and early twentieth centuries were scarcely "preracial" peoples who lacked their own preformed racial worldviews. And certainly the post-1965 immigrant groups from Latin America and Asia are not preracial. Rather, each of them brings a set of racial schemas, a culture of race, that is *different* than the dominant one operant in the United States. What then transpires is an encounter between different cultures of race, from which a new synthesis may emerge. To be sure, the groups do not have equal power to enact their racial schemas, but it does not follow that the definitions of the dominant culture will prevail absolutely. As Sohrabi writes about the clash of two cultures of the state in Iran at the turn of the century, the "new emergent culture" of race is not the "result of a linear, one-way diffusion" of the dominant culture, "but a synthesis that emerge[s] out of the clash of two cultures" of race (Sohrabi, in press). We illustrate this idea by examining the racial classification of Latinos in the United States.

We have seen that, despite their multiple ethnic origins, the state currently defines Chinese, Japanese, Koreans, Indians, Filipinos, Guamanians, Vietnamese, and so on, as belonging to the same race. Similarly, "blacks" include not only descendants from the original African slave population but also more recent immigrants from Africa or the Caribbean. In the case of the equally multiethnic category of "Hispanics," however, the state, rather than designating this category as a "race," refracts it along those categories the state officially recognizes as "races": white, black, and, to a lesser extent, Native American, and Asian. Faced with this official classificatory scheme in census questionnaires, significantly high percentages of Latinos simply opt out of it by reporting their racial status as "Other" (Toro 1998).

The unique features of the U.S. Latino population's multiracial composition are rooted in Spanish colonialism, during which the colonial states imposed racial hierarchies more gradational and fluid than those in their northern counterparts. More so than in the English colonies, Spanish colonization in Cuba, Mexico, Puerto Rico, and elsewhere in Latin America entailed widespread miscegenation among the Spanish, Indian, and African populations, but the "mixes" varied by region. The racial order in Mexico was organized primarily around Spanish/Indian miscegenation, while the racial order in the Caribbean was organized in Spanish/African terms. These patterns, in addition to the differences in the timing of the subsequent colonization by the United States in the mid– and late nineteenth century, have factored centrally in the complex reracialization of the Latino population in the United States. At the point of their respective colonization by the United States, Mexican, Puerto Rican, Cuban (and Filipino) populations had already experienced centuries of Spanish colonial rule. In these earlier colonial contexts, local hierarchical racial orders had emerged that were far more fluid than the U.S. white/black distinction based on hypodescent.

In Mexico, it is estimated that, by 1900, *mestizos* (individuals of Spanish and Indian ancestry) comprised 85 percent–90 percent of the population; Indians comprised 8 percent–10 percent; and Europeans, mainly Spanish, made up the remainder (Morner 1967). In the Spanish Caribbean during the eighteenth century, the Spanish (free) and black (slave) populations were fairly even in number (Williams 1970, 109). By 1898, when Puerto Rico and Cuba passed into U.S. hands as a result of the Spanish-American War, the largest racial category in the islands was *blanco* (white); an intermediate stratum (variously defined as *mulatto* or *trigueno*) was the next largest, and the smallest, but discernible, category was *negro* (black). In 1910, for example, 65.5 percent of Puerto Ricans were identified in the Puerto Rican census as *blanco* (as opposed to *mulatto* or *negro*), a figure which continued to rise throughout the century. Indicating that the *blanco* category was not intended to be "unmixed," as was the white category was in United States, Virginia Dominguez (1989, 273) explains that "when given the choice to identify themselves as either white or black, most Spanish-speaking people from the Caribbean identify themselves as white."

The different ways that the racial lines were drawn during the Spanish colonial period, and then later remapped under U.S. rule, are central to the racial dilemmas Latinos confront to the present day. In the American Southwest, prior to its annexation by the United States at the conclusion of the Mexican American War of 1846–48, there existed a racial order that was similar to those established elsewhere in the Spanish colonial world. Ramon Gutiérrez's highly acclaimed *When Jesus Came, the Corn Mothers Went Away* explores with deep insight its initial construction and transformation in colonial New Mexico from the sixteenth to the mid–nineteenth century.

> Throughout colonial Spanish America, race functioned as a metalanguage: with few exceptions, a person's occupation and status was often quickly deduced by simple appearance. For

such visual evaluations of race to be correct, a close correlation had to exist between all constituting elements of racial definition: legal color, actual physical color, and phenotype. When such a correspondence existed, it meant that in the daily life of face-to-face community, race was a visual metonymic sign of a person's position in the social division of labor, symbolic of a propinquity to the infidel, or in the case of slaves, dishonor and social death. (Gutiéreez 1991, 202–3)

Racial and religious lines in New Mexico revolved along a relational axis that privileged the conquering Spaniards (who were Christian, "civilized," and white) at one end and the vanquished Amerindians (who were deemed heathen, "uncivilized," and dark) at the other.

The above racial order in what is now the American Southwest had important consequences for the way that the Mexican population was reracialized under U.S. colonial rule in the mid–nineteenth century. Those living in the territory ceded by Mexico, for example, were initially defined as honorary "whites" through the Treaty of Guadalupe Hidalgo, which officially ended the war. The treaty formally extended to them access to U.S. citizenship, a privileged status that was reserved only for "free white persons" at the time (Almaguer 1994; Martinez 1998). While the mixed Spanish/Indian background of most Mexicans was a basis of derision, antipathy, and ambiguity, the fact that they were not of African ancestry factored centrally in their attaining an "honorary" white status at this time. As discussed above, the late antebellum period was a time of drawing a stark distinction between white and black through the ever stricter enforcement of the hypodescent rule. Hence, we can see that even at this initial point, the U.S. state was trying to capture Mexicans symbolically with its classification system centered on whites and blacks.

At the same time, however, the newly conquered Mexicans—especially the elites—were attempting to assert their own culture of race. For example, in making the case that Mexicans were white during the California State Constitutional Convention in 1849, a prominent Mexican *ranchero* from Santa Barbara passionately argued that the term was a reference to European ancestry and social standing, as it was understood under Spanish and Mexican rule, not merely to skin color. Don Pablo de la Guerra, a delegate to the convention, maintained that "it should be perfectly understood in the first place, what is the true significance of the word 'white.' Many citizens of California have received by nature a very dark skin; nevertheless, there are among them men who have heretofore been allowed to vote, and not only that, but to fill the highest public offices. It would be very unjust to deprive them of the privileges of citizenship merely because nature had not made them white." In drawing attention to the Californio elite's European ancestry, de la Guerra strategically downplayed the predominantly *mestizo* backgrounds of most Mexican Californians, closing his eyes to the Indian and perhaps African blood flowing in their veins. Moreover, he apparently allayed Anglo concerns over Mexicans attaining an "honorary" white status by reassuring them that if they used the word white as a term intended to "exclude the African race" from the franchise, de la Guerra was in full agreement with this usage (Almaguer 1994, 55–56).

The synthesis resulting from the clash of the two cultures of race was a racial order that recognized the "whiteness" and hence citizenship rights of some Mexicans but denied them to others. The latter was particularly true in the case of working-class or darker Mexicans, who were often denied their legal rights by being categorized summarily as Indians (as were the Chinese at one point), despite the Mexicans' own racial antipathy toward Indians. A notable example involved Manuel Dominguez, a dark-skinned *mestizo*, who served as an elected delegate to the California State Constitutional Convention of 1849 and as a member of the Los Angeles County Board of Supervisors. In 1857, he traveled to northern California to enter testimony in a San Francisco courtroom. Before Dominguez could testify, however, the Anglo lawyer for the plaintiff objected to his taking the witness stand. The lawyer argued that Dominguez was an Indian and, therefore, ineligible to enter testimony in the state. Despite Dominguez's high social standing among Mexican Californians, the judge upheld the objection, and Dominguez was dismissed (Almaguer 1994, 57).

But the above synthesis was not permanent, most notably as large numbers of Mexicans of working-class origins began to immigrate to the Southwest. With continual immigration from Mexico, and the heated politics around it, a new synthesis has yet to fully emerge. Examining the census categories applied to people of Mexican origin throughout the twentieth century reveals the state's ambivalence toward the racial status of Mexicans. After classifying Mexicans as "white," at least in theory, for a lengthy period of time, the 1930 federal census listed "Mexican" as a racial category for the first time. Then, the category was absent once again just ten years later. In 1950 and 1960, Latinos appeared as an "ethnic" category with the designation, "persons of Spanish mother tongue." In 1970, the appellation for the category changed to "persons of both Spanish surname and Spanish mother tongue." And in 1980 and 1990, the "Hispanic" category emerged (Omi and Winant 1994, 82). But from 1950 to the present day,

Table 1   Latinos by Ethnicity and Race in the 1980 U.S. Census (%)

Race	Mexican	Puerto Rican	Cuban	Other Hispanic	Total
White	55.4	48.3	83.8	63.4	57.7
Black	1.9	3.5	2.9	4.5	2.7
American Indian	.7	.2	.1	.1	.7
Asian/Pacific Islander	.3	.6	.2	4.7	1.2
Other	41.7	47.5	13.1	26.4	37.7

Source: U.S. Census Public Use Microdata Sample (PUMS), 1980.

Table 2   Latinos by Ethnicity and Race in the 1990 Federal Census (%)

Race	Mexican	Puerto Rican	Cuban	Other Hispanic	Total
White	50.4	45.8	83.6	50.9	51.6
Black	.9	5.9	3.8	7.3	2.9
American Indian	.8	.2	.1	.7	.7
Asian/Pacific Islander	.5	1.0	.3	2.5	1.0
Other	47.4	47.2	12.2	38.5	43.9

Source: U.S. Census Public Use Microdata Sample (PUMS), 1990.

the Latino category was to be marked *in conjunction with* one of the state's recognized racial categories. As the state imposed these changes in racial/ethnic categorization vis-à-vis Mexicans (and other Latinos), people of Mexican origin tried to make sense of the changes in their own cultural terms, by either declaring themselves to be white (whereas neither the state nor the society may share this view) or opting out of the categories altogether. For example, more than 40 percent of people of Mexican origin in 1980 and nearly 50 percent in 1990 opted out of the state's predetermined racial categories (see tables 1 and 2).[14]

The situation reflects a clash between two cultures of race, as a Latino population, racialized according to one racial logic, is reracialized in the United States according to a different racial logic. Similar ambiguities of race within the Latino population are also vividly captured in the way that these lines are configured among Puerto Rican migrants in the United States. According to the sociologist Clara Rodriguez, Puerto Ricans bring with them a more complex understanding of racial categories than the categories recognized by the U.S. state. Her review of the scholarly literature on this issue suggests that there exists among Puerto Ricans a variegated continuum of racial types. These include individuals who are defined "as *blanco* (white), *indio* (dark skinned and straight haired), *moreno* (dark skinned but with a variety of negroid or Caucasian features and hair forms), *negro* (black or African-American in appearance), and *trigueno* (brown or wheat colored), a term that can be applied broadly to each of the foregoing types except for the very blond *blancos*" (Rodriguez 1996, 133; see also Rodriguez-Morazzani 1996). Eduardo Bonilla-Silva suggests a less differentiated racial classification scheme among Puerto Ricans, one that contains three principal categories—white, *trigueno,* and black—with the first two being the major categories and the latter a smaller, subordinate one (personal communication, 1998).

Either way, Rodriguez and Bonilla-Silva agree that, as in the rest of Latin America, one can be racially reclassified through class mobility and other mitigating factors, and that persons within the same family may identify and be identified as belonging to different races based on somatic features such as skin color or hair texture. Unlike racial classification in the United States—which depends, above all, on descent and hence is perceived as immutable—racial classification in Latin America is more fluid. Hence, Rodriguez concludes about Puerto Rican racial practices, "Members of the same kin groups can be identified with varying racial terms, and an individual might change racial status with changes in class or education" (1996, 134).

One plausible reading of the U.S. census vis-à-vis Puerto Ricans is that while the state recognizes their distinctness or "Latino-ness" with the "Hispanic" category, it nonetheless attempts to impose a choice between the black and white racial categories, an act that has roots in the historical enforcement of the hypodescent rule. But, like their Mexican counterparts, Puerto Ricans in the U.S. assert their own understandings of race, their culture of race, within the strictures of the state-sanctioned categories. Hence, we see that although a large majority of Puerto Ricans may be perceived by the state and the society at large as "black," only 3.5 percent of Puerto Ricans identified themselves as being "black" in the 1980 federal census, whereas 48.3 percent and 47.5 percent identified as "white" and "other," respectively. Similarly, ten years later, 45.8 percent, 5.9 percent, and 47.2 percent of Puerto Ricans identified themselves as "white," "black," and "other," respectively.

The racial classification scheme in Cuba is similar to that of Puerto Rico, as it recognizes three racial categories—black, white, and mulatto (*trigueno* in Puerto Rico)—and also takes phenotype and social class into consideration (Pedraza 1996, 274). The similarity between the two, however, is not replicated among the Cuban and Puerto Rican populations in the United States. The intervening variables are the open borders between the United States and Puerto Rico, a U.S. commonwealth, and the relatively closed borders between the United States and Cuba, a U.S. political foe. Consequently, immigration from Cuba has been in distinct waves and has been less racially (and politically) reflective of Cuba than the migration from Puerto Rico. Hence, the relatively recent arrival of the Marielitos in the 1980s was the first major wave of Cuban immigrants with a sizable number of blacks. According to Pedraza, "Over 91 percent of the refugees who came over in the first wave, Cuba's elite, were white. But the proportion of whites declined quite markedly during the second wave. From 14 to 19 percent of those who immigrated from 1965 to 1979 considered themselves as 'other.' The Marielitos had the lowest proportion white of any wave (77 percent) while 16 percent considered themselves 'other' and 6 percent considered themselves Black" (1996, 274–75). As with the Puerto Ricans' usage of the census categories, the numbers of "whites," "blacks," and "others" are probably reflective of the Cubans' understandings of these racial categories, not the state's.[15]

Conclusion

This chapter has argued that the state is a major (re)producer of racial categories, continually alchemizing the seemingly arbitrary into the seemingly natural, the biologically unreal into the socially real. By looking to the ambiguities of the distant past and the present, we have shown that even the most rigid "color line" between whites and blacks, long governed via the unforgiving one-drop rule with the backing of the state, is not immutable. By examining the interethnic instabilities within the contemporary racial category "Asian or Pacific Islander," the boundary of which was largely a state invention, we saw the outlines of possible reconfigurations of the category. By rethinking the concept of racialization—not (only) as a unilateral imposition of racial categories onto preracial peoples but as a synthesis of differing cultures of race—we demonstrated the ongoing process of synthesis of the state's attempts to capture Latinos with its official racial/ethnic categories and the Latinos' divergent understanding of race. And although for analytical purposes we paired each of the three themes with a particular group, there were obvious overlaps. The classificatory implications of intermarriages and multiracial identities, the interethnic instabilities within panethnic categories, and the reconceptualization of racialization as the clash of differing cultures of race are, in varying degrees and varied ways, relevant to the study of all three groups discussed in this chapter as well as the ones we did not.

For almost the entirety of U.S. history, the (re)production of racial categories, in general, and the state's formative role in it, in particular, have been inextricably tied to the structuring of racial domination. However, in the past several decades, the preceding statement has become somewhat ambiguous. The racial social movements of the 1960s and 1970s transformed the nonwhite racial categories into meaningful political identities, and the state responded, in part, by instituting race-conscious programs to redress past and present discrimination. As a result, the racial distinctions that were used to subjugate are now partially the tools with which to resist subjugation.

What are the implications of this paradoxical shift for social scientific research? Paralleling antiracist politics of race, social scientific study of race cannot simply abandon "race" on the grounds that it is biologically groundless or "merely" an ideology. Both in politics and scholarship, "color blindness" does not present us with a compelling choice, which would only leave us blind to the vast racial inequalities that remain with us. On the other hand, social scientists also cannot merely ratify and reify the state's official racial categories and become complicit in their naturalization. This analytic route only leads us back to treating race *as if* it were biologically tenable. Because "one of the major powers of the state is to produce and impose . . . categories of thought that we spontaneously apply to all things of the social world," Pierre Bourdieu writes, "when it comes to the state, one never doubts enough" (1994, 1). As social scientists, we should vigilantly doubt the racial categories we employ in our scholarly research. Historical analyses must always be mindful of the historical specificity and mutability of the boundaries and the meanings of racial categories. Likewise, contemporary analyses must contextualize race and theoretically justify the racial categories they use. In the process, the important project of studying the powerful effects of the "color line" must be closely tied to the study of the construction of the "color line" itself.

Notes

1. As Barrett and Roediger (1997, 186) argue, e.g., "The power of the national state gave new [European] immigrants both their firmest claims to whiteness and their strongest leverage for enforcing those claims. The courts consistently allowed new immigrants, whose racial status was ambiguous in the larger culture, to be naturalized as 'white' citizens."

2. In recent years, there has been a surge of interest and scholarship on the making of "whites," seeking to study this hegemonic and hence previously unproblematized racial category. While we agree with this line of research, the racialization of whites in

general and the state's attempts to categorize them in particular are beyond the scope of this chapter. Similarly, there is a growing literature on the post–World War II formation of a supratribal American Indian identity, which we do not address in this chapter. See Allen (1994), Frankenberg (1993, 1994), Ignatiev (1995), Roediger (1991, 1994), Sacks (1994) and Saxton (1991) for recent writings on white racial formation and Cornell (1984, 1988), Nagel (1995, 1996), Nagel and Snipp (1993), and Snipp (1986, 1989) for recent writings on Native American racial formation.

3. Here, we are not confining our criticism to the unquestioning usage of race as a categorical variable in quantitative survey research (which not coincidentally mirrors the state practice of the census). Historically-minded social scientists have a tendency to project today's racial categories onto the past and also become complicit in naturalizing the categories in the process. For example, Barrett and Roediger (1997) point out that many contemporary analysts are retroactively dismissive of historical evidence, including coeval social scientific evidence, in which turn-of-the-century European immigrant groups are referred to as races (e.g., Italian race), thereby treating them as if they *arrived* in the United States as "white" ethnic groups. Similarly, the recent historical scholarship on prestatehood Hawai'i tends to falsely assume that "Asian" or "Asian American" was a meaningful racial category (Jung, in press).

4. Obviously, the Africans brought to the New World did not think of themselves as "African," "Negro," or "black." They were of diverse ethnic groups who spoke different languages, practiced different customs, and were not necessarily even on peaceful terms with one another.

5. In this part of the chapter, we draw extensively on F. James Davis's important book, *Who Is Black?* According to its author, this is the only book-length study of blacks and the hypodescent rule (see also Williamson 1980).

6. Televised and written about for weeks, Fuzzy Zoeller's exact remarks to a Cable News Network reporter were, "That little boy is driving well, and he's putting well. He's doing everything it takes to win. So, you know what you guys do when he gets in here? You pat him on the back and say 'Congratulations' and, 'Enjoy it' and tell him not to serve fried chicken next year. Got it. Or collard greens or whatever the hell they serve."

7. The directions for the 1990 census, as in the past, clearly indicated that only one racial category could be claimed by a person: "Fill *one* circle for the race that the person considers himself/herself to be."

8. For example, in the 1990 census, under the heading of Asian or Pacific Islander (API), respondents could check one of nine ethnic entries (Chinese, Filipino, Hawaiian, Korean, Vietnamese, Japanese, Asian Indian, Samoan, and Guamanian) or select "other API," writing in another unlisted nationality, e.g., Hmong, Fijian, Laotian, Thai, Tongan, Pakistani, and Cambodian (U.S. Census 1990).

9. Because Japan was a growing international power, the United States did not take a unilateral approach but negotiated a "gentlemen's agreement" with the Japanese government, which simply stopped issuing passports thereafter. The Japanese government had already stopped the emigration of Koreans in 1905, after it occupied that country.

10. In addition to its particular effect on Asian Indians, the case finally resolved a point of long ambiguity: the intermittent conflict between "scientific" and "social" understandings. These federal decisions to exclude Asians from citizenship also shaped the language of laws at the state level. Among the more discriminatory measures against Asians were the alien land laws, which prohibited the purchase or lease of land by "aliens ineligible to citizenship." Enacted first in California in 1913, they were followed

236   TOMÁS ALMAGUER AND MOON-KIE JUNG

by similar laws in Arizona, Washington, Louisiana, New Mexico, Idaho, Montana, Oregon and Kansas. Later, during World War II, Utah, Wyoming, and Arkansas (three of the states containing concentration camps for Japanese internment) passed similar laws as preventive measures.

11. By 1924, unlike in 1917, the Supreme Court had definitively decided that Asian Indians were "ineligible to citizenship." This law also severely restricted the immigration of Southern and Eastern Europeans.

12. An indication of the marginalization of Filipinos can be found in Asian American studies, the name of which is in itself noninclusive in this regard. The two most comprehensive historical surveys of Asian America to date, Sucheng Chan's *Asian Americans* and Ronald Takaki's *Strangers from a Different Shore: A History of Asian Americans*, do not give much coverage to Pacific Islander groups. And, noting that "pan-Asian American . . . ethnicity has taken root primarily among Asian Americans," Espiritu (1992, xi) purposely uses "the term Asian American rather than Asian Pacific American" in her book. She attributes the "Filipino-Asian split" to the "cultural distance between Filipinos and other East Asian groups" and, perhaps more important, the "class cleavages" between the better-off Asian Americans and Filipino Americans who have not fared as well in the labor market (1992, 107–9). There is a third factor, namely, the impact of U.S. colonization of the Philippines. E. San Juan, Jr., a cultural theorist who advocates disengaging Filipinos "from the sweeping rubric of 'Asian American,'" has repeatedly emphasized that the "reality of U.S. colonial subjugation and its profoundly enduring effects . . . distinguish Filipinos from the Chinese, Japanese, Koreans, and others from the Asian continent" (1994, 206). Although there is not much sociological or historical literature on the "enduring effects" of U.S. colonization on Filipino Americans, San Juan's comments warrant further investigation. Certainly, controlling for education and other relevant factors, Filipino Americans have fared worse than other Asian Americans, perhaps because they faced a qualitatively different form of racism. For example, in prestatehood Hawai'i, Filipinos, as colonial subjects of the U.S., faced a racism different in character than the one faced by the Japanese, which placed and kept the former at the bottom of the racial order (Jung, in press).

13. Of course, "white" itself is not a natural racial identity. In anglophone North America, the English and other Europeans initially imagined this new identity into being in the late seventeenth century, in the course of their interactions with Africans and American Indians (Jordan 1968).

14. We gratefully acknowledge the valuable research assistance of Sylvia Orduno of the Department of Sociology at the University of Michigan in compiling the census data used in this chapter. The data are drawn from the 1980 and 1990 U.S. Census Public Use Microdata Sample (PUMS), a 5 percent weighed sample. Reynolds Farley also provided valuable advice and guidance in answering various questions we had about the data set.

15. The distorting impact of the Cubans' more selective immigration to the United States is reflected in the federal census, as Cuban Americans are by far much more likely than Puerto Ricans (or Mexicans Americans) to identify themselves as white. For example, according to the 1980 and 1990 censuses, 83.8 percent and 83.6 percent of Cuban Americans, respectively, identified themselves as "white." The comparable figures for Puerto Ricans were 48.3 percent and 45.8 percent (see tables 1 and 2).

References

Allen, Theodore. 1994. *The Invention of the White Race*. London: Verso.

Almaguer, Tomás. 1994. *Racial Fault Lines: The Historical Origins of White Supremacy in California*. Berkeley: University of California Press.

Barrett, James R., and David Roediger. 1997. "Inbetween Peoples: Race, Nationality and the New Immigrant Working Class." In *American Exceptionalism? U.S. Working-Class Formation in an International Context*, 181–220. New York: St. Martin's Press.

Blumer, Herbert. 1958. "Race Prejudice as a Sense of Group Position." *Pacific Sociological Review* 1:3–7.

Bonilla-Silva, Eduardo. 1997. "Rethinking Racism: Toward a Structural Interpretation." *American Sociological Review* 62:465–80.

Bourdieu, Pierre. 1994. "Rethinking the State: Genesis and Structure of the Bureaucratic Field." *Sociological Theory* 12:1–18.

Chan, Sucheng. 1991. *Asian Americans: An Interpretive History*. Boston: Twayne Publishers.

Cornell, Stephen. 1984. "Crisis and Response in Indian-White Relations, 1960–1984." *Social Problems* 32:44–59.

———. 1988. *The Return of the Native: American Indian Political Resurgence*. New York: Oxford University Press.

Daniel, G. Reginald. 1993. "Review of *Who Is Black?*" *Contemporary Sociology* 22:178–79.

Davis, F. James. 1991. *Who Is Black? One Nation's Definition*. University Park: Pennsylvania State Press.

Delgado, Richard, ed. 1995. *Critical Race Theory: The Cutting Edge*. Philadelphia: Temple University Press.

Dominguez, Virginia R. 1986. *White by Definition: Social Classification in Creole Louisiana*. New Brunswick, N.J.: Rutgers University Press.

Espiritu, Yen Le. 1992. *Asian American Panethnicity: Bridging Institutions and Identities*. Philadelphia: Temple University Press.

Frankenberg, Ruth. 1993. *White Women, Race Matters: The Social Construction of Whiteness*. Minneapolis: University of Minnesota Press.

———. 1994. "Whiteness and Americanness: Examining Constructions of Race, Culture, and Nation in White Women's Life Narratives." In *Race*, edited by Steven Gregory and Roger Sanjek, 62–77. New Brunswick, N.J.: Rutgers University Press.

Genovese, Eugene D. 1976. *Roll, Jordan, Roll: The World the Slaves Made*. New York: Vintage Books.

Goldberg, David Theo. 1997. *Racial Subjects: Writing on Race in America*. New York: Routledge.

Gutiérrez, Ramon A. 1992. *When Jesus Came, the Corn Mother Went Away: Marriage, Sexuality, and Power in Colonial New Mexico, 1500–1846*. Stanford, Calif.: Stanford University Press.

Hall, Stuart. 1992. "New Ethnicities." In *"Race," Culture, and Difference*, edited by James Donald and Ali Rattansi, 252–59. London: Sage Publications.

Haney López, Ian F. 1996. *White by Law: The Legal Construction of Race*. New York: New York University Press.

Harris, Marvin. 1964. *Patterns of Race in the Americas*. New York: W. W. Norton.

Hing, Bill Ong. 1993. *Making and Remaking Asian America through Immigration Policy, 1850–1990*. Stanford, Calif.: Stanford University Press.

Hodgkinson, Harold L. 1995. "What Shall We Call People? Race, Class, and the Census for 2000." *Phi Delta Kappan*.

Ignatiev, Noel. 1995. *How the Irish Became White*. New York: Routledge.

Jordan, Winthrop D. 1968. *White over Black: American Attitudes toward the Negro, 1550–1812*. Chapel Hill: University of North Carolina Press.

Jung, Moon-Kie. In press. "No Whites, No Asians: Race, Marxism, and Hawaii's Preemergent Working Class." *Social Science History*.

Lowe, Lisa. 1991. "Heterogeneity, Hybridity, Multiplicity: Marking Asian American Differences." *Diaspora* 1:24–44.

Martinez, George A. 1998. "Mexican Americans and Whiteness." In *The Latino/a Condition: A Critical Reader*, edited by Richard Delgado and Jean Stefancic, 175–79. New York: New York University Press.

Massey, Douglas S., and Nancy A. Denton. 1987. "Trends in the Residential Segregation of Blacks, Hispanics, and Asians: 1970–1980." *American Sociological Review* 52:802–25.

Morner, Magnus. 1967. *Race Mixture in the History of Latin America*. Boston: Little Brown.

Nagel, Joane. 1995. "American Indian Ethnic Renewal: Politics and the Resurgence of Identity." *American Sociological Review* 60:947–65.

———. 1996. *American Indian Ethnic Renewal: Red Power and the Resurgence of Identity and Culture*. New York: Oxford University Press.

Nagel, Joane, and C. Matthew Snipp. 1993. "Ethnic Reorganization: American Indian Social, Economic, Political, and Cultural Strategies for Survival." *Ethnic and Racial Studies* 16:203–35.

Omi, Michael, and Howard Winant. 1994. *Racial Formation in the United States: From the 1960s to the 1980s*, 2d ed. New York: Routledge.

Pedraza, Silvia. 1996. "Cuba's Refugees: Manifold Migrations." In *Origins and Destinies*, edited by Silvia Pedraza and Rubèn Rumbaut, 263–79. Belmont, Calif.: Wadsworth.

Rodriguez, Clara. 1994. "Challenging Racial Hegemony: Puerto Ricans in the United States." In *Race*, edited by Steven Gregory and Roger Sanjek, 131–45. New Brunswick, N.J.: Rutgers University Press.

Rodriguez-Morazanni, Roberto P. 1996. "Beyond the Rainbow: Mapping the Discourse on Puerto Ricans and 'Race.'" *CENTRO* 8 (1, 2): 151–69.

Roediger, David R. 1991. *Wages of Whiteness: Race and the Making of the American Working Class*. London: Verso.

———. 1994. *Towards the Abolition of Whiteness: Essays on Race, Politics, and Working Class History*. London: Verso.

Sacks, Karen Brodkin. 1994. "How Did Jews Become White Folks?" In *Race*, edited by Steven Gregory and Roger Sanjek, 78–102. New Brunswick, N.J.: Rutgers University Press.

San Juan, Epifanio, Jr. 1994. "The Predicament of Filipinos in the United States: 'Where Are You From? When Are You Going Back?'" In *The State of Asian America: Activism and Resistance in the 1990s*, edited by Karin Aguilar–San Juan, 205–18. Boston: South End Press.

Saxton, Alexander. 1991. *The Rise and Fall of the White Republic: Class Politics and Mass Culture in Nineteenth-Century America*. London: Verso.

Snipp, C. Matthew. 1986. "Who Are American Indians? Some Observations about the Perils and Pitfalls of Data for Race and Ethnicity." *Population Research and Policy Review* 5:237–52.

———. 1989. *American Indians: The First of This Land*. New York: Sage.

Sohrabi, Nader. In press. "Revolution and State Culture: The Circle of Justice and Constitutionalism in 1906 Iran." In *State/Culture: New Approaches to the State in the Social Sciences*, edited by George Steinmetz. Ithaca, N.Y.: Cornell University Press.

Stoler, Ann Laura. 1995. *Race and the Education of Desire: Foucault's "History of Sexuality" and the Colonial Order of Things*. Durham, N.C.: Duke University Press.

Takagi, Dana. 1993. *The Retreat from Race: Asian American Admissions and Racial Politics*. New Brunswick, N.J.: Rutgers University Press.

Takaki, Ronald. 1989. *Strangers from a Different Shore: A History of Asian Americans*. Boston: Penguin Books.

Toro, Luis Angel. 1998. "Race, Identity, and 'Box Checking': The Hispanic Classification in OMB Directive no. 15." In *The Latino/a Condition: A Critical Reader*, edited by Richard Delgado and Jean Stefancic, 52–59. New York: New York University Press.

Wacquant, Loïc J. D. 1997. "For an Analytic of Racial Domination." *Political Power and Social Theory* 11:221–34.

Williams, Eric. 1944. *Capitalism and Slavery*. Chapel Hill: University of North Carolina Press.

———. 1970. *From Columbus to Castro: The History of the Caribbean, 1492–1969*. New York: Vintage Books.

Williamson, Joel. 1980. *New People: Miscegenation and Mulattoes in the United States*. New York: Free Press.

CHAPTER FOURTEEN

Second Generations: Past, Present, Future

ROGER WALDINGER AND JOEL PERLMANN

Thirty years after the Hart-Celler Act marked the renewal of mass immigration to the United States, the immigration research agenda is slowly shifting from the newcomers to their children. The timing is right because it has only been within the past decade that immigrants' children have become a sizable presence in American schools and still more recently that they have moved from the schools into the labor market. But the tenor of the times is clearly not good. America is in the throes of another debate over immigration, and this time, the parties that would narrow, if not close, the door to immigration seem to have the upper hand. An unhealthy brew of popular anxiety whipped up by politicians who can never stoop too low in search of votes lies behind the emerging trend toward restriction. Nonetheless, there are also scholarly reasons to worry. Many of the newcomers arrive with low levels of skill and converge on a handful of metropolitan areas that lack the resources needed to support the process of immigrant adaptation. And these days, even the friends of immigration will concede that serious questions have been raised about immigrants' prospects and about the costs associated with absorbing the many newcomers who have moved to the United States over the past fifteen years.

Not surprisingly, then, the emerging scholarship on the "new second generation formed by children of immigrants born in the United States or brought at an early age from abroad" (Portes and Rumbaut 1996, 232) has begun on a note of inflected pessimism.[1] Leading students of American ethnic life (e.g., Gans, Portes, Rumbaut, and Zhou) outline, with clarity and acuity, the reasons for concern. Today's non-European newcomers are visibly identifiable and enter a mainly white society still not cured of its racist afflictions. Shifts in the structure of the economy aggravate the impact of discrimination: while poorly educated immigrant parents have little trouble starting at the very bottom, the shift toward knowledge-intensive jobs means that the next generation will have to do well in school if it wishes to surpass the achievements of the foreign-born. With big-city schools in more trouble than ever before, the outlook for successful passage through the educational system seems dim. And because second generation expectations are likely to rise, we can count on a mismatch between the aspirations of immigrant children and the skills required by the jobs which they seek.[2]

So our leading sociological commentators on ethnicity are worried about "second generation decline" (Gans 1992). Their anxieties, however, take a very different form from that voiced in the popular press, which worries that the children of today's immigrants are failing to assimilate, in supposed contrast to their predecessors of earlier in the century. The scholarly literature assures us that the new second generation is assimilating, all right, but in a "segmented" fashion, with some large, though so far undefined, proportion likely to converge with the "urban underclass" (Portes and Zhou 1993).

This new perspective on the second generation emerged just as the topic of immigrants' children showed up on the scholarly radar screen. As such, it seems likely to have been designed for agenda-setting purposes, laying out a set of leads and sensitizing concepts for subsequent researchers to modify, extend, alter, and systematize as empirical work on the new second generation moved ahead. But these ideas have struck a particularly deep chord; consequently, the hypotheses of "second generation decline" or "segmented assimilation" have already assumed canonical form. As can be seen from the articles appearing in the special issue of the *International Migration Review*, entitled "The New Second Generation," or from any perusal of this rapidly growing literature, the research community has taken the new perspective as conventional wisdom.[3]

While the new views present a powerful case, the core contentions rest on a set of assumptions neither adequately specified nor beyond reproach. The anxiety about emerging second generation trends is also notably broad brushed. While one can argue that some portion of today's second generation is either stalled or headed downward, the relative size of that portion is never addressed. And the underlying case for pessimism relies on a set of analogies to the experience of other contemporary minorities that have not yet received much attention and may not bear up under scrutiny.

This chapter thus takes a doubting, if friendly, look at the hypotheses of second generation decline and segmented assimilation. We begin by reviewing the basic approach, outlining the logic of the argument, and specifying the central contentions. We then assess the empirical background against which the second generation problematic has been framed and inquire into both the characteristics of those children of immigrants who might find themselves at risk and the precise source of any such peril.

Second Generation Decline?

There is little question that many, possibly even most, immigrant children are heading upward, as exemplified by the large number of Chinese, Korean, South Asian, and other Asian-origin students enrolled in the nation's leading universities. Some are the children of workers, others the descendants of immigrants who have moved right into the middle class. This rapid ascent evokes parallels with the past, most clearly the first and second generation East European Jews who began appearing at New York's City College and then at Harvard, Columbia, and other prestigious schools in numbers that discomfited the WASPs then dominating those institutions. As Steinberg (1981) pointed out some years ago, it was the Jews' good fortune to have moved to America just when the educational system was expanding and moving away from its classical past and to have converged on the Northeast where opportunities to pursue schooling were particularly good. But even so, *schleppers* greatly outnumbered scholars, and the proportion of Jews who made their way to Harvard or to its proletarian cousin, the City College of New York, was dwarfed by those who moved ahead as skilled workers, clerks, or owners of small businesses. In this light, the Asian advance into higher education remains phenomenal. In the Los Angeles region, for example, in every Asian group (including Vietnamese who arrived after age 10) young people between eighteen and twenty-four years old attend college at a rate that exceeds native-born whites, with U.S.-born Asians far ahead of U.S.-born whites on this count (Cheng and Yang 1996, 315). And ironically, the efforts to eliminate affirmative action seem likely to accelerate rather than reverse this trend—quite a different turn of events than that which transpired in the Ivy League seventy years ago.

Even though some portion of today's second generation is rapidly ascending, others appear to be left behind. It is this latter group that has attracted scholarly interest and concern, and it is around their fate that a "second generation problematic" has been framed. As we read the emerging literature, the obstacles to progress appear to stem from a complex of intersecting economic, social, and psychological factors. The starting point is race. Since the European immigrants, as Portes and Zhou (1993, 76) write, were white, "skin color reduced a major barrier to entry into the American mainstream." Like beauty, however, skin color lies largely in the eyes of the beholder, and Gans reminds us that white Southern and Eastern European immigrants were earlier characterized as "other" races. Henry Adams, E. A. Ross, and others of their type were certainly convinced that the swarthy masses arriving at the turn of the century were of a different kind. Since Portes and Zhou are quite right in arguing that race, or rather the meanings associated with it, "is a trait belonging to the host society," one wonders whether levels of xenophobia and racism are indeed higher today than they were in the 1920s or 1930s when the last mainly European second generation came of age. Still, many agree with Gans (1992, 176) that the "ethnic and racial discrimination" suffered by contemporary dark-skinned and non-European immigrants seems "more permanent."[4]

Perhaps this is true. But the argument has more to do with second generation response than with the mainstream's problems with race. While the parents are far more distinct than their offspring in self-presentation and cultural attributes, they are also more likely to lead a segregated existence, working within ethnic niches and living within immigrant neighborhoods. By contrast, their children are more likely to cross ethnic boundaries and head for the mainstream. More important, the children respond differently. They have a heightened perception of discrimination and its prevalence (Rumbaut 1997a) and react to actual and perceived discrimination by rejecting the dreams that impelled their parents.

But how to account for this distinctive second generational response? Answer: the advent of the second generation yields an attitudinal shift, which in turn, stems from varying sources. One derives from the immigration process itself. Following Piore (1979), we can call this a "second generation revolt." The immigrants arrive willing to do jobs natives reject; however low these jobs may fall in the U.S. hierarchy, they still offer wages and compensation superior to the opportunities back home. Having been exposed to different wage and consumption standards from the start, the children want more. Consequently, the question is whether their "careers . . . keep pace with their U.S.-acquired aspirations" (Portes and Zhou 1993, 85).

For Piore, the generational shift in immigrant aspirations was inherent in the processes of migration and settlement and thus a recurrent phenomenon. This would suggest greater continuity between the second generations of yesterday and today, but Portes, Zhou, and Gans all argue that the mismatch between aspirations and opportunities is greater today than ever before, and therefore the greater likelihood of frustration as well (shades of Merton). The conundrum of the contemporary second generation lies in the continuing transformation of the U.S. economy. The manufacturing economy of old allowed for a three- and possibly four-generational move beyond the lowest positions to which immigrants were originally consigned. Even though low-skill jobs persist, occupational segmentation has "reduced the opportunities for incremental upward mobility through well-paid, blue-collar positions" (Portes and Zhou 1993, 85). The declining viability of small business reduces possibilities for advancement through expansion of businesses established by the immigrant generation. And the general stalling of mobility reduces the chances for ethnic succession. Jews and Italians followed the Irish into the public sector as the latter moved on to more lucrative pursuits. Today's civil servants are unlikely to enjoy the same options, which will close off this path of mobility to today's second generation.

Of course, the manner in which the comparison is constructed heightens the contrast between the experience of the earlier and the later second generations. On the one hand, the divisions of yesterday pale before those of today. Then, "joining society's mainstream was seen ... as both proper and inevitable" (Portes and Rumbaut 1996, 267). Second generation children could reject the ways of their parents but still "join the American mainstream, at least that tail end formed by the white industrial working class of the time" (Portes and Rumbaut 1996, 247). On the other hand, options were also different, since the children of the European immigrants could automatically move up the ladder, taking over the "relatively secure but low-status blue- and white-collar jobs that WASPs and the descendants of earlier immigrants would no longer accept" (Gans 1992, 177).

Historical considerations aside, the advent of the hourglass economy confronts today's immigrant children with a cruel choice: either they acquire the college or other advanced degrees they need to move into the professional/managerial elite, or they accept the same menial jobs their parents held. Given the aspirational shift entailed in second generation revolt, the latter possibility is not in the cards.

> If the young people are offered immigrant jobs, there are some good reasons why they might turn them down. They come to the world of work with American standards, and may not even be familiar with the old-country conditions ... by which immigrants ... judged the urban job market. Nor do they have the long-range goals that persuaded their parents to work long

hours at low wages; they know they cannot be deported and are here to stay in America, and most likely they are not obliged to send money to relatives left in the old country. From their perspective, immigrant jobs are demeaning; moreover, illegal jobs and scams may pay more and look better socially— especially when peer pressure is also present. (Gans 1992, 182)

The scenario has the ring of plausibility, but note the slippage in the argument. One need not have discriminating employers and "poor young men with dark skins" (Gans 1992, 182) for the hourglass economy to yield the same effect. As long as the parents arrive with very little schooling (consider the fact that 10 percent of Mexican immigrants in the Los Angeles region report *zero* years of schooling) and doing better requires a substantial increment of formal education, immigrant children who drop out of high school or learn little or nothing while attending school will do poorly—even in a world of color-blind and benevolent employers.

Gans links aspirational change to the process of settlement. That element appears in Portes and Zhou as well, but they place greater emphasis on contingent factors. The new immigrants converge on central cities where they live in close contact with earlier established, native minorities. Proximity to African- and Mexican-Americans yields two effects. One has to do with outsider categorization: oblivious to finer distinctions of nativity and ethnicity, whites simplify reality, identifying immigrants with their native-born homologs. More important, propinquity yields exposure to the "adversarial" norms of "marginalized youth." As immigrant children come into contact with the reactive subculture developed by native minorities, they undergo a process of "socialization" that "can effectively block parental plans for intergenerational mobility" (Portes and Zhou 1993, 83).

In all likelihood, factors inherent to the migration process as well as those of a more contingent nature are at work. At the very least, however, theoretical clarity requires that we distinguish between the two. Empirical research needs to assess their relative importance. While both explanations yield the same effect, second generation revolt does not require the presence of native minorities and their oppositional subculture. By contrast, it is not clear whether exposure to a preexisting oppositional subculture would work in equally insidious ways, were there not an immigrant predisposition toward that point of view born out of the frustration produced by the hourglass economy. Historical evidence is germane to this question, since it would allow us to determine whether or not an "oppositional subculture" is sui generis to the situation of contemporary immigrants, for whom the "proximal host" is a visible, stigmatized, native-born minority.

Both explanations also highlight a similar factor: namely, exposure to influences outside the immigrant communities. The argument for inherent factors underlines the impact of the broader society and its culture of consumption. By contrast, the argument for contingent factors underlines the impact of a subsociety and its distinctive subculture; to the extent that the subculture reflects the broader culture in its emphasis on individualism, acquisitiveness, and materialism, the two lines of influence may be highly intertwined.

It is also worth recalling that the type of immigrants around which Piore organized his theoretical framework began as temporary migrants and came from peasant societies. It is precisely those origins and circumstances that account for the divergence between first generation expectations and the wage and consumption standards of the native-born. Although the argument is never developed, it would follow that the diffusion of consumption norms from host to sending countries could alter expectations prior to migration and therefore would also accelerate the process of second generation revolt. In that case, the new immigration may differ from the old in the degree of premigration cultural change. If the Old World communities were more isolated and more attached to traditional modes of scarcity-bound consumption, the influence of U.S. consumption patterns may have worked with a more delayed effect, making second generation revolt less intense than it is today.

In sum, the recent attempts to conceptualize the dilemmas the second generation have the great merit of laying out an important research agenda and directing our attention toward hypotheses that can be measured and assessed. While these conceptual efforts suffer from the usual drawbacks of logical consistency, adequacy of evidence, and appropriateness of the comparative frame, the main problem may simply be that the effort is premature. The children of today's immigrants may well be star-crossed, but we should be cautious before consigning them to oblivion.

Second Generations Today and Tomorrow

Who is at risk? The theory of segmented assimilation is almost certainly right in identifying multiple, divergent paths of second generation adaptation. But the importance of that discovery is bound up with the matter of the relative size of the cohorts following the different paths, a question that is never addressed. Considering today's situation in light of the historical experience of immigration puts the issue in an entirely different light. While America's new immigrant population is extraordinarily diverse, its overwhelmingly largest component—the Mexicans—falls at the very bottom of the skill ladder. As of 1990, Mexicans accounted for just over one out of every five immigrants, but they made up one out of every three children of immigrants. Put somewhat differently, Mexicans are overrepresented by 50 percent among the second generation relative to their share among the foreign-born. If Mexicans are omitted, today's second generation bears a much closer resemblance to the rest of the American population in socioeconomic characteristics. Those characteristics are not sufficient to guarantee satisfactory adjustment to the economy of the next generation, but the same can be said for young, third-generation-plus Americans of any ethnic stripe. And a very large proportion of the second generation begins with a substantial edge over their third-generation-plus counterparts.

By contrast, at the turn of the century, no single group could have altered the generalization that most immigrants were much more likely than natives to start out near the bottom. At the early part of the twentieth century, immigrants were a relatively homogeneous population of persons narrowly concentrated at the bottom of the occupational scale. True, there were entrepreneurs among the immigrants of old—mainly persons with a background in trade (as among the Jews) or unskilled laborers who somehow managed to move into entrepreneurial endeavors. Nonetheless, in 1910, immigrants from all major groups except the English were far more likely to work at the least skilled jobs than were native whites of native parentage, and all were less likely to work in white-collar jobs, whether at high or low levels. Italians, Poles, and other Eastern and Southern Europeans disproportionately fell into jobs at the very bottom of the occupational ladder. Low levels of literacy (just over half of the "other Eastern and Southern Europeans" reported that they could read, and just over half of the Italians could not speak English) also distinguished these groups from the newcomers from Western and Northern Europe. Although the Jews entered America at a level above their counterparts from elsewhere in Southern and Eastern Europe, they still began with quite a disadvantage, in clear contrast to the highly skilled immigrants of the post-1965 period.

To be sure, the adult second generation of the time found itself at less of a disadvantage, although the English and the Germans—and even the Irish immigrants of an earlier wave—began with advantages that the newcomers of the turn of the century never possessed. Even so, immigrant adolescents of all national origins were less likely than natives of native parentage to remain in school. The gap in school attendance is surely worth recalling: fourteen- to eighteen-year-old male children of Polish, Italian, and other Eastern and Southern European origin were about three times less likely to attend school than were native whites of native parentage.

Of course, there has been heterogeneity among immigrant flows in every period. There were highly skilled Germans and English immigrants coming in large numbers in the 1890–1920 period, for example. Similarly, the literate, English-speaking, although low-skilled Irish remained important up to the shutting off of immigration in the 1920s. But the skill level of the skilled today is very much higher than it was in the past, and the situation of one especially large and especially low-skilled group, the Mexicans, is unique. Contrasting past and present thus brings out the contemporary importance of the Mexican-origin component, even though it does not make it *all*-important. Clearly, there are individuals in every group (including the children of native whites) who are "at risk" in the sense of having little education and access to few resources of a parental or neighborhood kind. Nor are the Mexicans the only origin group among whom many are at risk. But a comparison of Mexicans with Cubans, a group that has received great attention in the literature, puts the matter in sharp relief.

Cuban immigrants are a much smaller group than Mexican immigrants relative to the share of all immigrants (only 3.7 percent in 1990); Cubans are especially underrepresented among children of the foreign-born (just 2 percent in 1990). Moreover, the Cuban population is growing slowly, characterized by a high median age and low fertility. While it may well be the case that second generation Cubans are moving rapidly, if incompletely, into the middle class, either through a path mediated by the enclave economy or through assimilation, classical style, the quantitative import is relatively slight and is destined to decline, given lower fertility and reduced immigration. By contrast, in the six years since 1990, Mexicans have grown from 22 to 27 percent of the foreign-born, with no evidence that the most recent immigrants are any more skilled or better educated than their predecessors. The key point, therefore, is that no group is at all similar to the Mexicans in being simultaneously the lowest skilled of all the major immigrant groups and the overwhelmingly largest part of the total immigrant population.

Specifying the at-risk component of the second generation and understanding the dynamics behind its growth are important for other reasons. The segmented assimilation hypothesis takes the presence of at-risk populations for granted, contending instead that shifts on the demand side are the key factors changing the opportunities for the offspring of the foreign-born. But even if the demand side conditions are changing just as the theory of segmented assimilation would predict, the impact would be a good deal less severe if Mexican-origin children were not so heavily overrepresented among the children of the foreign-born. That fact has little to do with the considerations of changing economic structure emphasized in the literature, but rather with the age structure of the Mexican immigrant population, its fertility, and the timing of its moves to the United States—factors that no one has yet unpacked. Moreover, second generation outcomes do seem to vary with other demographic factors: whether a child was born abroad or in the United States; the presence of other foreign-born children in the household; and the nativity status of parents. We suspect that these factors differ among immigrant groups, with the result that the assimilation process will be more advanced among some groups than among others, simply because the timing of migration reduces the likelihood of a child's birth occurring outside the United States and the characteristics of household structure provide less exposure to foreign-born persons.

Educational Attainment and Labor Market Outcomes

The possibility that we have a new expanded underclass in the making lends the edge to research on today's second generation. In our view, applying the "underclass" concept to issues of second generation adaptation is not especially helpful since the concept has been more successful in generating debate than in shedding light in the area where it originated—namely, in the discussion of the problems of the urban, African-American poor. But whatever the problems of the concept when used on its home territory, it has traveled poorly and has been employed inconsistently.

More important, the invocation of the concept serves the rhetorical device of implying identity between an evolving underclass of immigrant origins and an African-American underclass, a comparison made plausible mainly because the latter's existence is presumed to be a matter of fact. Whatever one's view of the applicability and usefulness of the underclass concept, there is clearly slippage in the explanation as it applies to immigration. The African-American underclass is generally ascribed to structural changes in the environment (as in Wilson's [1996] account), whereas the advent of a second generation underclass results from cultural diffusion, notwithstanding a very different environment.

The chapter "Growing up American" in Portes and Rumbaut's new edition of their justly influential *Immigrant America* (1996) exemplifies both the tenor and the cast taken by today's discussion. On the one hand, today's immigrants mostly converge on poor areas of central cities where they come "into close contact with the urban underclass" (Portes and Rumbaut 1996, 248). To be sure, Portes and Rumbaut note that the making of this urban underclass results from discrimination and the changing economic structure of the cities, but to these causes they ascribe "the development of an adversarial outlook toward middle-class *culture*" (248; emphasis added). They also see no need to explain what the underclass is and how it differs from a lower or poor working class of the past.

In any case, geographic proximity to the underclass matters because it presumably encourages second generation children to associate with the "wrong crowd," from which they pick up the "wrong attitudes" of their native-born peers. (This argument implicitly revives earlier theories from the deviance literature on differential association.) Native-born underclass youth "exercise a powerful influence on newly arrived youth by reinterpreting for them the difficult conditions of adaptation . . . creating the conditions for a problematic mode of dissonant *acculturation*. . . . [Through a] *socialization* process [newcomers' loyalties] shift toward the common adversarial stance of their native-born peers" (Portes and Rumbaut 1996, 248–49; emphasis added).

Children who adopt the adversarial stance are unlikely to do well in school. Of course, this does not necessarily translate into labor market disaster: after all, there are the supposedly abundant low-level jobs occupied by their parents. But the parents are caught in a deadend mobility trap. And educationally unsuccessful immigrant children "run the risk of being trapped into the same low-paid occupations held by their parents, confirming the dismal portrayals of a *permanent underclass*" (Portes and Rumbaut 1996, 250; emphasis added).

Although it borrows language and concepts from Wilson's work on the black underclass, the explanatory framework underlying the segmented assimilation hypothesis differs significantly. For Wilson, the underclass is the product of the disappearance of the factory sector, the out-migration of the black middle class, and the resulting social isolation of the poor. Lacking the regulative structure of work, as well as the institutions, informal connections, and role models provided by the more complete ghetto community of old, contemporary ghetto dwellers alter their behavioral patterns and attitudes. They respond to the changes around them in self-defeating and self-reproducing ways.

Thus, in Wilson's formulation, subculture serves as a factor that perpetuates the reproduction of the underclass, but the formation of the underclass itself ultimately derives from the "disappearance" of work. However, work has hardly disappeared from the immigrant communities where second generation immigrants are said to stand at risk. We concede that the level of economic activity differs among the less skilled immigrant groups, but among Mexicans—the largest and paradigmatic group of contemporary labor migrants—employment rates among first generation men are extremely high. Almost everybody works. From the Wilsonian perspective, this pattern should make work normative, with consequences felt by the U.S.-born or -raised children of Mexican immigrants.

Moreover, the hypothesis of segmented assimilation involves particularly strong assumptions about the importance and power of cultural diffusion. After all, the null hypothesis would simply be class reproduction: the children of working-class immigrants will take up the same type of positions as occupied by their parents. Stratificationists might change the terms still further. Starting so far at the bottom, the children of working-class immigrants have a greater likelihood of moving ahead than they do of falling yet further behind. It is worth recalling that the immigration literature emphasizes the importance of the informal group resources developed through the migration process. As Massey and his colleagues have argued, the information and support mechanisms built up through the development of migrant networks have a transforming effect, so that landless peasants may start out "poor in financial resources" but arrive "wealthy in social capital, which they can readily convert into jobs and earnings" (Massey et al. 1987, 171). Is it realistic to assume that the social capital developed by the immigrant generation, which embeds job seekers in informal networks that also transmit skills once jobs are acquired, will be obliterated by the time that the second generation comes of age?

Granted, we are describing a first generation phenomenon, and one can certainly imagine a scenario characterized by intergenerational discontinuity as suggested by the hypothesis of segmented assimilation. But we caution against going down that road too fast. The analogy is clearly overdrawn: East Los Angeles bears little resemblance to the South Side of Chicago, either in its past or present incarnations. If the concept of social capital has any meaning at all, it implies that social structure has an independent effect. Since the children of less skilled immigrants are far more likely than comparable African-Americans to live in neighborhoods with dense job networks, and also to grow up in households where the head is employed, we would expect higher employment rates among second-generation school-leavers or high school completers, as compared to their African-American counterparts.

It is also worth recalling that the embedding of immigrant communities is, at least in part, a response to employers' favorable views of the work ethic and behavior of the foreign-born; for that reason, one might expect that immigrant children enter a reception context quite different from that encountered by their African-American counterparts. The penetration of immigrant networks is also now very deep, which, in the Los Angeles case at least, means that there are still plenty of Mexican sweepers and sweatshop workers, but also quite a few foremen and skilled workers, which in turn provides the second generation with access to job opportunities well above the bottom of the ladder. As immigration itself generates ample needs for bilingual speakers, whether in hospitals, department stores, or factories, it creates positions for which the children of immigrants are ideally suited (Waldinger 1996a, 1996b, 1997; Waldinger and Bozorgmehr 1996).

But could this all be undone by the workings of the famous "oppositional culture"? Perhaps, but we note that an oppositional culture has historically been a characteristic of working-class communities. In the past, it emerged from the immigrant experience *without* exposure to a "proximal host" composed of visible, stigmatized, native-born minorities (see Perlmann and Waldinger 1997). The oppositional culture of the traditional kind had its origins in the disarticulation between schools, on the one hand, and the world of manual work to which immigrant children were destined, on the other. That disconnection bred revolt: working-class children correctly perceived that school had little to do with their chances in life; they also reacted against the middle-class culture of the school and its denigration of working-class life and labor. Moreover, the world of the factory legitimates values quite different from those of the classroom—physicality, toughness, labor—the themes sounded by Paul Willis ([1977] 1981) in his ethnography of working-class "lads" in Britain, but which reappear in Douglas Foley's description of lower-status, Mexican *vatos* in a South Texas high school:

> Most aspired to working class jobs like their fathers', such as driving a tractor, trucking melons, fixing cars, setting irrigation rigs, and working in packing sheds. Some wanted to be carpenters and bricklayers, or work for the highway road crew. Being able to survive on a blacktopping crew during the summer heat was considered a very prestigious job. . . . It was dangerous, dirty, heavy work that only "real men" did. It was a true test of a young man's body and character. . . . The vatos preferred . . . rough physical work. . . . They considered working with their hands honorable. . . . In contrast, school work was seen as boring, sissy stuff. (Foley 1990, 87)

As this quote suggests, the opposition between working-class students and their schools is also gendered—no surprise, as it is prefigured in earlier ethnographic work (see, e.g., Gans 1962). Relative to the factory, the high school is a more "feminine" institution, one in which women play a prominent role. Because the high school also transmits skills that are more likely to be immediately valued by the employers of women than by the employers of men, male working-class adolescents are more likely to drift into revolt than their female counterparts.

We concede that, in the past, school could be flaunted with relative impunity as long as there was a vibrant factory-based economy that unsuccessful students could access through the help of relatives and neighborhood-based friends. The stronger the industrial economy, the greater the value placed on manual work and the more influential its subculture, which in turn sanctioned youth rebellion and gave it a ritualized form. But to make the point this way also implies that any oppositional culture, if so it should be characterized, was a transitional phenomenon associated with the passage from adolescence to adulthood and fading in salience as attachment to work progressed.

While it is one thing to concede that today's factory sector is no longer so strong as in the past, it is another to note that neither manufacturing nor other forms of manual work have disappeared, especially in such areas of immigrant concentration as Texas or California. Though the literature is fragmentary, it appears that both the traditional working-class oppositional culture and its related pattern of protracted settling down into the labor market persist, albeit in attenuated form, in the remaining ethnic working-class enclaves in the Northeast and Midwest. And for all the reasons noted above, an oppositional culture may therefore remain an aspect of the second generation, working-class transition to adulthood and not involve resocialization into the underclass.

Although the implicit worry surrounding the literature on the second generation is that the children of immigrants face a fate similar to the one visited upon African-Americans, we are also struck by the fact that the comparison, while implicit in all the discussions, has not squarely been framed. The conventional wisdom strikes the underclass note in a second way, through historical analogy, implying that the at-risk children of today's immigrants may recapitulate the earlier black (or Puerto Rican) experience not so much for the reasons of cultural diffusion mentioned above, but because of similarity in the historical experiences. The latter groups got stuck due to discrimination and diminishing opportunities for workers with few skills. As Portes puts it (1996, 5), the "perpetuation of these negative conditions eventually led to an interrelated set of urban pathologies."

This characterization faithfully echoes the basic Wilsonian view, but the underlying similarity of experience requires a second look. Certainly, contrasts abound, at least if the relevant characterizations involve comparing African-American migrants from the South, circa 1940–1965, with the low-skilled immigrants of today and if we can use Los Angeles as a case in point. African-Americans occupied a marginal position in the urban economy, were still heavily dependent on the traditional service occupations en route to a concentration in the public sector, and enjoyed only limited success in finding manufacturing jobs. By contrast, Mexican immigrants, exploited as they are, have nonetheless moved into a wide swath of the region's economy from which they are unlikely to be dislodged. In this respect, the most oppressed of America's new immigrants occupy a position of structural centrality quite unlike the marginal role relegated to urban African-Americans at a comparable point in their movement to urban centers. For that reason, the children of today's Mexican immigration will probably have a better chance of finding positions up the job ladder than did the children of the Great Migration.

The descendants of the most recent great immigration to the United States have now moved far up the totem pole. From the perspective of the 1990s, it is hard to imagine that their adaptation to America could have turned out differently. But this view of an inexorable climb up the social ladder is certainly not how the children and grandchildren of the European immigrants experienced the process themselves. Their beginnings were not particularly promising, nor were the established

groups of the time ready to accept the newcomers and their descendants. And there is every reason to think that the earlier second generation movement upward involved a variety of patterns and strategies
sufficiently complex to defy a characterization as dependent on good
manufacturing jobs alone.

At a minimum, this portrait of the past suggests that the children of
the post-1965 immigration begin with disadvantages no greater than
those encountered by immigrant children before. This generalization
is probably too cautious. On the one hand, the immigrants' class composition is far more heavily weighted toward the middle class than was
true earlier in the century. And on the other hand, American society is
more receptive to immigrant incorporation—in large measure due to
the efforts by earlier groups of outsiders to widen access to opportunity.

Although America's new immigrant population is extraordinarily diverse, its overwhelmingly largest component—the Mexicans—falls at
the very bottom of the skill ladder, and Mexicans are even more heavily
represented among the immigrants' children. With their exception, today's second generation looks little different from the rest of the American population in socioeconomic characteristics. Those characteristics
are not sufficient to guarantee satisfactory adjustment to the economy
of the next generation, but the same can be said for young, third-
generation-plus Americans of any ethnic stripe. The immigrant children most at risk are the Mexicans, and it is the presence of this very
large group, so far below the others in skills, that distinguishes today's
from yesterday's second generation. However, we note that the advent
of the new economy means trouble for the children of the native-born
members of America's working class as well; they also find themselves
in conflict with the middle-class values and expectations of schools.
These are the main reasons why we should worry about the future for
the offspring of Mexican immigrants and of other less skilled newcomers.

Notes

1. As one might expect, basic definitions of the subject in question are still in flux.
For the purposes of this discussion, we accept the definition of the "second generation,"
formulated by Portes and Rumbaut (1996) in their influential interpretation. Accepting
their definition seems appropriate, first because Portes and Rumbaut's account has already assumed canonical status and second because the debate we seek to engage defines the phenomenon in precisely this way. As Zhou (1997, 64–65) notes in her recent

article in the *Annual Review of Sociology,* the "emerging literature on the new second generation" has discussed not only U.S.-born children (the true second generation), but also contemporary immigrant children who arrived in the United States before reaching adulthood. The prevailing definition, then, construes the phenomenon broadly; narrower definitions, distinguishing between the native-born children of foreign-born parents, and their foreign-born counterparts of comparable age, might be preferred. Rumbaut, in particular, has suggested an intermediate category, nicknamed the "1.5 generation," referring to those children born abroad but entering the host country before the age of 12. More recently (Rumbaut 1997), he has argued for the utility of more refined breakdowns, distinguishing between a 1.25, 1.5, and 1.75 generation, the last referring to foreign-born children brought to the host society prior to age 6; the second referring to children brought to the host society between ages 6 and 12; the first referring to those children who enter the host society after age 12.

Space does not allow us to pursue this discussion at greater length. However, now, as in the past, the great majority of the children of immigrant parents are born in the United States. As of 1990, 76 percent of children of immigrants were U.S.-born; an additional 15 percent qualified for Rumbaut's 1.75 generation; and, by Rumbaut's definition, only 9 percent could be considered 1.5 generation and a mere 1 percent as 1.25 (data recalculated from Landale and Oropesa [1997, 437]). Later we emphasize the disproportionate size of the Mexican second generation; this population is also disproportionately composed of children who fall into either the 1.75 or the second generation categories, the latter containing the greater portion of the group.

We note that the utility of these various distinctions has not fully been established. Interest in social psychological patterns of adaptation explains part of Rumbaut's motivation; age at migration strongly influences the flexibility of response to the culture of the host country. But that same consideration pushes the 1.75 generation toward convergence with the "true" second generation—which is exactly how the matter has been dealt with in the literature. Thernstrom (1973, 120) referred to foreign-born children who nonetheless grew up in the United States as a *"de facto* second generation"; Piore (1979, 66) argued that the critical distinction between first and second generation "appears not to be the place of birth but the place where one grows up, and in particular spends his or her adolescence"; Zhou and Bankston's (1998) book on Vietnamese-American youth defines the second generation as including both the U.S.-born and those foreign-born children who arrived in the United States prior to age 5.

2. For the purposes of this discussion, the central texts cited are Gans (1992), Portes and Zhou (1993), Portes and Rumbaut (1996), Portes and Zhou (1993), and Zhou and Bankston (1998). These texts reveal a common theme, even though each author speaks with a distinct voice. Rumbaut (1994), in particular, strikes an optimistic note, as does Zhou (1997), although to a lesser degree. Nonetheless, both use the terminology of segmented assimilation and, in their empirical work, both have noted that sizable components of today's second generation seem headed for trouble.

3. This special issue of the *International Migration Review* was republished as *The New Second Generation* (Portes 1996). Zhou (1997) provides a thorough review of the literature—a valuable exercise, but one that we will not attempt, given our objectives.

4. Among immigrants from the Caribbean, for example, skin color does play a role in the "sifting" of individuals into white, brown, and black social categories.

References

Cheng, Lucie, and Philip Yang. 1996. "Asians: The 'Model Minority' Deconstructed." In *Ethnic Los Angeles*, edited by Roger Waldinger and Mehdi Bozorgmehr, chap. 11. New York: Russell Sage Foundation.

Foley, Douglas. 1990. *Learning Capitalist Culture: Deep in the Heart of Tejas*. Philadelphia: University of Pennsylvania Press.

Gans, Herbert. 1962. *The Urban Villagers*. New York: Free Press.

———. 1992. "Second-Generation Decline: Scenarios for the Economic and Ethnic Futures of the Post-1965 American Immigrants." *Ethnic and Racial Studies* 15 (2): 173–92.

Landale, Nancy, and R. S. Oropesa. 1997. "In Search of the New Second Generation: Alternative Strategies for Identifying Second Generation Children and Understanding Their Acquisition of English." *Sociological Perspectives* 40 (3): 427–54.

Massey, Douglas, et al. 1987. *Return to Aztlan*. Berkeley: University of California Press.

Perlmann, Joel, and Roger Waldinger. 1997. "Second Generation Decline? The Children of Immigrants, Past and Present: A Reconsideration." *International Migration Review* 31.

Piore, Michael. 1979. *Birds of Passage*. New York: Cambridge University Press.

Portes, Alejandro, ed. 1996. *The New Second Generation*. New York: Russell Sage Foundation.

Portes, Alejandro, and Ruben G. Rumbaut. 1996. *Immigrant America*, 2d ed. Berkeley: University of California Press.

Portes, Alejandro, and Min Zhou. 1993. "The New Second Generation: Segmented Assimilation and Its Variants among Post-1965 Immigrant Youth." *Annals*, no. 530, 74–96.

Rumbaut, Rubén. 1994. "The Crucible Within: Ethnic Identity, Self-Esteem, and Segmented Assimilation among Children of Immigrants." *International Migration Review* 28 (4): 748–94.

———. 1997. "Ties that Bind: Immigration and Immigrant Families in the United States." In *Immigration and the Family: Research and Policy on U.S. Immigrants*, edited by Alan Booth, Ann C. Crouter, and Nancy S. Landale, 3–46. Mahwah, N.J.: Lawrence Erlbaum Associates.

Steinberg, Stephen. 1981. *The Ethnic Myth*. New York: Atheneum.

Thernstrom, Stephen. 1973. *The Other Bostonians*. Cambridge, Mass.: Harvard University Press.

Waldinger, Roger. 1996a. *Still the Promised City? New Immigrants and African-Americans in Postindustrial New York*. Cambridge: Harvard University Press.

———. 1996b. "Who Makes the Beds? Who Washes the Dishes? Black/Immigrant Competition Reassessed." In *Immigrants and Immigration Policy: Individual Skills, Family Ties, and Group Identities*, edited by Harriet Orcutt Duleep and Phanindra V. Wunnava. Greenwich, Conn.: JAI Press.

———. 1997. "Black/Immigrant Competition Re-Assessed: New Evidence from Los Angeles." *Sociological Perspectives* 40 (3): 365–86.

Waldinger, Roger, and Mehdi Bozorgmehr, eds. 1997. *Ethnic Los Angeles*. New York: Russell Sage Foundation.

Willis, Paul. (1977) 1981. *Learning to Labor: How Working-Class Kids Get Working-Class Jobs*. New York: Columbia University Press.

Wilson, William Julius. 1996. *When Work Disappears*. New York: Knopf.

Zhou, Min. 1997. "The New Second Generation." *Annual Review of Sociology* 23:63–95.

Zhou, Min, and Carl Bankston III. 1998. *Growing Up American*. New York: Russell Sage.

Immanuel Wallerstein

This book grows out of a project of introspection by the world sociological community. As president of the International Sociological Association from 1994 to 1998, I hoped to encourage serious discussion on
the theme of the 1998 World Congress: "Social Knowledge: Heritage,
Challenges, Perspectives." I thought that one way to encourage such
serious discussion was to prepare it by holding a series of regional
colloquia prior to the congress, and then making those papers available
for congress participants. This book is the final outcome of the North
American regional colloquium.

I had asked all the regional colloquia to discuss the basic question
of the heritage of sociology and the future of the social sciences in the
twenty-first century from the perspective of the region. It is a measure
of how difficult it is for all sociologists, and not merely those in North
America, to emerge from their provincial cocoons that almost everyone
discussed this question not from the perspective of the region but
rather in the region. I consider that our most urgent task intellectually
in the coming decades is to reframe our analyses and assumptions
such that we consider our data, our methods, and our theorizing as
though we were actually living in the single world-system in which
we find ourselves.

Having said that, this volume represents a serious reflection on the
reality of North America. As such, the most striking thing I find is how
much the continuities and the cutting edges are the same. One hundred years ago, the United States was primarily concerned with two
issues: its place in the world-system and how to overcome the legacy
of slavery. Canada was concerned with analogous issues: its place as
an autonomous state in the same world-system, and how to overcome
the legacy of the British defeat of the French in the Seven Years' War.
This volume demonstrates how current these concerns of yesteryear
still are.

Furthermore, the metatheorizing on these issues seems to me to have remained remarkably the same. Both we and our predecessors treat these central social issues in the light of three underlying intellectual debates or dilemmas. The first arises out of the reformist agenda that has underlain so much of social science, and of sociology in particular. We wish to analyze where the world is heading in order better to ensure that it will head in the right direction. Second, we worry about the adequacy of our concepts to analyze the social realities we face. That is, we worry whether our intellectual tools and the ways in which we conceive the issues are in fact relevant to their solution. And third, we worry about the appropriate relationship between facts and values and how indeed we can reconcile what we consider to be our scientific role and what we hold dear as our human priorities. Throughout this book, these three issues are discussed and debated.

Ramkrishna Mukherjee, in an unfortunately neglected book,[1] put forward the four fundamental questions one should answer to appraise any variation in social reality: What is it? How is it? Why is it? and What will it be? He argued that it was in fact possible to go beyond description and explanation to diagnosis, that is, to the understanding of the process in the middle of which we find ourselves and in which all of us, including of course the analysts, are inextricably involved.

I shall not add my voice here to those in this volume, to the analysis of contemporary so-called globalization nor to the analysis of what goes under the label of racism/ethnic conflicts/gender/multicultural realities. I have written on both of these subjects elsewhere. I have no doubt that our concerns for the future do and should center around these two issues, that the concepts we have been using have not been sufficiently adequate for their analysis, and that it is not plausible to say we can separate the perception of social facts and value orientation in our work on these issues.

I would rather take up one theme from the essay by Joel Levine, the mathematical social scientist in our ranks. He says "science requires jeopardy." I could not agree more. This is very close to what Isabelle Stengers, chemist and philosopher of science, has been arguing in her works about the centrality of risk to science. Stengers argues that science should be seen not as a set of "requirements" (exigencies) but as a set of obligations:

> The theme of "rationality" has a different meaning if it is taken as implying requirement, in which case it is most often a vector of arrogance and infamy, or if it is taken as implying obligation, in which case it becomes the synonym of risk and

of being put to the test, a test not of the general public or of the non-competent but of the one who has chosen to commit himself to a practice that makes the claim [of rationality].[2]

This idea of risk or jeopardy in science, which Joel Levine illustrates so well in his essay, is crucial for all three metaconcerns: the shape of the future, the adequacy of our concepts for diagnosis, and the relationship of facts and value orientations. Jeopardy or risk involves the courage of clear assertion about verifiable realities and realistic choices. And such jeopardy enters the picture at all moments of our scholarly exercise: in the choice of the problem, in the choice of the kind of data we shall consider pertinent, in the choice of the concepts we use, in the interpretations we proffer for the data we claim as objective (i.e., claimed to be non-self-serving fantasy but rather replicable by others). The scientific choices and the moral choices turn out to be identical, or it is not defensible science.

If I insist on world-systems analysis in my work, it is certainly not because I am asking myself or anyone else to look only at macrophenomena. Far from it. It is because I do not believe one can make relevant, meaningful analyses of the data (at whatever level from which they are drawn) if one omits significant contextual variables that can only be derived and evaluated at the level of the historical system under analysis. Groups of any size (from casual duos, to ongoing families, to large-scale organizations, to state structures) operate within an evolving historical system and can only be understood if carefully placed within that system, its pressures and constraints, its multiple actors and their actions, its possibilities and limits.

Sociology for the twenty-first century? We have accomplished much in the past century. But we have also accomplished very little. It might be better to concentrate on the latter sober reminder than on the former self-congratulation. We have learned a lot about formal rationality, but almost nothing about substantive rationality. But does formal rationality exist?[3] Concern with substantive rationality underlies many, if not most, of the essays in this volume. It needs to move into the center of our scholarly debates, as we seek to make sociology (or rather social science) truly scientific and truly relevant to our social world.

Notes

1. Ramkrishna Mukherjee, *What Will It Be? Explorations in Inductive Sociology* (Durham, N.C.: Carolina Academic Press, 1978).

2. Isabelle Stengers, *Cosmopolitique, I: La guerre des sciences* (Paris: La Découverte, 1996,

90). She explains further: "It is clear that 'requirement' (exigence) and obligation, as their prefixes indicate, form a sort of topology. 'Ex' implies addressing oneself to an 'outside,' a relation of exteriority, whereas 'ob' implies a face-to-face relationship. One requires something of something or someone. One is obliged by, and is obligated to [another], noting, in some cases, the degree of this gratitude, something insisted upon by [the grammar of] the Portuguese language" (89).

3. See my presidential address to the International Sociological Association,"The Heritage of Sociology, the Promise of Social Science" (*Current Sociology* 47 [1999]: 3).

Janet Abu-Lughod is professor emerita of sociology and historical studies in the Graduate Faculty of the New School for Social Research and of Northwestern University. Among her most recent books are *Before European Hegemony: The World System, A.D. 1250–1350* (1989); *Changing Cities* (1991); *From Urban Village to East Village: The Battle for New York's Lower East Side* (1994); and *New York, Chicago and Los Angeles: America's Global Cities* (1999). She is currently writing an analysis that compares race riots in those three cities.

Tomás Almaguer is Arthur F. Thurnau professor and associate professor of sociology and American culture at the University of Michigan, where he directs the Center for Research on Social Organization. He is the author of *Racial Fault Lines: The Historical Origins of White Supremacy in California* (1994).

Giovanni Arrighi is professor of sociology at Johns Hopkins University. He received the Award for Distinguished Scholarship of the Political Economy of the World-System Section of the American Sociological Association for *The Long Twentieth Century* (1994). His latest book, coauthored with Beverly Silver, is entitled *Hegemonic Transitions: Chaos and Governance in the Modern World System.*

Gilles Bourque is professor of sociology at the University of Quebec at Montreal, where he specializes in political sociology and political discourse analysis. His published works deal largely with the national question and the state. The recipient of many awards, he received the Richard-Ares award for *L'Idendité fragmentée* (1996), which he coauthored with Jules Duchastel.

Randall Collins is currently professor of sociology at the University of Pennsylvania. His books include *Conflict Sociology* (1975), *The Credential*

Society (1979), *Weberian Sociological Theory* (1986), and *Theoretical Sociology* (1988). His most recent work is *The Sociology of Philosophies: A Global Sociology of Intellectual Change* (1998).

Jules Duchastel, professor of sociology at the University of Quebec at Montreal, specializes in the fields of culture, political sociology, and methodology of discourse analysis. He directs the Interdisciplinary Research Centre on Social and Economic Regulations and Transformations (CRITERES). His most recent book, *L'Identité fragmentée* (1996), coauthored with Gilles Bourque, received the Richard-Ares Award.

Joe R. Feagin, Graduate Research Professor in sociology at the University of Florida in Gainesville, has conducted considerable research on racial and gender discrimination. The most recent of his three dozen published books are *Racial and Ethnic Relations, Living with Racism: The Black Middle-Class Experience,* and *White Racism: The Basics.* He served as scholar in residence at the U.S. Commission on Civil Rights, and his 1973 book *Ghetto Revolts* was nominated for a Pulitzer Prize. Two of his recent books won the Gustavus Myers Center's Outstanding Human Rights Book Award. He is president-elect of the American Sociological Association.

Harriet Friedmann is professor of sociology at the University of Toronto, where she teaches sociology and international relations. Her publications explore various aspects of the international political economy of food. Former chair of the ASA Section on the Political Economy of the World-System, she recently cochaired the Toronto Food Policy Council, which works for a socially just and sustainable regional food system.

Pierre Hamel is a professor at the University of Montreal and a member of the Center on Social and Economic Regulations and Transformations. He is responsible for the center's series, Politique et Economie, at the University of Montreal Press. His research focuses on social movements and urban policy.

Moon-Kie Jung is a Ph.D. candidate in sociology at the University of Michigan. His dissertation, tentatively titled "Toward the 'One Big Union': Race and the Making of Hawaii's Working Class," focuses on the prestatehood formation of Hawaii's interracial working class.

Joel Levine is professor and chair of Mathematical Social Sciences at Dartmouth College in Hanover, New Hampshire. Among his innovative books on methodology are *Exceptions Are the Rule: An Inquiry into Methods in the Social Sciences* (1993) and *Rules of Evidence: Introduction to Data Analysis* (a Web book, 1997). His latest work is *Data without Variables: Analysis of Attributes with or without the Use of Exclusive and Exhaustive Variables* (forthcoming).

Henri Lustiger-Thaler is an associate professor at Ramapo College. Among his coauthored or edited books are *Political Arrangements: Power and the City* (1994), *Urban Lives: Fragmentation and Resistance* (1995), and *Artful Practices: The Political Economy of Everyday Life* (1995). His forthcoming book with Margit Mayer and Pierre Hamel is entitled *Urban Fields and Global Movements*.

Louis Maheu is professor of sociology and dean of the graduate school at the University of Montreal. He currently chairs the Research Committee on Social Movements and Social Classes of the International Sociological Association. Among his recent publications are the edited volume *Social Movements and Social Classes: The Future of Collective Action* (1995) and "Social Movements in Quebec: Environmental Groups as a Cultural Challenge to the Neo-Corporatist Order," in *Quebec Society: Critical Issues* (edited by M. Fournier et al., 1997).

Joel Perlmann is senior scholar at the Jerome Levy Economics Institute of Bard College and Levy Institute Research Professor of History at Bard College. A historian and sociologist, he is the author of the award-winning book, *Ethnic Differences: Schooling and Social Structure among the Irish, Italians, Jews, and Blacks in an American City, 1880–1935* (1988), as well as numerous articles on immigration and education.

Saskia Sassen, formerly professor of urban planning at Columbia University, is currently professor of sociology at the University of Chicago and a Fellow of the American Bar Foundation. Among her most recent books are *Losing Control? Sovereignty in an Age of Globalization* (1996), *Globalization and Its Discontents* (1998), which deals with immigration policies in a world economy, and *Guests and Aliens* (1999).

Gideon Sjoberg is professor of sociology at the University of Texas at Austin. His long, distinguished career is bracketed by his classic study, *The Preindustrial City* (1960), and his most recent book (with Roger

Nett), *A Methodology for Social Research: With a New Introductory Essay* (1997). His current interests focus on bureaucratic capitalism, human rights, and democracy.

Dorothy E. Smith is a professor in the department of Sociology and Equity Studies, Ontario Institute for Studies in Education/University of Toronto. Among her numerous publications are *The Everyday World as Problematic: A Feminist Sociology* (1987); *The Conceptual Practices of Power: A Feminist Sociology of Knowledge* (1990); *Texts, Facts, and Femininity: Exploring the Relations of Ruling* (1990). In 1998 she published *Writing the Social*.

Roger Waldinger is professor of sociology, University of California at Los Angeles. He is the author of four books, of which the most recent are *Still the Promised City? African-Americans and New Immigrants in Postindustrial New York* (1996) and *Ethnic Los Angeles,* coedited with Mehdi Bozorgmehr (1996). He has written numerous articles and book chapters on immigration, ethnicity, and urban change.

Barry Wellman is professor of sociology at the University of Toronto and conducts his research at the Centre for Urban and Community Studies. Wellman founded the International Network for Social Network Analysis in 1976 and headed it for a dozen years. He is currently chair of the ASA Section on Community and Urban Sociology. He has edited *Social Structures: A Network Approach* (rev. ed., 1997) and *Networks in the Global Village* (1998); he has also published a large number of articles based on his Toronto research.